The Wisdom of George the Third

W. Hogarth invᵗ et del.

C. Grignion sculp.

Et spes & ratio Studiorum in Cæsare tantum.

Published according to Act of Parliament May 7.1761.

Juv.

THE WISDOM

OF

GEORGE THE THIRD

Papers

from a Symposium at

The Queen's Gallery, Buckingham Palace

June 2004

Edited with an Introduction by

Jonathan Marsden

Royal Collection Publications

This publication has been generously supported by
THE LECHE TRUST
THE PAUL MELLON CENTRE FOR STUDIES IN BRITISH ART

Published by
Royal Collection Enterprises Ltd
St James's Palace,
London SW1A 1BQ

For a complete catalogue of Royal Collection publications, please write to
the above address or visit the website at www.royal.collection.org.uk.

ISBN: 1 902163 72 9

British Library Cataloguing in Publication Data: a catalogue record of this
book is available from the British Library.

Cover typography by Alan Kitching RDI using Caslon Old Face, c.1720.

Text set in 11 point Bembo
Printed in the United Kingdom by Henry Ling Limited, at the
Dorset Press, Dorchester DT1 1HD

Opposite title page: C. Grignion, after William Hogarth, frontispiece to the
Catalogue of Pictures exhibited in the Spring Gardens, May 1761.
Engraving, 301 x 187, 2005

Contents

CONTENTS

Introduction

Among those responsible for creating a popular view of George III that has persisted to some extent to this day, the West Country cleric John Wolcot (1739–1819) could be singled out as one who made this activity his full-time profession. His doggerel verses, published under the pen-name Peter Pindar, poked fun at every aspect of the King's life and interests, and to a lesser degree those of Queen Charlotte. The King depicted in Pindar's verses is very much the bluff, impatient figure memorably portrayed by Nigel Hawthorne in Alan Bennett's film *The Madness of King George* (1994), adapted from Bennett's earlier stage play, with his repeated 'what, what?'. He visits Whitbread's brewery and peers into the barrels, lecturing those around him about the processes of brewing, and elsewhere he cross-questions a kitchen-maid as to how she has made an apple appear inside a dumpling. He feeds the wrong foodstuffs to his livestock at Windsor, and his Handel programmes at the Concerts of Ancient Music '. . . drove half to doors, the other half to slumber.'[1] The King also comes across as haughty, and not merely frugal but positively mean; according to Pindar several leading musicians, including Nancy Storace (Mozart's original Susanna), declined to perform at Buckingham House because they would not be paid.

Some time after 1810 when his target had begun finally to recede into solitary madness at Windsor, Wolcot was asked what he really thought of the King. He replied that he thought him 'an excellently good man, but also a clever man'. When asked why, then, he had devoted so much of his life to saying the opposite in print, the satirist replied, 'Oh, that is a matter of mere business. I want to sell my writings, that I may live; and if I had written against a bad man, though all might have been very true, nobody would have purchased.'[2] Whatever the brilliant caricaturist James Gillray thought of the King – or of the Queen, for he showed her no mercy with his pen – he, like Pindar, found in George III a perfect, and lucrative, target. The King's achievements as a collector and connoisseur were turned to political purpose by Gillray in his print of the King squinting at Samuel Cooper's miniature of Oliver Cromwell (fig. 1), and something as apparently inconsequential as a visit to a farm tenant became an image of irreconcilable division between kings and commoners (fig. 2).

These contemporary jibes have probably had less significance for the King's historical reputation than three other factors: the 'Mad-Business'; the intense concentration by historians on the nature of constitutional monarchy in the first two decades of the reign; and the question of America. This book does not set out to deny the twenty-eight crimes attributed to George III in the Declaration of Independence, or to debate its proposition that 'the history of the present King of Great Britain is a history of repeated injuries and usurpations all having in direct object the establishment of an absolute Tyranny over these states.' Its aim is rather to provide further evidence of the King's achievements outside these areas, and on his activities during the period of his reign – amounting to almost fifty years – when he was not in any sense mad.

The seventeen papers published here were given at a symposium held at The Queen's Gallery at Buckingham Palace in conjunction with the exhibition *George III & Queen Charlotte: Patronage, Collecting and Court Taste* (March 2004– January 2005). The first such event to take place in the new Gallery since its completion in 2002, the symposium opened on George III's birthday, 4 June. By a happy chance it was followed only a few days later by the astronomical phenomenon that had most captivated the King, the transit of Venus, occurring for only the second time since his reign on 8 June. The symposium was held for two related reasons: first, the exhibition was selected and arranged, and the catalogue written, entirely by the curatorial staff of the Royal Collection, a practical and not unusual restriction but one which did not allow a fully interdisciplinary[3] approach to the subject.

A CONNOISSEUR examining a COOPER.

1. James Gillray, *A Connoisseur examining a Cooper*, 1792. Engraving, published by H. Humphrey. RCIN 809343

Secondly, although it was intended that the 500 works of art selected from the Royal Collection should represent the widest possible range of the King and Queen's interests, it had to be acknowledged that there were subjects which the exhibition could not fully address. The successive gifts to

2. James Gillray, 'Affability' (George III and Queen Charlotte), 1795. Engraving, published by H. Humphrey. RCIN 814399

other institutions of the King's naval and topographical models in 1822, his library (including coins and medals) in 1823, his scientific instruments in 1841, and his music library in 1957, meant that these important areas were under-represented. Nor was an art exhibition the best way in which to evoke the

3. Nigel Hawthorne as George III in the film *The Madness of King George*, 1994.

incessant musical activity of George III's court, the details of his dietary regime, or his intense interest in the Royal Navy. Equally, one of the very greatest works of art produced for his use, the State Coach, although on public display nearby in the Royal Mews, could not for practical reasons be included. Furthermore, despite the intention expressed in the exhibition's title, Queen Charlotte remained somewhat under-represented, due to the comprehensive sales of her collections in 1819, and the subsequent dispersal of her jewels.[4]

The symposium was organised by Marion Carlisle and Trish Popkin of the Royal Collection's Education service, assisted by their curatorial colleague Kathryn Jones. The success of this experimental venture was thanks as much to their efforts as to the quality of the contributions from the podium. That we have been able to bring the proceedings to a wider public is due to the generous support of the Leche Trust and the Paul Mellon Centre for Studies in British Art, and this is very gratefully acknowledged. The publication has been guided with wisdom and care by Marie Leahy, Editor, while Kathryn Jones has borne the brunt of the editing and picture research.

In the pages that follow, the contributions of twelve leading scholars in many disciplines from museums, universities and other walks of life are joined by some further reflections by those who worked on the exhibition. The first section reveals the climate of optimism, particularly in the arts, that prevailed at the time of George III's accession, as John Harris examines the King's artistic DNA and Francis Russell reveals the extent of the influence of the Earl of Bute. My own contribution expands on an earlier examination of the King's State Coach as a vehicle not only for his person but for political and artistic ideals, while Marcus Köhler presents an invaluable German perspective, in which the source of the King's all-embracing interest in the minutiae of the life of his subjects is traced to earlier continental theories of good government and good husbandry.

The second part of the book provides further detailed analysis of the King's personal patronage and collecting, in the contributions of Christopher Lloyd, Jane Roberts and Hugh Roberts, while Stephen Roe's paper, which was originally conceived as part of a performance by the ensemble *Charivari agréable*, adds the vital dimension of music and allows us to discern a further strand of difference in taste between the King and the Queen.

The value of interdisciplinary debate is fully brought out in the third section, where Clarissa Campbell Orr makes an entirely convincing case for Queen Charlotte as a patroness of literature, revealing the cosmopolitan nature of her circle but at the same time the self-sufficiency of the court. The symposium provided several glimpses of Queen Charlotte's activity in what were hitherto unknown areas. Her taste for Sèvres porcelain (which she was among the first in England to appreciate), for Indian and Chinese textiles, lacquers and furniture have long been apparent from the 1819 sale catalogues, but her other preoccupations as Bluestocking, botanist, musician, 'scientist', and collector of 'curiosities' must now also be taken into account. And Judy Rudoe's painstaking reconstruction of a lost collection enables us for the first time to appreciate not only the magnificence but the extreme sophistication of Queen Charlotte's jewellery. To read this paper in conjunction with Matthew Winterbottom's account of the King and Queen's dining arrangements reminds us of George III's very subtle understanding of the art of kingship. In one of his essays for Lord Bute he writes that 'The Prince . . . will be feared [and] respected abroad and adored at home by mixing private economy with public magnificence.'[5]

Flora Fraser concentrates on the private domain, and on those of biography and art history. While her observations on the boundaries between these disciplines are well made, her contribution reminds us that historians of art, furniture, ceramics or silver can become so caught up with whether the shape of a leg or handle is advanced for its date, or with the way in which the paint is built up in successive glazes on a canvas, that the identity and character of anyone who might have sat to the painter, on the chair, or made use of the coffee pot or tureen, can be lost from view. Biographers can introduce beating hearts to the scene.

Taken together, the seventeen separate but complementary papers form a picture that is more complex, with more contrasts and more paradoxes than can be found in any biography or political history of George III or Queen Charlotte. There is for example in the King's life the coexistence of magnificence – as revealed by the State Coach, the services of plate ordered for London and Hanover, and the lavish use of ancestral silver furniture at Windsor – and economy – the 'frugal meals', the parsimony and the disdain for 'unhealthy' carpets at Buckingham House. There is the King's interest in public virtue of a kind epitomised not by *ancien régime* monarchs but by republicans such as Cromwell (whose bust by Wilton the King admired) and Thomas Hollis (whose hero was Brutus and who devised the iconography of the State Coach), or by Regulus, as portrayed by the King's favourite painter, the American Quaker, Benjamin West. The

King who took an active and financial interest in attempts to assess the size of the solar system never travelled beyond the shores of his own kingdom, and seldom very far within them. Peter Barber provides an enthralling *tour d'horizon* of the King's vast topographical collections, which prove that his outlook was anything but insular. The collection with its universal scope calls to mind that earlier Paper Museum formed in the seventeenth century by Cassiano dal Pozzo, which George III acquired (in the form of 6,000 drawings) from Cardinal Alessandro Albani in 1762 (see p. 107).

The topographical collection provides ample evidence of the vast expansion of Great Britain's sphere of influence during George III's reign, a phenomenon which is borne out by another simple art-historical fact: the studio of Allan Ramsay produced at least 179 versions of the King's state portrait of 1761 (plate I), of which more than half were destined for the rapidly expanding diplomatic service, reaching posts as far afield as Russia, America, India and the West Indies as well as many parts of Europe.[6]

In the final section of the book the King's relationships with scientific, military and artistic institutions are explored. Holger Hoock explains just how closely the King was involved in the creation of the Royal Academy of Arts and portrays the Academy as a theatre for cultural politics. Celina Fox and Jane Wess present two examples of the King's passion for the mechanical, both of which also provided scope for his collecting instincts. Celina Fox's paper offers some compensation for W.H. Pyne's failure to commission a view of the Marine Gallery at Buckingham House, with its ship and harbour models, at the same time as he made those (e.g. fig. 45) of the other component rooms of the King's Library, which though interesting cannot have been as picturesque.

The last word is David Watkin's. Here, as in his book *The Architect King: George III and the Culture of the Enlightenment* (2004), Professor Watkin makes a compelling case for a radical reconsideration of George III, and it is to be hoped that these papers, grouped under a deliberately revisionist title, may go some way further in establishing both King and Queen in their proper place in the history of this country, and in particular its cultural life.

Jonathan Marsden

NOTES

1. 'Brother Peter to Brother Tom. An Expostulatory Epistle', *The Works of Peter Pindar Esq.*, 3 vols., 1794, vol. II, p. 73.
2. W. Craig, *Memoirs of Her Majesty Queen Charlotte of Great Britain*, Liverpool, 1818, p. 555.
3. This term can only be used here with an apology to George III, who would not have recognised the modern demarcation of separate areas of study.
4. See Matthew Winterbottom's very helpful résumé of the destination of Queen Charlotte's property after her death in *George III & Queen Charlotte*, pp. 385–9.
5. RA GEO Add. 32/818–819.
6. A. Smart, *Allan Ramsay. A Complete Catalogue of his Paintings*, ed. J. Ingamells, New Haven and London, 1999, no. 192. Only around a dozen versions are known of the official portrait of George II by John Shackleton, of which only one went overseas, to Massachusetts. See Millar 1969, nos. 567 and 568.

Abbreviations for frequently cited sources

Architect King
　D. Watkin, *The Architect King: George III and the Culture of the Enlightenment*, London, 2004

Bibliothecae Regiae Catalogus
　F.A. Barnard, *Bibliothecae Regiae Catalogus*, 5 vols., London, 1820

BL
　British Library, London

Brooke
　J. Brooke, *King George III*, London, 1972

Burney Diary
　Diary and Letters of Madame d'Arblay (1778–1840), ed. Charlotte Barrett and A. Dobson, 6 vols., London, 1904–5

Bute
　Francis Russell, *John, 3rd Earl of Bute, Patron and Collector*, London, 2004

Crown Jewels
　The Crown Jewels, ed. C. Blair, 2 vols., London, 1998

Diaries of a Duchess
　The Diaries of a Duchess. Extracts from the Diaries of the First Duchess of Northumberland (1716–1776), ed. James Grieg, London, 1926

Enlightenment
　Enlightenment: Discovering the World in the Eighteenth Century, ed. K. Sloan with A. Burnett, London, 2003

Farington Diary
　The Diaries of Joseph Farington, ed. K. Garlick, A. Macintyre and K. Cave, 16 vols., London and New Haven, 1978–84 (Index vol., 1998)

George III & Queen Charlotte
   George III & Queen Charlotte, Patronage, Collecting and Court Taste, exh. cat., The Queen's Gallery, London, 2004

King's Purchase
   A King's Purchase: King George III and the Collection of Consul Smith, exh. cat., The Queen's Gallery, London, 1993

King's Works
   The History of the King's Works, ed. H.M. Colvin, 6 vols., London, 1963–73

Levey
   M. Levey, *The Later Italian Pictures in the Collection of Her Majesty The Queen*, 2nd edn, Cambridge, 1991

Millar 1963
   O. Millar, *The Tudor, Stuart and Early Georgian Pictures in the Collection of Her Majesty The Queen*, 2 vols., London, 1963

Millar 1969
   O. Millar, *The Later Georgian Pictures in the Collection of Her Majesty The Queen*, 2 vols., London, 1969

Papendiek
   C.L.H. Papendiek, *Court and Private Life in the Time of Queen Charlotte: Being the Journals of Mrs Papendiek, Assistant-Keeper of the Wardrobe and Reader to Her Majesty*, ed. Mrs Vernon Delves Broughton, 2 vols., London, 1887

Princesses
   F. Fraser, *Princesses: The Six Daughters of George III*, London, 2004

RA
   Royal Archives, Windsor Castle

RCIN
   Royal Collection Inventory Number

RL
Royal Library Inventory Number (drawings and
watercolours in the Royal Collection)

Royal Residences
W.H. Pyne, *The History of the Royal Residences of Windsor
Castle, St James's Palace, Carlton House, Kensington Palace,
Hampton Court, Buckingham House, and Frogmore*, 3 vols.,
London, 1819

Sir William Chambers
Sir William Chambers, Architect to George III, exh. cat.,
Courtauld Gallery, London 1996

Sophie in London
Sophie von la Roche, *Sophie in London, 1786; being the diary
of Sophie V. la Roche*, London, 1933

Survey of London
Survey of London, London County Council, 45 vols., 1900–
(in progress)

TNA, PRO
The National Archives, Public Record Office, Kew

Walker
R. Walker, *The Eighteenth and Early Nineteenth-century
Miniatures in the Collection of Her Majesty The Queen*,
Cambridge, 1992

Walpole Correspondence
The Yale Edition of Horace Walpole's Correspondence, ed.
W.S. Lewis, 48 vols., New Haven and London, 1937–83

NOTE

All paintings illustrated are oil on canvas unless otherwise stated.

I

GEORGE III in 1760

4. Attributed to William Hogarth, *Frederick, Prince of Wales*, c.1737.
RCIN 400592

I

George III's parents: Frederick and Augusta

JOHN HARRIS

The parents of Frederick, Prince of Wales (1707–51; fig. 4) were Georg August (1683–1760), who became Elector of Hanover in 1698, and Caroline of Brandenburg-Ansbach (1683–1737).[1] They married in 1705, produced Frederick in the Leineschloss at Hanover in January 1707, and would become King George II and Queen Caroline of Great Britain in 1726. To discover the artistic influences that might have passed genetically from Frederick to George, Prince of Wales – our George III – we must first examine the artistic credentials of Frederick's great-grandparents: Ernst August, of the House of Brunswick-Luneburg (1629–98), created Duke of Hanover in 1679, and Sophia (1630–1714), the grand-daughter of James I, and daughter of Elizabeth, the Winter Queen, the wife of the ill-fated Frederic, Elector Palatine of Heidelberg – where, in the castle, Sophia married Ernst August. Both Ernst and Sophia were enthusiasts for European culture. In particular they spent much time every year in Italy, stayed frequently in a Venetian palazzo, and kept abreast of architecture and artistic happenings in Venice and North Italy. Sophia was a renowned scholar, philosopher and connoisseur. They made their court at Herrenhausen a hotbed of culture, reflecting their passion for the arts and architecture, literature, gardening and music. Of course, we can exaggerate the influence of the remarkable Sophia on a young Frederick who was only seven at her death. Nevertheless, we cannot dismiss the influence of Herrenhausen as a vortex of all that German culture. Genetic gifts would surely filter down to George III, via Frederick, whose education was centred on Herrenhausen, where he spent the first twenty-one years of his life.

Sophia would have become Queen Sophia of Great Britain had she not died a few months before Queen Anne in 1714. In the event, George, Elector of Hanover was proclaimed King George I, and it was to him that Colen Campbell dedicated the first volume of *Vitruvius Britannicus* in 1715. Even if from a distance, Frederick must have become aware of the English reassessment of Palladio and Inigo Jones. Certainly there were connections between the cultural ambience of Herrenhausen and the court of Johann Wilhelm, the Elector Palatine, at Dusseldorf, and particularly at nearby Schloss Bensberg, where around 1710 English neo-Palladianism found one of its sources in Giacomo Leoni (1686–1746) and his anglophile master Matteo Alberti.[2] The wings added to the Neues Schloss at Bensberg, designed in 1703, could be confused for Lord Burlington's Westminster Dormitory (1721); and Alberti's Schloss Eifel of 1711 with the later Palladian works of William Adam in Scotland. Nevertheless, whatever Frederick learned of English Palladianism – and he would be in the thick of it in 1729 – the status quo in Herrenhausen, with its opulent gilded German Baroque interiors matched by dazzling formal gardens outside, must have been far more important. We shall observe that a taste for this rich gilded style passed down to Frederick, as witnessed in his Kentian palace at Kew and the Kentian interiors at Leicester House.

What comes to the fore is the traditional Hanoverian dislike between father and son: George I and his son George, George II and Frederick, and even the politically twisted Queen Caroline, who would call Frederick a wretch and villain. One marvels at the lack of communication between the Queen in her palace at Richmond Lodge and Gardens and her son in Kew Palace, as if the dividing public footpath, ironically named Love Lane, between those two domains, was a Caroline Wall. When at last Frederick was allowed to come to London in 1728, he first briefly camped in Leicester House, where his father as George, Prince of Wales had established a centre for *his* opposition party to George I, and where Colen Campbell was the prince's architect. Frederick's tenure of his father's palace was brief. He also stayed briefly in St James's Palace and he was soon seeking a palace that he could call his own. It is the story of his search that enables us to recognize his unusual artistic and intellectual attributes. A King George or a Queen Anne would rely upon the Office of Works to choose an architect, but not Frederick. In 1729 he made an architectural tour,[3] which can be seen as prophetic of his son's interest in architecture. He visited Cliveden in Buckingham-shire,[4] which he would rent in 1739, and where Giacomo Leoni had made designs in 1727 for a new house; then Clandon in Surrey, also by Leoni, and at that time under construction. This prompts us to ask whether he knew of Leoni through those Herrenhausen contacts with Schloss Bensberg. Next Frederick visited 'Lord Ashburnhams';[5] then to Pope's villa at Twickenham, Middlesex, and discourse with Alexander Pope, all of whose published works the Prince possessed in his distinguished library; then to the Duke of Newcastle's Claremont in Surrey, where William Kent's first gardening works were in train; and finally to Chiswick Villa, where he met Lord Burlington and was no doubt transfixed by him whom Pope called 'the little rogue Kent'. So when Frederick bought his estate at Kew in 1729, its gardens jostling those at Richmond Gardens, there was surely osmosis across the Caroline Wall, for on the Queen's side Kent was at work on her Hermitage and Merlin's Cave at exactly the same time as he was building Frederick's own Kew Palace. Indeed, as Kent's work for the formidably intellectual Caroline occupied the years from 1730 to 1735, including her great library in St James's Palace, maybe the wit and amiability of *il signor* contributed to the late thaw that occurred in the previous frosty relations between mother and son.

The White House (fig. 5), so called because it was painted white, was Kent's first big architectural commission, and from

5. William Woollett after Sir William Chambers, *Kew Palace, a view from the lawn in the Royal gardens*, 1763. Engraving. RCIN 501385

the bills and from descriptions it was clearly a remarkably integrated design, with Kent attending to all decorations and furnishings, with much gilding. The garden at this time was still the old formal one with geometrical parterres. Indeed it remained so, as we may see on the engraving by John Rocque of his *Plan of Richmond Gardens* of 1748. From 1732 the Prince's gardener was John Dillman, who throughout Fred's life maintained the gardens at Kew, Carlton House, Leicester House and Durdans. By 1735 Kew[6] would serve as the headquarters of Frederick's cultural renaissance and with Carlton House, and later Leicester House, would accommodate his growing collection of paintings.[7] The collection must surely have been inspired not only by that of Charles I, but also by that of Charles's brother, the equally ill-fated Henry, Prince of Wales. Carlton House was occupied from 1732 following a lease drawn up between the Prince and Lord Burlington.[8] The house is shown in two views: John Kip's engraved *A Prospect of the City of London, Westminster and St James's Park* of 1720, and an anonymous painting, *View of*

6. William Woollett, *A view of the gardens of Carlton House* (detail), 1760. Engraving. RIBA, London

Carlton House with a Royal Party in the Grounds of *c.*1733–4 (Tate Britain). Here Frederick kept his library, for book collecting was his passion, a passion inherited by his son. Here too in 1734 Kent laid out his celebrated flower garden (fig. 6),[9] remarked on by Sir Thomas Robinson at the end of that year:

> There is a new taste in gardening just arisen, which has been practised with so great success at the prince's garden in town, that a general alteration of some of the most considerable gardens in the kingdom is begun, after Mr Kent's notion of gardening, viz to lay them out, and work without either level or line.[10]

I cannot believe Kent planned this extraordinary garden without close consultation with an enthusiastic gardening prince. There is a clutch of bills[11] submitted on 31 August 1736 for the Octagon Temple there, a Chiswick Villa in miniature. We might speculate whether the Octagon Temple might have been a wedding present for Princess Augusta of Saxe-Gotha, who arrived in England the previous April. It would be nice to think so, for the dome features prominently in Philip Mercier's portrait of the prince in 1736 (National Portrait Gallery). But what is significant is that Kew and Carlton House, and later Leicester House, are demonstrations of Fred's patronage of Kent and his most advanced notions of architecture and gardening. It is tempting to wonder if Kent was involved with the gardening at Cliveden, where Frederick laid out a flower garden, built two aviaries, and built a 'Coffee Room adjoining the Thatched House'.[12] Surely it is at Carlton House that we may recognise the source of Princess Augusta's own passion for gardening. And it is significant, too, that Kew in particular would be the setting for the education of the future George III, born in 1738.

If we are to assess what the young George might have absorbed from his father we have to recognise that the sands of time were running out, for just thirteen years were left of Frederick's life. Nevertheless, there are a few identifiable achievements to which Prince George might have responded. I refer, for example, to 1737 when Fred took in a fellow Freemason, John Theophilus Desaguliers, and gave him a large room, seemingly behind the pediment of the White House, in which to house his mathematical instruments and set up a planetarium; here Desaguliers lectured on Natural Philosophy. Can we recognise a link between Desaguliers's planetarium, which remained at Kew for many years, and George III's Observatory built in 1768 by Sir William Chambers in old Richmond Gardens? Was Desaguliers's collection of mathematical and scientific instruments a starting point for George's own scientific collections? We must also remember that Frederick's future mentor, John, 3rd Earl of Bute, was also a distinguished collector of scientific instruments and had his own laboratory at Luton.[13]

In order to accommodate his growing family (plate II), Frederick leased Norfolk House, St James's Square, in 1737, and it was here that George, Prince of Wales was born in

1738. Norfolk House was given up in 1741, being too small, and in 1743 Leicester House was reacquired and expensively decorated and furnished. It is tantalising that we have accounts only for the new interiors,[14] for it would seem that Fred and Augusta refashioned the whole of the first floor, conjuring up a rich gilded interior in the Kew Kentian style, and indeed Kent was paid £300 in April 1743 as a 'Free Gift and Bounty'.[15] The Kent team is here, including Benjamin Goodison, cabinet-maker, and John Boson, carver. It was all lavishly fitted up, even to the State Cradle with Indian quilts, gold lace, fringe and crimson lustring cover. The staircase that preceded the sequence of state rooms was obviously spectacular and grand, hung with John Wootton's *Siege of Tournay* and *Siege of Lille* in Boson's carved frames gilded by Paul Petit.

It is not necessarily apocryphal that Frederick was a gardener who used a spade; or visited cottages and cottagers at Cliveden and Kew; or took ale in local pubs. Are not these habits prophetic of our Farmer George? Cliveden, where much internal work was carried out in 1738 and 1739, including the hanging of a Chinese paper with green poppies on white, and miscellaneous works at nearby Hedsor, used as a lodging, remind us that Fred was peripatetic thanks to his acquisition of country estates: in 1738 he leased Park Place, Henley, for hunting,[16] and Durdans near Epsom in the following year; there, Frederick and his crony Lord Baltimore loved the racing, as would George III. But it is surely at Kew, right at the end of Frederick's life, that the young George would inherit those interests that, had Frederick lived, father and son would have shared. Of course, there is the enigmatic role of Augusta, who is artistically a shadowy figure before Fred's death in 1751. In 1747 there had occurred that eventful meeting at the Egham races of Frederick with Lord Bute. Both shared passions for architecture, horticulture, botany, books, scientific instruments and music, and in particular the last named, for Frederick possessed many mechanical organs, and these were one of Bute's passions. We surely must assume that Bute was involved with Frederick's new plans for an enlarged Kew, as was that other lover of planting and botany, Bute's uncle, Archibald, 3rd Duke of Argyll. Alas, we have no visual evidence to document what Bubb Dodington referred to when stating that Frederick had 'approv'd' the 'plan' for Kew by the French architect and stage designer, Giovanni Niccolo Servandoni,[17] to whom payments were made in December 1751. This must refer to what George Vertue recorded on 12 October 1750, when he observed Frederick:

> directing the plantations of trees [and] exotics with the workmen – advising and assisting where we were received graciously and freely walking attending the Prince from place to place – for 2 or three hours, seeing his plantations, told his contrivances, designs of his improvements in his Gardens, water works, canal, etc. great numbers of people, labouring there, his new Chinesia Summer hous, painted in their style & ornaments. The story of Confucius & his doctrines, etc.[18]

Frederick had purchased another 42 acres in 1749 or 1750, and by 1751, 32 more had been planted. We can only conjure up the making of an L-shaped lake with a pseudo-Renaissance Mount Parnassus, with a bust of Archimedes paired with one of Newton, Aeschylus with Shakespeare, Horace with Pope, and Vitruvius with Jones, leading us to wonder if Frederick knew of Henry, Prince of Wales's Mount Parnassus at Richmond Palace. In addition there is a record of building in exotic styles. We know that Frederick had a Chinese-papered bedroom at Cliveden; that George's eleventh birthday, 25 May 1749, was celebrated with a Regatta on the Thames in the new Chinese barge, the watermen in Chinese dress; that payments were made to Frederick's Cabinet Painter, Joseph Goupy, for the design of various chinoiserie decorations in the gardens, although there is no record of Goupy being paid for the barge, or for the disputatious matter of the House of Confucius,[19] built in the spring of 1750, the one building taken over by Augusta for her new garden, the Kew of Sir William Chambers. All we know is that in 1750 Johann Heinrich Müntz designed an Alhambra at Kew that preceded

7. Edward Rooker after William Marlow, *Kew Palace, a view of the Wilderness, with the Alhambra, the Pagoda and the Mosque*, 1763. Engraving. RCIN 702947s

the one by Chambers by eight years (fig. 7); that Müntz sent this design to Bute through the intervention of Chambers, also then in Rome; and that it is Chambers in Rome, and only Chambers, who made designs for 'poor Fred's' mausoleum in 1751–2.[20] All this suggests that Bute, and I suspect Carl Linnaeus, Bute's Swedish gardening correspondent, fully conversant with what Chambers had recorded in China, arranged for Chambers to meet Frederick and Augusta that summer of 1749 when our architect was in England en route from Gothenburg to Paris and Rome. All this explains[21] why Chambers, the Anglo-Swede, should be chosen by Augusta to be her architect at Kew and Carlton House, and the Prince's tutor in architecture.

This link to the Kew of Augusta (fig. 8) crosses unknown territory. If only we knew more of Augusta's doings during those interim years between the death of the prince on 20 March 1751, and 1757; years of Bute's growing influence, and the influence too of the Duke of Argyll, another who knew

8. Jean-Etienne Liotard, *Augusta, Princess of Wales*, 1754. Pastel.
RCIN 400892

Linnaeus well. They would both have joined with Peter Collinson in lamenting that 'Gardening and planting have lost their best friend and encourager; for the Prince had delighted in that rational amusement a long while: but lately, he had a laudable and princely ambition to excel all others'.[22] We must assume that Augusta terminated poor Frederick's gardening projects and tidied things up. This is implied in the estimate of June 1753 of Robert Greening, who by then had succeeded

Dillman in charge of Kew: 'To Planting the Mount', and finishing the digging of his lake. In March 1757, on the cusp of the new Kew Gardens, we have a reference to the gardens extending from the house to 'the Hedge which goes from the Little Mount in Love Lane to the Chinese Arch by the Road'.[23] On 22 August 1757 Robert Wood, of Palmyra and Baalbec fame, whom I suspect was an *éminence grise* at Kew, congratulated Chambers 'upon the compliments paid you by the Prince & upon Lord Bute's friendship'. As Chambers replied to Wood:

> My hands are full of work, but my pockets are not full of money. The prince employs me three mornings in a week to teach him architecture; the building [and] other decorations at Kew fill up the remaining time. The princess has the rest of the week, which is scarcely sufficient as she is forever adding new embellishments at Kew, all which I direct the execution [and] measure the work. I have also the care of the house there, Carlton House in London with three other habitations occupied in different parts of the town by her attendants, for which I am rewarded with fifty pounds a year punctually paid by the prince and one hundred by the princess.[24]

This implies initiatives by Augusta. What matters is that there was a partnership between Augusta and Bute in the creation of this famous garden. The future Knight of the Polar Star would teach Prince George architecture in circumstances that were unique among monarchs or princes:[25] to be taught architecture on a building site. No doubt His Royal Highness The Prince of Wales envies that aspect of his ancestor's upbringing.

NOTES

1. My interest in Frederick and Augusta was at first engendered by my studies of Sir William Chambers in the 1960s, which led me into communication with the late Frances Vivian, an eccentric if ever there was one, whose passion in life was Viking Warrior, a

racehorse, to whom she wrote love letters. Frances was a doughty old-fashioned scholar, whose latter years were dedicated to the life of Frederick. Her manuscript has been edited by Roger White under the superintendence of the Royal Librarian for publication. To her I owe much of my knowledge of Frederick, and indeed to her memory I dedicate this paper.

2. J. Gamer, *Matteo Alberti*, Dusseldorf, 1978, pp. 57–115 and fig. 12. This is the only biography of this uncommonly interesting architect.

3. BL, Add. MS 24401, f. 5, warrants for coach bills, Midsummer to Christmas 1729: 27-8 May to Lord Orkney at Cliveden; 1 August to Lord Ashburnham's; 13 August to Twickenham; 21 August to Claremont; 3 September to Chiswick.

4. Reported in *Gloucester Journal*, 5 August 1729.

5. This could have been either Ashburnham House, Westminster, or perhaps Ampthill Park, Bedfordshire.

6. For this period of Kew's growth see R. Desmond, *Kew: The History of the Royal Botanic Gardens*, London, 1995, chapters 1–3; and J. Harris, *Sir William Chambers, Knight of the Polar Star*, London, 1970, pp. 32–40.

7. Frederick as a collector is discussed by K. Rorschach, 'Frederick, Prince of Wales (1707–51) as Collector and Patron', *Walpole Society*, LV, 1989–90 (1993), pp. 1–76.

8. *King's Works*, V, pp. 138–9, quoting *Survey of London*, pp. 71–2; but see also David Coombs's excellent article, 'The Garden at Carlton House of Frederick Prince of Wales and Augusta Princess Dowager of Wales', *Garden History*, XXV, no. 2, winter 1997, pp. 153–70.

9. J. Harris, 'A Carlton House Miscellany: William Kent and Carlton House Garden', *Apollo*, October 1991, pp. 251–5.

10. Sir Thomas Robinson, letter to Lord Carlisle, 23 December 1734. HMC *Reports*, Castle Howard, VI, 1897, pp. 143–4.

11. Duchy of Cornwall Archives, Household accounts vouchers of Frederick, Prince of Wales, in particular VI, ff. 1, 293, but also f. 258d and f. 260d; also *King's Works*, V, 1976, pp. 262–82.

12. Duchy of Cornwall Archives, Household accounts of Frederick, Prince of Wales, VII, ff. 142 and 355, and XIX, f. 48. Thatched garden buildings were one of Kent's specialities.

13. For Bute I rely upon Francis Russell's magisterial *John, 3rd Earl of Bute, Patron and Collector*, London, 2004.

14. Duchy of Cornwall Archives, Household accounts of Frederick, Prince of Wales, XV, ff. 351–3.
15. *Survey of London*, vol. 34, p. 447.
16. The subject of three canvases by John Wootton which remain in the Royal Collection (RCIN 406898, 400507 and 400505).
17. For Servandoni, see H. Colvin, *A Biographical Dictionary of British Architects 1600–1840*, New Haven and London, 1995, pp. 858–9; and in the forthcoming 4th edition.
18. Vertue Notebooks, *Walpole Society*, XXX, 1955, p. 153.
19. Rorschach makes an uncertain case for Goupy designing the House of Confucius, but the truth is there are no payments to him, whereas there are regular payments for other lesser chinoiserie decorations at Kew. See also the forthcoming biography by Vivian, chapter 18, part 3, 'Architecture is Frederick's Last Delight'.
20. Harris 1970, chapters 2 and 3; see also *Sir William Chambers*.
21. Harris 1970, pp. 18–32; and see also J. Harris, 'Exoticism at Kew', *Apollo*, August 1963, pp. 103–8.
22. W. Darlington, *Memorials of John Bartram and Humphry Marshall*, London, 1849, pp. 184, 367.
23. Desmond 1995, chapter 2, 'Prince Frederick at Kew', pp. 20–29.
24. Royal Academy of Arts archives, London.
25. Such as Gustavus III of Sweden, Prince Franz of Anhalt-Dessau at Wörlitz, or Frederick the Great.

Inside the painting (inscription panel):

John third Earl of Bute
Knight of the Thistle and of the Garter
appointed
First Lord of the Treasury
1762
when he concluded the Treaty of Peace called
Peace of Paris
This, the original Picture painted by order of
The Prince of Wales, afterwards George
the Third, was given by His Majesty in
1763 to John Lord Mountstuart.

9. Allan Ramsay, *John, 3rd Earl of Bute*, 1762. Bute House, Edinburgh

2

Lord Bute and King George III

FRANCIS RUSSELL

The elder surviving son of James Stuart, 2nd Earl of Bute and his wife, Lady Anne Campbell, John Stuart (fig. 9), styled Viscount Mount Stuart, was born at Edinburgh in 1713.[1] Much of his childhood was, however, passed in and near London. His father's early death in 1723 left Bute, as he now became, a minor of nine, under the guardianship of curators including his mother, who returned to Scotland, and her brothers, John, 2nd Duke of Argyll and 1st Duke of Greenwich, and Archibald, Lord Ilay, later 3rd Duke of Argyll. It was to their houses that Bute was sent in holidays from Eton, and their influence was of immense importance. Both brothers were outstanding patrons of architects: Argyll, like so many of Marlborough's associates, was a serious collector of pictures, as also of china; his brother was a determined bibliophile, with a voracious taste for architectural drawings, and one of the greatest collectors of plants of the age. Bute's experience of Sudbroke, and presumably of Adderbury, the Duke's houses, and Ilay's Whitton with its outstanding garden, helped to form his own tastes.

Perhaps because one of his father's brothers lived in Jacobite exile in Rome, Bute was not sent on a Grand Tour. Instead he went to Groningen and subsequently to Leiden before returning in 1734 to take control of his inheritance. He centred his life on his father's new house, Mount Stuart, on the Isle of Bute, just off the west coast of Scotland. In 1735 he made what was described as a 'runaway' match with Mary Wortley Montagu (fig. 15). For a decade they lived for the most part in Scotland. Minor architectural works, described in detail in correspondence with his Eton friend Thomas Worsley,[2] the laying out of an ambitious garden and a programme of planting were among the activities of these years. Too poor to live in appropriate style in London, Bute was rich enough to form a serviceable library and clearly came to study its contents with a passionate determination: architecture, the history of painting, and natural history were strongly represented, as the catalogue of his books at Mount Stuart proves.[3] And there can be little doubt that after ten years of near exile on his island, Bute was immeasurably better informed on such subjects than the vast majority of his contemporaries. The Butes' plans to return to London were resisted by her parents, the immensely rich Edward Wortley Montagu and the celebrated Lady Mary – whose intelligence Lady Bute inherited to the full, but to which she added a tact altogether lacking in her mother – but they did so in 1746. Ilay, himself childless and more understanding, eventually secured them the reversion of Kenwood, formerly occupied by the 2nd Earl, where Bute was to create the second of his great gardens. To begin with, however, the couple moved between Twickenham and White Waltham. It was at this stage that chance intervened. Bute was given a lift to Egham Races by an apothecary, and met the Prince of Wales:

> The weather proving rainy, it was proposed in order to amuse His Royal Highness before his return home, to make a party at cards, but a difficulty occurred about finding persons of sufficient rank to sit down at the same table with him.[4]

Bute was called on to make up numbers. By the time play finished, the apothecary had gone and the Prince took Bute to Cliveden. The Earl quickly became an habitué of the Prince's court, whether at Leicester House, at Kew or at Cliveden. Acting was one mutual interest, but Bute's other artistic interests must also have drawn him to the flamboyant, and in some ways unreliable, Prince and to many of his associates. Not all of these will have recognised how different in

10. Allan Ramsay, *Augusta, Princess Dowager of Wales,*
*c.*1764. Private Collection

character from Frederick was his wife, Augusta of Saxe-Gotha
(fig. 10), unassuming yet determined, most certain in her sense
of duty. The Butes evidently did not; and by 1748 Lady Bute
was known to be a friend of the Princess.

Bute's advent as a courtier was marked in 1749 by his
appointment as a Lord of the Bedchamber; his salary from the

post must have been as welcome as the trust this implied. The Prince's death in 1751 came as a massive blow to the disaffected politicians who had attached themselves to him in hope of future preferment; Lady Mary was eloquent in her expression of sympathy to her daughter – and of course Bute's salary lapsed. The Butes' discretion and that of Princess Augusta meant that the world was quite unaware that the result of the Prince's death was vastly to increase the Earl's role at Leicester House. Princess Augusta's faith in Bute is perfectly expressed in a brief note that survives in the Bute archives.

> I desire Lord Bute to be my partner
> Augusta[5]

It was one thing for the Prince to accept Bute as a companion for amateur theatricals and garden projects, but quite another for the Princess to extend her trust in whatever way this note implies.[6]

What of the – in some ways backward – 13-year-old George, now Prince of Wales? His official advisers, chosen by his grandfather, had to yield place to an unofficial mentor, to whose position the conventional designation of tutor does inadequate justice. The very fact of his mother's trust must have counted for much; and the shared experience of the premature loss of their fathers was another bond. The Prince clearly recognised a disinterested devotion: he instinctively sympathised with the essentially non-partisan political views that Bute had perhaps developed during his 'exile' at Mount Stuart, and shared his strong sense of duty and his essential moral standpoints. The Prince responded equally instinctively to Bute's way of life: his belief in the benefits of equestrian exercise and sea water, his personal frugality and lifelong need for time for his studies. What is of more interest to us is that Bute fired the Prince's enthusiasm for his own interests: architecture, the visual arts, botany (Bute's 'darling' subject), music and books. No doubt such interests were latent in the princely genes, but it was unquestionably Bute – addressed from 1757 as 'My Dearest Friend' – who unlocked their secrets for the Prince of Wales. Neither man was cut out to be a social favourite. And the fact that both were in some respects shy can only have strengthened a bond which from the mid-1750s alarmed both King George II and his ministers, and was given public recognition with the Earl's appointment as Groom of the Stole to the Prince in October 1756.

Bute's mission was to prepare the Prince for kingship. Neither the Prince nor his mother was entitled to the financial resources of the Duchy of Cornwall which Frederick, Prince of Wales had spent with such energy.[7] Only one of Frederick's projects was pursued with vigour: the botanical gardens at Kew. The Princess was committed to this, but Bute's was the controlling mind, both where planting was concerned and in architectural matters. Chambers's great volume about the buildings at Kew of 1763 would be dedicated to the King, but in the splendid album of drawings for the publication he presented to Bute, Chambers states that the gardens and buildings were 'Plan'd by His Lordship, and executed under his Inspection.'[8] Although Kew was the Princess Dowager's project, it must, I think, be assumed that Bute sought to interest the Prince in it at every stage.

The *George III & Queen Charlotte* exhibition at The Queen's Gallery in 2004, and its catalogue, allowed us to see how Bute's influence was felt. It is impossible to tell what role he had in Princess Augusta's patronage of Jean-Etienne Liotard, although the artist's later correspondence with him might imply an earlier acquaintance. But with the botanical drawings acquired in Dr Mead's sale in 1754 and with the Avercamps sold in 1759 we are, perhaps, on firmer ground. From 1756, when a 'Separate Account' was opened with Bute's bankers, Campbell and Coutts, the evidence is irrefutable. Henceforward, until well after Bute's political retirement in 1763, it was he who set the course of his master's taste.

The return from Italy of Allan Ramsay in 1757 inaugurated a new phase of royal portraiture. Prince and Earl exchanged

11. Allan Ramsay, *George III when Prince of Wales*,
1757–8. Private Collection

portraits and, as Bute no doubt anticipated, Ramsay's whole length of the former (fig. 11) was the most sophisticated English Royal portrait since the era of Van Dyck. It led directly to the celebrated state portrait of the young King (plate I), of which an early version was given to Bute.

Although Richard Dalton had been patronised by Frederick, Prince of Wales, Bute was evidently responsible for his appointment as Librarian to the Prince's son in 1755. The Earl's passion for books meant that he would inevitably have taken a close interest in Dalton's activities. In 1758 Dalton returned to Italy with instructions to secure drawings and gems – both considered natural adjuncts of the library. The letters in which he reported on his activities to Bute are balanced by recorded payments from the Separate Account.[9] The Royal Collection was transformed by the drawings Dalton secured, supplemented by James Adam's purchase of the Albani collection (the importance of which Dalton had underestimated), by those secured by a young Scottish painter, Jakey Seton, who reported to Bute and indeed painted his son, and, of course by those included in the collection of Consul Joseph Smith, the acquisition of which was the single most important artistic coup of the new reign. Here too Bute's was the decisive contribution. His kinsman General William Graeme had alerted him in 1760 to the likely availability of the collection, and Bute took the initiative, as he later told Sir James Wright: 'When I employ'd my Brother to make the purchase of Mr Smith's noble Collection, I had nothing to traverse me. I was permitted to act as for my self.'[10]

Bute's brother, James Stuart Mackenzie (?1719–1800), was the British envoy at Turin and is known to have been in contact with Smith. His letter book survives to document the ebb and flow of their correspondence, and on 28 January 1763 the transaction was completed, Dalton signing receipts for the collection.[11] Smith's remarkable library subsequently passed to the British Museum, as did his coins, but the pictures permanently transformed the character of the Royal Collection, dominated as this was by dynastic portraiture and the surviving group of renaissance pictures from the collection of King Charles I, supplemented by the old masters secured by Frederick, Prince of Wales. Smith's unrivalled group of Canalettos is justly celebrated, but the depth of the Consul's holdings of other Venetian *settecento* masters including Ricci, Longhi and Zuccarelli, an artist of whom Bute himself was a determined patron, was almost equally remarkable. Smith's old masters were also impressive – as the Vermeer and the late Bellini portrait attest.

Although himself a voracious collector of pictures, choosing to concentrate on the Dutch masters, it is doubtful whether Bute would have encouraged the King to secure Smith's pictures if he had not known that there was space for them. It is therefore significant that the acquisition coincided with an equally momentous purchase of 1762, that of Buckingham House. Here, too, Bute proves to have been the moving spirit, as a recently published letter from the King reveals.

> My Dearest Friend's description of Bucks. House does not in the least exceed what I found on seeing it; there seems to Me but little necessary to make it habitable; as to the Furniture, I would wish to keep nothing but the Picture in the Middle panel of the Japan Room, & the four glasses in the Room, they all having Japan frames, as to the Picture over the Chimney, I don't wish to have it.
>
> All I have to recommend is dispatch that I may seen get possession of it, this will be on my Dearest Friend for Worstley already makes fifty difficultys about getting Sir Charles out; to me it appears as easy for him to be out in a fortnight as in six months; he means to send his family to Col. Sabines for the Summer, & as to his goods, they may as well now be mov'd to an Auctioneers as at any time, & indeed better, the Town being still full, consequently the more probability of selling them well; I send with this the plans of it; the only thing that appears to me necessary to be bought except what is mentioned before, is the trees in the two Green houses; which I find from Worstley are movables.[12]

Although he had arranged the appointment of his old friend Thomas Worsley (1710–78) to the Office of Works, Bute himself was closely involved in the fitting up of the Queen's House – as Buckingham House was renamed – as a note referring to grates proves. He also was the intermediary through whom Lancelot Brown's work at Kensington, and presumably elsewhere, was managed.

12. Johan Zoffany, *The Ladies Anne, Caroline and Louisa Stuart*, c.1763–4.
Tate Britain, London

The most celebrated picture of the Queen's House is of
course Zoffany's portrait of Queen Charlotte (plate III). While
this, like other interiors by the artist, was in no sense a literal
representation, it is a very clear statement of the intended
function of the house as the private royal residence. The
choice of artist is also telling. Zoffany had, as it were, been
discovered by the actor David Garrick. Bute was, however,
quick to recognise his talents, as the two group portraits of his
younger children recently acquired by the Tate demonstrate
(fig. 12). Here again the sovereign followed the taste of his
mentor, who was by now in uneasy and incomplete retreat
from public life but still, two years after his resignation as
Minister in 1763, in private communication with the King.
The great series of pictures commissioned by the King and

Queen from Zoffany thus constitutes a coda to the commissions with which the Earl was associated. Like Bute, the King had reservations about Reynolds, although he had insisted on pre-empting the double portrait of the Earl with his secretary, Mr Jenkinson, commissioned by Lord Eglinton (fig. 13). It is not unreasonable to speculate that the later royal predilection for Gainsborough was partly due to the King's recognition that he was as sensitive a portraitist as Ramsay, with an equal delicacy in the description of drapery. However, after Ramsay's effective retirement from portraiture, it was to Sir Joshua that Bute went in the 1770s for whole lengths of himself and his wife intended as overmantels for Luton (figs. 14 and 15).

There is another intriguing parallel between Bute and the King as picture collectors. Bute was passionately interested in pictures and an exceptionally disciplined collector, but when his walls at Luton were worthily dressed in the mid-1770s he, at least temporarily, gave up shopping. One sees a similar pattern in King George III's collecting. The Smith pictures were appropriately absorbed in the royal palaces, and as the hanging plans for the Queen's House show,[13] the King evidently thought out their arrangement with due care. The abandonment of the project for a new palace at Richmond – where Bute more than coincidentally held the Rangership of the Park – meant that there were fewer walls to fill than would have been anticipated in the mid-1760s. This lack of need for pictures must help to explain the King's slackening pace of acquisition and increasing concentration on books, for which his appetite continued to be as inexhaustible as Bute's in his chosen fields. It may also explain the decision to dispose of many of the Smith pictures, including such outsize masterpieces as the greatest of Ricci's classical *capricci*, now in an English private collection. Dalton is sometimes seen as the villain of such sales. But he could hardly have acted without the King's sanction. The King's intervention was certainly evident in the return to the family of the great Ramsay portrait of Bute and the Reynolds double portrait (figs. 9 and

13. Sir Joshua Reynolds, *John, 3rd Earl of Bute with his secretary, Charles Jenkinson*, 1763. Private Collection

13). The latter was the most ambitious of all ministerial portraits of its century; a work which, as Sir Walter Scott wrote of Reynolds's *Lord Heathfield*, approaches 'those confines

14. Sir Joshua Reynolds, *John, 3rd Earl of Bute*, 1773.
Private Collection

where portrait painting and historical composition meet'.[14] It is ironic that this, the first major picture that King George III acquired on his own initiative, celebrates a man who may be seen to have failed as a minister, but was surely the most civilised mentor in artistic matters who ever advised an English monarch. Without in any way denying the personal

15. Sir Joshua Reynolds, *Mary, Countess of Bute*,
*c.*1777. Private Collection

achievement of King George III, one can see the constructive
influence of Bute in every facet of his artistic and intellectual
life: in the portraits of Ramsay and Zoffany, in the Smith
pictures, in the prodigious acquisitions of old master drawings,
in the books, in the furniture of Vile and the silver of
Hemming, in the great barometer by Cumming – who

supplied similar if less elaborate instruments to Bute and to his son-in-law, Sir James Lowther – and, not least, in the architectural projects of the early years of the reign.[15] The King was indeed well served by his 'Dearest Friend'.

NOTES

1. Francis Russell, *John, 3rd Earl of Bute, Patron and Collector*, London, 2004 (hereafter *Bute*): unless otherwise indicated the information set out below is drawn from this, and quotations are from the Bute MSS at Mount Stuart.
2. Hovingham MSS; see *Bute*, pp. 10–15.
3. *Bute*, pp. 12–14.
4. Sir Nathaniel Wraxall, quoted in *Bute*, p. 17.
5. *Bute*, p. 20.
6. This is to some extent open to interpretation; it is not impossible, for example, that the note might refer to a dance. That it should be the only communication from the Princess preserved among the well-known series of letters and notes to Bute from her son suggests, however, far greater significance.
7. Only the eldest son of a reigning monarch is entitled to the Duchy of Cornwall revenues.
8. *Bute*, p. 31.
9. *Bute*, p. 38; the full letter is published in the appendix, p. 239.
10. Letter of 21 August 1767, quoted in *Bute*, p. 55.
11. Bute MSS.
12. Harrowby MSS (in *Bute*, p. 51).
13. See F. Russell, 'King George III's picture hang at Buckingham House', *Burlington Magazine*, CXXVIII, 1987, pp. 524–31.
14. Sir H. Grierson, ed., *The Letters of Sir Walter Scott*, London, 1932–7, XI, p. 290 (slightly misquoted by the present writer in *Portraits of Sir Walter Scott*, London, 1987, p. 19).
15. As a conversation with Jonathan Scott at the symposium prompted me to realise, Bute's influence can be sensed also in the *lacunae* of the King's taste: for example, his lack of interest in classical sculpture. Bute passed on the Egyptian antiquities he received from his errant brother-in-law to the British Museum, evidently not sharing Worsley's enthusiasm for such things; apart from a set of copies intended for the façade at Luton, he bought no significant works of sculpture.

Plate I. Allan Ramsay, *George III*, 1761–2. RCIN 405307

Plate II. George Knapton, *The Family of Frederick, Prince of Wales*, 1751. RCIN 405741

Plate III. Johan Zoffany, *Queen Charlotte with her two eldest sons*, c.1765. RCIN 400146

Plate IV. George III's State Coach in the Royal Mews, Buckingham Palace

Plate V. Attributed to John Wootton, *George III's procession to the Houses of Parliament*, 1762. RCIN 402002

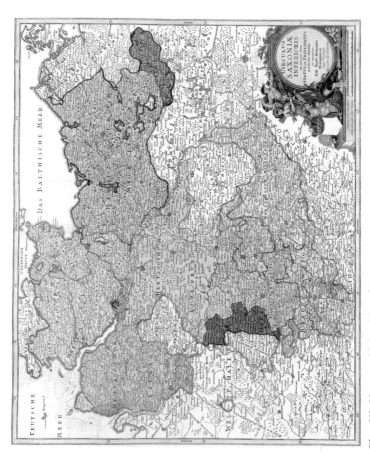

Plate VI. Homann Heirs, *Map of Lower Saxony*, 1784. Hanover is highlighted in the west, Mecklenburg in the east. British Library, London

Plate VII. Johann Ziesenis, *Queen Charlotte when Princess Sophie Charlotte of Mecklenburg-Strelitz*, 1760–1. RCIN 403562

Plate VIII. William Vile, *Jewel cabinet*, 1762. Mahogany, amboyna, rosewood, holly, olive, padouk, oak, ivory. RCIN 35487

3

George III's State Coach in context

JONATHAN MARSDEN

The context of my title is not a vehicular one. George III's
State Coach, which was commissioned at the end of 1760 and
completed two years later, has been studied in relation to
contemporary coaches by others far better qualified for the
task. My context is the rather more general one with which
this section of the book is concerned, the context in which
George III ascended the throne.[1]

The onset of a new reign is a suitable time for grand
gestures, for change, and for renewal, especially if the
preceding reign has been long, as it was in the case of
George II (ruled 1727–60). Certainly, a new state coach was
required, to replace one that had been in use since the reign
of Queen Anne and must by now have been both
unfashionable and scarcely roadworthy. The interesting
question is how this routine requirement was fulfilled by
what has been described as one of the very greatest collective
works of art of eighteenth-century England, in which the
several arts of architecture, painting and sculpture came
together to create something that was greater than all of
them (plate IV). We would surely be mistaken in believing
either that its design and complicated iconographical scheme
were conjured up by the young King himself, or that such
matters were considered for the first time when the official
order was placed in November 1760. Can it, in fact, be
regarded as a summation of some of the ideals and aspirations
that were being advanced as the new reign began? The
answer may be found by an examination of the particularly

close-knit circle of individuals responsible for creating the coach.

Among those involved, the artists – Sir William Chambers (1723–96), Joseph Wilton (1722–1803) and Giovanni Battista Cipriani (1727–85) – are the best known, for they were central figures in George III's artistic life in the 1760s: Chambers had been his architectural tutor and in 1761 was appointed as Joint Architect of the Board of Works; Wilton for his part was appointed 'Sculptor to His Majesty' in 1764; and Cipriani's profile drawing of the King's head, made in 1768, was widely used as an official likeness.[2] All three were among the founding members of the Royal Academy, of which Chambers was also the first Treasurer.

The State Coach was by no means their first or only collaboration. In 1756 they had worked together on the remarkable new teaching academy established by the Duke of Richmond in Whitehall. Chambers designed the building, while Wilton stocked it with exemplary casts of ancient and more recent sculptures from Rome and Florence, and was appointed jointly with Cipriani as the academy's keeper. More significantly, Chambers had introduced Wilton for the creation of the Gallery of Antiques at Kew, for which the sculptor supplied a number of classically inspired statues.[3]

The mechanics of their collaboration on the coach can be understood from the surviving drawings and other sources. As Chambers's first project for the new King, the coach reflected his studies of antiquities in Rome, and made use of the French neoclassical language that he had learnt in Paris. His symbolism, notably the palm branches and the corner trophies of 'decommissioned' weapons, brilliantly suited the national mood after the great Year of Victories of 1759. Comparison of the design from Chambers's office now in the Royal Library[4] with a drawing in Sir John Soane's Museum which must be by Wilton[5] reveals how the sculptor imparted a real sense of energy and propulsion to the four tritons. These figures – the younger ones on the front announcing the arrival of the Monarch of the Oceans, and those on the back (who are both more elderly and winged) spreading Good Government over the Empire – were modelled by Wilton and carved from an aggregated mass of small blocks of walnut by the ship carver Nicholas Collett. Cipriani's paintings, which were the very last ingredient to be finished and were undertaken in Wilton's studio in Newman Street, have most recently been interpreted as a cycle of the Four Elements.[6] If the coach can be seen as a triumphal 'peace chariot', it also fulfilled to an unprecedented extent the need for a travelling throne canopy or baldacchino for the display of the king's person in public. As originally configured, the coach was glazed with very large panels of glass on all sides.[7]

But Wilton, Chambers and Cipriani cannot take all the credit for this magnificent *gesamtkunstwerk*. In the background are two further figures, on whom it will perhaps be profitable to throw some light here. They were Francis Hastings, 10th Earl of Huntingdon (1729–89; fig. 16), the official who commissioned the coach, and Thomas Hollis (1720–74; fig. 20), nonconformist, collector, antiquary, iconographer, political advocate and patron, Dorset landowner, bibliographer, bibliophile, epigrapher, and universal benefactor. He was Cipriani's most enduring patron, and between June and October 1762 the two of them met at least seven times to discuss the iconography of the panels on the State Coach (fig. 17).[8]

The coach was 'ordered to be created' at the very start of the new reign, in November 1760. Almost six years earlier, at the beginning of 1755, four passengers had embarked for England from Italy, having lately been in Florence.[9] It seems that Chambers, Wilton and Cipriani set sail on the same vessel, together with G.B. Cappezzuoli, a Florentine sculptor who was one of those responsible for making the little presentation model of the State Coach now in the possession of the Worshipful Company of Coachmakers.[10] Late in 1754 Horace Mann, the British Resident at Florence, had reported to Horace Walpole the arrival of a young nobleman, the Earl of Huntingdon:

16. Sir Joshua Reynolds, *Francis Hastings, 10th Earl of Huntingdon*, 1754. Huntington Library, San Marino

who . . . will certainly make a great figure . . . [he] has that easy politeness that distinguishes those who have kept the best company . . . He has learned Italian to a surprising degree of perfection in a month, and which he studies for three hours every morning, and then passes as many more with Doctor Cocchi and his medals, after which he stays till half past four in the Gallery, to examine the statues and busts with Wilton.[11]

Walpole replied: 'Lord Huntingdon I know very well, and like very much; he has parts, great good breeding, and will certainly make a figure.'[12]

Dr Antonio Cocchi (fig. 18) was a good friend of Mann, and of Englishmen in general. A medical doctor by training, he was the Keeper of the Grand Ducal collections in Florence for twenty years from 1738. It was not uncommon for him and Wilton to show English visitors round the collections, but Huntingdon may have enjoyed special treatment because Cocchi had travelled extensively with his father thirty years earlier, and indeed had lived in London for a year as the 9th Earl's guest.[13]

Mann writes to Walpole at one point about Francis Huntingdon's and Cocchi's fondness for inventing inscriptions,[14] such as the one that appears on the magnificent bust of Cocchi which was commissioned from Wilton by Huntingdon in 1755.[15] After their return to England, Huntingdon commissioned his own portrait bust from Wilton (fig. 19), with another characteristic inscription.[16] Very happily these two busts, which stood together at Donington Park, Huntingdon's house in Leicestershire, are now reunited in the British Galleries of the Victoria and Albert Museum having been divided for many years.[17] The origins of Wilton's fine bust of Thomas Hollis are less certain, but we may suppose that it was commissioned by the sitter, shortly after Wilton's return from Florence.[18]

That Wilton was not only a client but a friend of Huntingdon and acquainted with Hollis invites us to suppose that the two sitters also knew one another. After all, Huntingdon was a member of the Council of the Society for the Encouragement of Arts, Manufactures and Commerce, where Hollis was an active committee member. But there is no mention of Huntingdon in Hollis's diary,[19] nor does Hollis appear as a correspondent among Lord Huntingdon's papers.[20] Despite this they had too many friends and acquaintances in common *not* to have known each other. For example they both corresponded over several decades with the Revd

17. Giovanni Battista Cipriani, *Preliminary sketches for the panels of the state coach*. Pen and ink. RL 17969

Theophilus Lindsey, vicar of Puddletown in Dorset;[21] Hollis sponsored the publication of Lindsey's religious tracts, while Huntingdon was patron of his living.

Descended from the Duke of Clarence, brother of Edward IV, and from Mary, sister of Henry VIII, Francis Hastings was the son of the redoubtable Selina, who gave her name to that branch of Methodism known as Lady Huntingdon's Connexion. We have already read Horace Mann's and Horace Walpole's estimations of him in 1755. Here is an extract from one of the famous letters from the Earl of Chesterfield to his son, five years earlier in date:

> next to you he is the truest object of my affection and esteem . . . His parts are as quick as his knowledge is extensive; and if quality were worth putting into an account . . . his is the first almost in this country: the figure he will make soon after he returns to it will, if I am not more mistaken than ever I was in my life, equal *his* birth and *my* hopes.[22]

After the death of the 9th Earl of Huntingdon in 1746, Francis Hastings had succeeded at the age of only 17, and Lord Chesterfield had decided to take on the role of mentor. There

(left) 18. Joseph Wilton, *Dr Antonio Cocchi*, 1755. Marble.
Victoria and Albert Museum, London
(right) 19. Joseph Wilton, *Francis Hastings, 10th Earl of Huntingdon*, 1761.
Marble. Government Art Collection, London.

is another considerable body of letters of advice from
Chesterfield to Huntingdon, covering twenty years.[23]

When Frederick, Prince of Wales died so unexpectedly in
1751, Chesterfield wrote to his protégé about the new Prince,
the 13-year-old future George III:

> that child, who will in two years be adolescent, and possibly
> King, ought not then to be a stranger to your name, your
> person, and, above all, to your abilities. You must be
> acquainted with him and about him, before he has taken all his
> habits and most of his early impressions.[24]

A serious Grand Tourist, Huntingdon acquired in Italy
(through Joseph Wilton) a substantial group of casts of antique
sculpture, and commissioned views of Florence from Thomas
Patch.[25] These were kept at Donington, where the Earl must
also have deployed the massive, 10,000-ounce silver wine
cooler by Abraham Portal of 1764, now in the Dallas Museum
of Art, which bears his arms and which in its design recalls the
work of Chambers. Although Huntingdon is not among the

architect's known patrons, we may recall the letter which Robert Adam wrote from Rome in February 1755 in which he gave his estimation of his future rival, and in which Adam specifically names Huntingdon as a likely future patron of Chambers, as someone who, as he put it, was 'determined to support him to the utmost of his power'.[26]

Huntingdon returned to England in 1756, the year in which the 18-year-old Prince of Wales was allowed his first official household appointments. Lord Chesterfield had prepared the ground with the Duke of Newcastle, and in October Huntingdon was appointed Master of the Horse. At the accession four years later he assumed the same appointment in the new King's Household. Huntingdon and Bute, the Groom of the Stole, were by some distance the first household appointments to be made. Huntingdon then succeeded Bute as Groom of the Stole in 1761, and in that position put in hand the arrangements for the coronation. At the coronation itself he carried the Sword of State.[27] It is perhaps worth reminding ourselves that the symbolic importance of the chief ornaments of the Regalia, including the Sword of State, is embodied by the elaborately carved cresting of the State Coach, where they are held aloft by three *genii* to ensure maximum visibility.

Thomas Hollis really is the quintessential *éminence grise*. Among the many designs he commissioned from Cipriani is an engraving of 1767 (fig. 20), in which Hollis appears twice: as a Roman in the roundel on the obelisk and in contemporary dress at the bottom right. The long inscription is from Plutarch's life of Brutus. An image such as this, in which Hollis identifies himself with the tyrannicide republican, would seem to sit oddly with an apparent interest in royal ceremonial.

Hollis, as a Dissenter, was barred from Oxford and Cambridge and was therefore privately educated. He was admitted to Lincoln's Inn and although he did not pursue his legal career he long afterwards styled himself 'Of Lincoln's Inn'. Having inherited two substantial fortunes, from his father

20. Giovanni Battista Cipriani, *Allegorical portrait of Thomas Hollis*,
1767. Engraving. Houghton Library, Harvard University

and grandfather, he resolved on a career of private, often
anonymous, patronage, in pursuit of what he referred to as his
'Plan of Public Service', the precise details of which he seems
never to have set down, but which was clearly devoted to the
promotion of Whig principles.[28] He was a discriminating
collector. Consul Smith sent him books and an introduction

to Canaletto, from whom Hollis commissioned six views of Venice and London, including the famous interior of the Rotunda at Ranelagh now in the National Gallery,[29] and the well-known view of Old Walton Bridge now at Dulwich.[30] Both privately and as a Committee member of the Society of Arts, Hollis commissioned medals, mostly to designs by Cipriani, commemorating the victories of 1759, and the accession of George III.[31] His connections with artists were very extensive. He advised Nollekens and Wedgwood (whom he allowed to copy his collection of antique vases), and corresponded with Piranesi, to whom he presented a set of drawing instruments in 1769 and who in turn gave him a set of his engravings, which Hollis duly gave to the Society of Antiquaries. Hollis was a patron of printers and publishers, and one of the chief contributors to the restocking of the library of Harvard University after a disastrous fire had carried off many of the books which his grandfather, also Thomas Hollis, had donated. His work as a designer of inscriptions can be seen on the title page of Robert Adam's great publication on the ruins of Diocletian's palace at Spalatro.

As a propagandist, Hollis contributed pseudonymously to periodicals, in particular the *London Chronicle*, and sent donations to editors 'for services to freedom'.[32] It was in the *London Chronicle* that the explanation of Cipriani's painted coach panels was published, in the report of the coach's first public appearance in November 1762 (plate V), and it seems certain that this explanation, which has been officially reprinted at each subsequent coronation, was written by Hollis.[33] In passing it is worth pointing out that the *Chronicle*'s identification of the scene on the central door panel on the 'far' side of the coach, 'Industry and Ingenuity giving a Cornucopia to the Genius of England' (fig. 21), is at best inexact. The fact that this mistake has gone unnoticed for 240 years is a salutary reflection on the public comprehension of painted allegories, or perhaps specifically those painted allegories that are continuously moving four feet from the ground in front of a dense crowd.

21. Giovanni Battista Cipriani, offside centre panel of the State Coach

How do the foregoing remarks affect the way we regard the State Coach? To begin to answer that question we should refer to what Hollis wrote in his diary following the death of George II and the accession of George III. He says of the new king:

May his pattern be ALFRED, as historiated by the incomparable John Milton; and may he be supported effectually in his counsels and undertakings throughout a long and glorious reign, by wife and faithful parliaments and ministers, and by the affections of his people, that the constitution may be preserved,

22. Joseph Wilton, *Oliver Cromwell*, *c*.1762. Marble.
Government Art Collection, London

the age re-formed, science and art encouraged, posterity
adhered to, mankind in general benefited.[34]

Hollis's heroes were Alfred, Milton and Cromwell, the heroes
in fact of the Whig 'patriots'. Cromwell might seem a dubious
hero, but as Francis Blackburne, author of the *Memoir* of
Hollis published in 1780, put it, Cromwell 'had a proper
regard for the honour of his country, which has been seldom
carried higher than it was during his administration.'
Cromwell was more than a cult figure in the eighteenth
century, as the numerous newly made portraits testify.[35] The
most significant of these for the present argument was the
marble bust commissioned from Wilton by the Earl of
Huntingdon (fig. 22). This portrait, inspired at least partly by

54

the death mask of Cromwell in the Bargello at Florence, was placed in the Hall at Donington Park, along with those of Huntingdon himself, Dr Cocchi and Pythagoras (also commissioned from Wilton). The Cromwell bust is described at Donington by J. Throsby in his *Select Views in Leicestershire* of 1790, and he adds that this bust 'secured the artist an honourable employment under his present Majesty'. The bust was exhibited at the Society of Artists' Exhibition in 1761, which must have been where the King saw it, and Throsby is most probably referring to Wilton's appointment as 'Sculptor to His Majesty' rather than to his commission for the coach. It cannot have been the first time the King had come across Wilton, who was working for the Royal Family at Kew in 1757.

George III's admiration of the bust, and Hollis's appeal to the 'pattern' of Alfred the Great, are reminders of the political principles under which the young King was educated. As John Brooke put it, he was nurtured on the pure milk of Whiggism, albeit flavoured by Lord Bute, and the effects of this can be seen in his student essays on history, where, for example, he credits the constitutional settlement of 1688 with having saved the nation 'from the iron rod of arbitrary power'.[36] Whilst alive to Cromwell's faults, the student prince calls him 'a friend of Justice and Virtue'.[37]

In 1747 the 'patriotic' poet Mark Akenside published an *Ode* dedicated to Lord Huntingdon, on his coming of age.[38] Huntingdon was one of three or four aristocrats of a new generation on whom the Whig Patriots placed their hopes:

> O Hastings, not to all
> Can ruling Heaven the same endowments lend:
> Yet still doth Nature to her offspring call,
> That to one general weal their different powers they
> bend,
> Unenvious.
>
> . . . The fate which form'd thee in a chosen mould,
> The grateful country of thy sires,
> Thee to sublimer paths demand . . .

> . . . This reign, these laws, this public care,
> Which Nassau gave us all to share,
> Had ne'er adorned the English name,
> Could Fear have silenced Freedom's claim.[39]

This survey of the individuals behind the creation of the coach has been intended to provide an argument for regarding it as a sort of three-dimensional mobile manifesto for the political principles held so strongly by those around the King at the moment of the accession, and sincerely also by the King himself. How happy we can feel that Huntingdon and Hollis were also such fine judges in the arts as to call on Chambers, Wilton and Cipriani to realise their plan.

Postscript

What happened to Huntingdon, and all his promise? When he died, suddenly, at the age of sixty, at the dining table of his nephew and heir Lord Rawdon in 1789, his obituarist in the *Gentleman's Magazine* wrote:

> The late Earl was a man whose virtues would reflect honour on his ancestors, had they been, in fact, more noble than they were. Those virtues were not, it is true, of the most shining nature; they were more useful than dazzling; they were the virtues of society . . .[40]

To the curious historian this seems to be glossing over something, but there does not appear to have been one particular, single reason why, following his dismissal from the office of Groom of the Stole in 1770, he took no further part in public life other than the Lord Lieutenancy of Leicestershire. He does not come across as a likeable character. A womaniser and a misogynist, he had a child by a Parisian dancer early on his Grand Tour, and everything suggests he was impossibly vain and conceited. All the flattery and encouragement he received from Walpole, Mann and Chesterfield seems simply to have gone to his head. He did fall out

with the King over several things, some small and some less
so. The King rebuked him for having allowed one of his
subordinates in the Mews to become involved in a duel, and
when Queen Charlotte gave birth to her first child, Huntingdon burst out to announce the happy event to the King,
unfortunately declaring that the future George IV was a fine
girl. Four years later, in 1766, Huntingdon launched an
unsuccessful claim on a royal title – that of Duke of Clarence
– on the strength of his own royal descent. Not the best way
to get on at court.[41]

NOTES

1. For a description of the coach with further references see J.
   Marsden and J. Hardy, ' "O Fair Britannia, Hail!": the "most
   superb" state coach', *Apollo*, February 2001, pp. 3–12.
2. e.g. *George III & Queen Charlotte*, no. 417.
3. For these undertakings see J. Coutu, 'William Chambers and
   Joseph Wilton', in *Sir William Chambers*, pp. 175–85, and ' "A
   very grand and seigneurial design": The Duke of Richmond's
   Academy in Whitehall', *British Art Journal*, I, no. 2, 2000, pp.
   47–54.
4. RL 17942. The drawing is somewhat enigmatically inscribed *WC.
   The Kings State Coach figures JB Cipriani 1760*.
5. Marsden and Hardy 2001, fig. 17.
6. See Marsden and Hardy 2001.
7. The extent of the glazing has subsequently been reduced. See
   Marsden and Hardy 2001, p. 8 and n. 47.
8. Meetings with Cipriani to discuss the subjects of the paintings on
   the coach are recorded on 24 and 27 June, 14, 15, 16 July, 10
   August and 28 October in Hollis's manuscript diary in the
   Houghton Library, Harvard University. All but the first meeting
   (whose location is unspecified) occurred in Wilton's studio,
   presumably in front of the coach. The paintings were finished by
   the time of the 28 October visit. I am grateful to William Bond
   and Susan Halpert for consulting the manuscript in connection
   with this paper. For Hollis's patronage of Cipriani and other

artists see W.H. Bond, *Thomas Hollis of Lincoln's Inn: A Whig and his Books*, Cambridge, 1990.

9. J. Fleming, *Robert Adam and his Circle*, London, 1964, pp. 135, 347–8.

10. The model is on long-term loan to the Victoria and Albert Museum.

11. *Walpole Correspondence*, XX, p. 457. Letter dated 13 October 1754.

12. *ibid.*, p. 461. Letter dated 9 January 1755.

13. T. Hodgkinson, 'Joseph Wilton and Doctor Cocchi', *Victoria and Albert Museum Bulletin*, III, no. 2, April 1967, pp. 73–80. See also D. Bilbey and M. Trusted, *Victoria and Albert Museum: British Sculpture 1470–2000*, London, 2002, no. 217.

14. *Walpole Correspondence*, XX, p. 480.

15. The inscription on Cocchi's bust ΑΝΤ.ΚΟΚΧΙΟΣ / ΞΑΨΝΕ ΓΗΡΑΣΚΩ ΔΙΔΑΣΚΟΜΕΝΟΣ was translated by Charles Avery for Hodgkinson's article as 'I go on learning as I grow old'.

16. ΖΗΘΙ / ΛΩΓΩΝ ΚΗΦΑΛΛΑΙΟΝ. 'Live! That is the sum of the matter'. I am grateful to Peter Howell for this translation.

17. The bust of Dr Cocchi was latterly in the collection of Sir Ian Walker-Okeover of Okeover Hall, Derbyshire. It was purchased by the Victoria and Albert Museum from Cyril Humphris Ltd in 1966. The bust of Huntington was purchased by the Ministry of Works from Montague Marcussen in 1947.

18. Sotheby's, 8 July 2003, lot 145. The bust is currently on loan to the National Portrait Gallery. See D. Wilson, 'A bust of Thomas Hollis by Joseph Wilton RA', *British Art Journal*, V, no. 3, 2005, pp. 4–26.

19. I am further indebted to William Bond for having searched his index to Hollis's diary.

20. HMC, *Report on the Manuscripts of the late Reginald Rawdon Hastings Esq., of the Manor House, Ashby de la Zouch*, III, London, 1934. These papers were subsequently acquired by the Henry E. Huntington Library, San Marino, California. The HMC calendar is not comprehensive and I am grateful to Mary Robertson, archivist at the Huntington Library, for undertaking a complete search on my behalf.

21. HMC *Hastings*, III, pp. 70ff; Bond 1990, p. 86.

22. Letter dated 22 October 1750 (*The Letters of Philip Dormer Stanhope, Earl of Chesterfield*, ed. J. Bradshaw, London, 1892, I, pp. 359–60).

23. *Letters of Lord Chesterfield to Lord Huntingdon*, with introduction and notes by F.A. Steuart, London, 1923.
24. *ibid.*, p. 43: letter of 8 April 1751.
25. F. Russell, 'Thomas Patch, Sir William Lowther and the Holker Claude', *Apollo*, August 1975, pp. 115–19.
26. Fleming 1964, p. 160.
27. In fact, he carried the Lord Mayor's sword because the Sword of State had been temporarily mislaid. See *Crown Jewels*, I, pp. 496–7.
28. For Hollis's extraordinary career see Bond 1990. See also the essays by Patrick Eyres and Dilys Hobson in *New Arcadian Journal* 55/56, 2003.
29. W.G. Constable, *Canaletto*, 2nd edn, revised by J.G. Links, 2 vols., Oxford, 1976, no. 420.
30. *ibid.*, no. 441.
31. J.L. Abbott, 'Thomas Hollis and the Society, 1756–1774', *Journal of the Royal Society of Arts*, CXIX, 1971–2, pp. 711–15, 803–7 and 874–8.
32. Bond 1990, pp. 83–4.
33. *The London Chronicle or Universal Evening Post*, 25–27 November 1762. See Marsden and Hardy 2001, pp. 9–10, n. 3.
34. MS Houghton Library, Harvard University; F. Blackburne, *Memoirs of Thomas Hollis Esq., F.R. and A.S.S.*, London, 1780, p. 98.
35. Original portrait busts of Cromwell were also made by Roubiliac, Rysbrack, Nollekens and Banks, and plaster casts proliferated.
36. RA GEO, Add. MS 32.
37. *ibid.*
38. 'Ode XVIII, To the Right Honourable Francis Earl of Huntingdon. 1747', *The Poetical Works of Mark Akenside*, London, 1835, pp. 190–98.
39. In 1761 Akenside was appointed Physician-in-Ordinary to Queen Charlotte, an appointment he may have owed to the intervention of Lord Huntingdon.
40. *Gentleman's Magazine*, LIX, 1789, p. 960.
41. For a good summary of Huntingdon's career, with further sources, see R. Asleson and S.M. Bennett, *British Paintings at the Huntington*, New Haven and London, 2001, no. 75.

4

The courts of Hanover and Strelitz

MARCUS KÖHLER

The search for a suitable German wife for the future George III had to be pursued in some haste in order to thwart the developing relationship between Lady Sarah Lennox and the king-to-be. A substantial dossier in the Royal Household Archives in Hanover reveals that, using secret channels, attempts were made to ferret out detailed information about various princesses of marriageable age from second-string German dynasties. For political reasons, princesses from Saxony, Prussia or Sweden seemed rather less suitable.[1]

Two favourites emerged, from the dynasties of Brandenburg-Schwedt and Hessen-Darmstadt. Count Schulenburg, who had been entrusted with the inquiries in Brandenburg, probably presented Princess Sophie Charlotte von Mecklenburg-Strelitz as an additional alternative, precisely at the point when the final selection between the other two was proving tricky. As early as March 1761, Schulenburg was to be found at Mirow, the family's summer residence in Mecklenburg. By May a detailed description of the princess had arrived in London, and the proposal of marriage followed in June. A few weeks later, surrounded by the tightest security because of the Seven Years' War, Sophie Charlotte arrived in Britain.

All the reliable contemporary sources available at the time spoke of an orphaned daughter of the penniless, non-ruling Duke Karl Ludwig Friedrich (1708–52) from the junior branch of the House of Mecklenburg, and the unimportant Duchess Elisabeth Albertine von Sachsen-Hildburghausen

(1713–61). Like other rulers of the smaller German states (for example Dessau, Schaumburg-Lippe or Zerbst), Charlotte's father had been obliged to accept military service in another state to ensure a regular income.

Moreover, when the search for a bride was taking place, the dukedom had been under the control of an external regent for seven years. The court consisted of only a small family of two widows and six young adults.[2] Without the secure income from the state of Ratzeburg and a share of the shipping duty from the River Elbe charged in Boitzenburg, the dukedom would have been unable to survive economically. The family did have more prosperous relations from the senior line in Schwerin, but they were pursuing such hapless political and economic policies in the first half of the eighteenth century that their fortunes were also languishing. So it is not surprising that building work on the palace of Ludwigslust (fig. 23) dragged on for twenty years. In later years Charlotte would present gifts of jewellery and mechanical devices to her cousin Duke Friedrich II in Schwerin, and he seems to have donated the plans for his residence Ludwigslust to the Royal Library along with his own design for a sluice gate. But Charlotte and Friedrich were not personally acquainted.[3] From a travel diary written by Duke Friedrich's son, the Hereditary Prince Friedrich Franz von Mecklenburg-Schwerin, we know he did not stay with the royal family when he was in London in 1782. Instead, he received a number of invitations from them, including one to attend a play performed for him by the children at Windsor Castle. The play texts and cast lists were copied by his travelling companion von Brandenstein.[4]

Understandably, Charlotte's family background gave rise to further inquiries on the part of St James's Palace. The first report to come back from Neustrelitz was a positive view of Charlotte's mother: 'she took great pains to educate her children in the best way.'[5] However, there were doubts whether this provincial princess would be equal to the demands of the English court. After all, following a visit to her

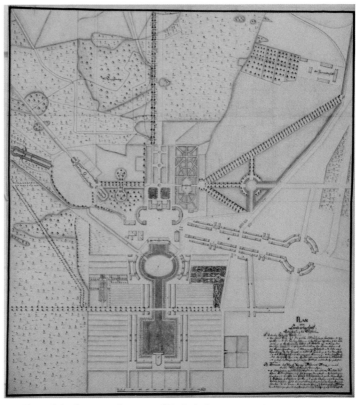

23. Plan of the house and estate of Ludwigslust, c.1750–80.
British Library, London

family at Canow Palace in 1736, even Friedrich II of Prussia
had commented:

> It is an absolute village, and the prince's manor house no more
> than a common hunting-lodge ... I took lodgings at the
> miller's house and had the maid announce me ... where the
> entire Mirow family was assembled ... [the Duke's] mother
> being the most intelligent of all present ... His lady wife is
> small, she was with child, but otherwise seems a very fine
> princess ... The discourse at table was of nothing but all the
> German princes who might be lacking in wisdom ... and after

the good gentleman was thoroughly inebriated, we rose and he, and all his family, promised to come and visit. No doubt he will! But how I am to rid myself of him, God only knows![6]

In spite of this unpromising situation, Charlotte's aunt, the ruling Duchess Sophie Dorothea, *née* Princess of Schleswig-Holstein-Sonderborg-Plön (1692–1765), attempted to create a small cultural hub in Neustrelitz. She kept a good orchestra, in which Johann Christian Hertel, Carl Philipp Emanuel Bach, Johann Friedrich Fasch, and Georg Anton Benda occasionally played. Charlotte's father, for his part, corresponded and played with Vivaldi.[7] Her uncle Friedrich Adolf III (1686–1752) extended the royal residence at Neustrelitz (fig. 24). With its star-shaped ground plan in the baroque style, it displayed similarities to major designs of the period such as the contemporary city plan of Karlsruhe. Following a fire in 1712, extensions to the palace and garden were laid out at some distance from the town by the architect and garden designer Christoph Julius Löwe, with work on the palace being carried out from 1726 to 1731. Along with the Fürstenberg Palace – built between 1745 and 1752, and used as a dower house by Charlotte's aunt Sophie Dorothea – and Sponholz manor house, this is regarded as one of Löwe's greatest achievements. He also built two palaces in Mirow. Of these, the more recent one, erected between 1749 to 1752, still exists. The older of the two, the house in which Charlotte was born, burnt down and was replaced by a new building.[8]

There are two surviving drawings of Neustrelitz Palace, possibly by Löwe, in the King's Topographical Library.[9] The palace also appears in the portrait of Charlotte painted by Johann Georg Ziesenis, the Hanover court painter, on the occasion of her engagement in 1761 (plate VII).[10] Both courtly and personal attributes are in keeping with the Baroque pathos in fashion at the time. The palace, which was her brother's residence, is seen from the courtyard side. A large number of coaches are depicted, possibly a reference to the Queen's departure for Mirow to see a firework display

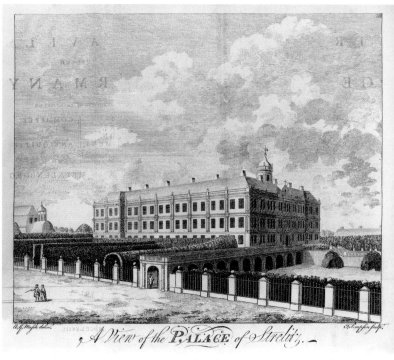

24. J. Simpson after J. Masch, *Neustrelitz Palace*, frontispiece to T. Nugent, *Travels through Germany*, 1768, vol. I. Engraving. British Library, London

before continuing on her journey to England.[11] The future queen is shown in a setting consisting of a drapery, a crown, and a column. When Zoffany, who was familiar with this picture, painted the King and Queen ten years later (plates X and XI), he drew on these elements:[12] unlike George III, Charlotte is shown sitting amidst furniture that is continental in style, beneath a hanging, with a view of an indeterminate landscape. So both portraits contain references to the English and continental backgrounds of the sitters. This distinction is entirely absent from a closely related pair of portraits, painted for the Leineschloss in Hanover (figs. 25 and 26), in which both the King and Queen appear in court dress.[13]

In fact, Charlotte never forgot her German background, just as she was never forgotten in her home country.[14] People prayed for her during her pregnancies, organised court celebrations following the births, and proudly displayed the Chelsea 'Mecklenburg Service'[15] in a garden room at Neustrelitz Palace. The court painter Daniel Wogen dedicated a book on antiquities to her and dared compare Strelitz with Herculaneum.[16] Again and again, aristocratic families from home are mentioned in her correspondence, and she had a particularly high opinion of Stephan Werner von Dewitz (1726–1800), a minister and Schlosshauptman at Strelitz, who had come to London in 1761 and again in 1763 as envoy extraordinary of both Mecklenburg courts. Thomas Nugent, who toured Mecklenburg in 1766 and published a diary, tells of a poem by the divine and antiquary Gottlob Burchard Genzmer (1716–71), rector of Stargard, addressed to the Queen and requesting a donation for his church, which had been destroyed by fire in 1758.[17] Nugent also paid a visit to the Queen's former governess, Frederike Elisabeth von Grabow, née von der Kettenburg (1705–79). She had once lived at court in Vienna, and the experience she gained there, along with her artistic gifts, had enabled her to publish a number of minor works. Working with Genzmer, she had instructed Charlotte in languages, theology and natural history.[18] This was the foundation that shaped the Queen's later interests, and which she was able to pass on to her daughters in particular.

Charlotte's parents must have been well aware that, given their modest circumstances, the only dowry they could pass on to their children was an aristocratic name and a good education. Their main aim was to bring up their children without pretensions, making it easier for them to face a life of privation – as a member of the military, as the wife of a penniless prince or even as a canoness. This education was along the lines of an ideal emphasised in the Universal Encyclopaedia published by Johann Heinrich Zedler in 1737, according to which children were not to be brought up in luxury.[19]

25. Johan Zoffany, *George III*, c.1771. Private Collection

Zedler's views were based on ideas propagated at the University of Halle, mainly by the scholars Christian Thomasius and Christian Wolff.[20] Clarissa Campbell Orr has rightly recognised that the educational ideal in the first half of the eighteenth century can be traced back to the ideas of the Enlightenment, which in turn derived from Protestant

26. Johan Zoffany, *Queen Charlotte*, *c*.1771. Private Collection

Pietism.[21] On this basis, Zedler also explained the role of women, as follows:

> Of course, it cannot be detrimental to a woman if her intellect be improved by the necessary scientific disciplines . . . they are to show their intelligence in household economy; indeed, it falls to them to educate the children, in all of which a virtuous

moral stance is essential. Furthermore, for their pleasure, they may also be permitted a kind of study, they may be poets, they may hold forth on the subject of morals, they may be engaged in botany ... Bringing up the children is the concern that governs everything they do or do not do.[22]

To assess the significance of Charlotte's education, we may look to another, comparable example. Princess Sophie Auguste Friederike von Anhalt-Zerbst (1729–96), the future Empress Catherine II of Russia, was also born into a family living in modest circumstances. Her father Christian August only held the post of Governor of Stettin. Nevertheless, both parents ensured that the child had a good basic education at the hands of a preacher named Wagner and a governess called Elisabeth Cardel. When, in 1745, Sophie took the name of Ekaterina and married Crown Prince Petr Fedorovich, heir to the Russian throne, her education served her well. Her memoirs, which cover her time as Crown Princess, are essentially reflections about herself of a kind that can be traced back to Pietistic theology.[23] The foundation of all the abilities she was later to display in literature and the sciences had been laid in Stettin. In the 1780s she actually took over the education of her eldest grandchildren, Alexander and Constantine. For Alexander, she wrote the *roman à clef*, *Tsarevitch Khlor*, which is based on Fénelon's *Les aventures de Télémaque, fils d'Ulysse* (1699). It is no coincidence that scenes from the story of Telemachus can be seen on the panel above the door in Zoffany's painting of Queen Charlotte and her two eldest sons (plate III), and that George, Prince of Wales is dressed in the costume of Telemachus himself. Some other elements in this picture should also be examined for possible educational references; such as the Queen at her dressing-table on a summer afternoon, the crane on the lawn, Lady Charlotte Finch's reflection in a mirror, the Queen flanked by two Chinese figures. So it seems that some of Charlotte's unique characteristics can be explained by reference to the typical education of a German princess. But research into this field is still in its infancy.[24]

In the context we are discussing here, it is also of interest to note that in Prussia this kind of education, which was indebted to Pietism and the Enlightenment, was mainly promoted by Friedrich Wilhelm I. As Martina Weinland has shown, his ideas were different from those of his wife Sophie-Dorothea, Princess of Hanover and sister to George II – she preferred a courtly, absolutist style of education.[25] These differences not only illustrate two different educational ideals in the first half of the eighteenth century; they also led to frequent tensions between the Prussian king and his son, the Crown Prince Friedrich.

George II, like his sister, supported the Hanoverian educational ideal. As in Prussia, the relationship between the King and his eldest son, the Prince of Wales, was marked by tension. But around 1750 this conflict between the generations resulted in a change taking place within the English royal family. In George III, it produced a new understanding of what it meant to be a ruler.[26] Let us first explore his circumstances more closely.

George II's last visit to Hanover took place in 1755. The state was administered via the German Chancery in London, which also co-ordinated its political direction with English policy if necessary. During the Seven Years' War, it became clear that the only way England's interests could be represented was for Hanover to adopt a line that was seen to be independent. The entanglement of English and continental imperial German policy was too opaque for the English parliament. When Friedrich Karl von Hardenberg (1696–1763) spent time in London as a Hanoverian diplomat during the peace negotiations in 1763, he was made painfully aware that he could expect no support or help from London. Hanover was on its own.[27]

The Hanoverian *Ceremonialbücher*, which correspond roughly to a court circular and are kept in the Royal Household Archive, give a good general overview of the court during this period.[28] In January 1763 the Queen's birthday was celebrated for the first time, followed by the

(left) 27. Johan Zoffany, *Prince Ernst of Mecklenburg-Strelitz*, 1772.
RCIN 406813
(right) 28. Johann Ziesenis, *Prince Carl II of Mecklenburg-Strelitz*, 1770.
RCIN 402463

King's birthday in June. In each case, around 120 people were invited to attend a ball and a dinner, with the seneschal presiding. In winter, there were also weekly concerts. Births were not celebrated. Occasionally aristocratic relatives were provided with accommodation, and at times court mourning was ordered. But the court itself only consisted of a small number of people.[29]

This remained the status quo until, following a trip to London, the Princes Carl and Ernst von Mecklenburg-Strelitz (figs. 27 and 28) became governors of Hanover and Celle respectively, and as such were obliged to undertake official duties on behalf of the court. They did not live at the palace, but moved into the *Fürstenhof* manor house, also called Beaulieu House.[30] Carl left no trace of his presence in Hanover. Instead, following his return from another trip to England in 1771, he invested all his energy in extending his family's country house of Hohenzieritz – reminiscent of

Nostell Priory – and into a garden designed by Archibald Thompson.[31] Ernst, on the other hand, built himself a manor house in Celle with a park that soon became famous.[32] For a time, Celle, which is thirty miles from Hanover, flourished thanks to the presence of George III's sister, Queen Caroline of Denmark, who was sent into exile there in 1772.[33]

The first member of the English royal family to take up residence in Hanover during George III's reign was Edward Augustus, Duke of York (1739–67), who was there from June to August 1765. William, Duke of Gloucester came to stay in 1769 and again in the summer of 1770, when he was accompanied by his mother. During this time, there were not only visits to the fortress of Wilhelmstein, the University of Göttingen and the spa Bad Pyrmont, but also evenings of making music with the Princes Ernst and Carl.[34] Another eleven years went by before William was followed by Frederick, Duke of York and Prince-Bishop of Osnabrück, who represented the Elector from 1781 to 1787. Before he arrived some initial changes were made at the Palace. To quote one record: 'All the table services stored in the court silver vault are of such antiquated design as to be unsuitable for use, given the current mode of serving.' That is why, starting in the early 1770s, the inventory of silver services was extended by ordering from French suppliers and purchasing the so-called Hardenberg service.[35] In addition the garden of the summer residence Montbrillant was landscaped in 1779. However, no changes were made to the baroque garden at Herrenhausen (fig. 29) with its famous fountain, which had been so admired for its high jet by early eighteenth-century travellers. This sense of historical reference can also be found in the portraits by Zoffany in his allusions to Van Dyck. Apparently, there was a willingness to accept the dated garden in order to represent a family tradition.

In the 1780s a new style of holding court led to regular visits by neighbouring princes. William was in Hanover from August 1783 to May 1785, Edward was in Lüneburg and Hanover from May 1785 to May 1787. And from July 1786

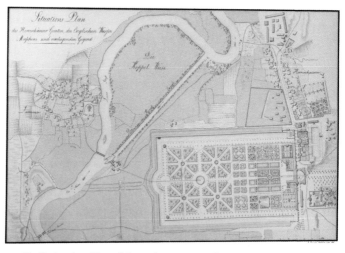

29. R. Reinecke, *Plan of the gardens at Herrenhausen*, 1808–18.
Pen and ink and watercolour. RL 29569

Ernest, Duke of Cumberland, Adolphus, Duke of Cambridge,
and Augustus, Duke of Sussex all studied at the university in
Göttingen (fig. 30). The former two stayed until the beginning of 1791, but Augustus left for Italy as early as October
1790.[36]

The *Ceremonialbuch* also gives detailed reports on concerts at
the Londonschänke inn, later known as 'Vauxhall' (in existence from 1768 to 1802), as well as dances held in Bad
Rehburg, which the princes attended until three o'clock in
the morning. The festivities in honour of the fiftieth anniversary of the founding of the state university at Göttingen are
described, as is a meeting of the royal princes at the home of
the Hardenberg family in July 1787. Yet in spite of this
modest flowering, the court failed to develop any significant
artistic activities. No major architectural projects were pursued, nor were interiors redesigned on a large scale or

30. The great hall of the University of Göttingen. John Bacon's marble bust of George III is surrounded by portraits of Kings George II, George IV and William IV, and of Kings Ernst and Georg of Hanover.

paintings commissioned.[37] Only the painter Johann Heinrich Ramberg (1763–1840) achieved a degree of fame when he was invited by George III to study (at the King's expense) at the Royal Academy from 1781 to 1789.

That is why – unlike Augustus the Strong, who, thirty years earlier, had flooded the kingdom of Poland and the Electorate of Saxony with artworks – George was thought, albeit wrongly, to lack interest. What actually happened was that, in the second half of the eighteenth century, the image of the ruler was changing on the Continent. Politics no longer drew on art as an instrument to represent a claim to power and legitimate authority. The artists were no longer depicting mythological apotheoses, but real people. In Otto Brunner's view, the monarch of the period no longer saw his role as arising from the divine right of kings, but derived it increasingly from the constitution or the law.[38]

Whereas on the Continent this growing awareness initially proceeded slowly, the English king occupied a defined place within the constitutional monarchy. However, for George I and George II, this presented considerable problems, since they saw themselves as princes in the baroque mould and were also able to act as such during their visits to Hanover. Frederick Louis, Prince of Wales turned his back on this view. But when Allan Ramsay painted the state portrait of George III in 1761, nothing appeared to have changed: again, we are presented with baroque pathos. But in the meantime, a change in education (or was it perhaps Lord Bute?) had shaped a new ruler: the 'Patriot King' and *Landesvater* (*Pater Patriae*).[39]

According to the typology of seventeenth- and eighteenth-century German courts developed by Volker Bauer, the court of George III corresponds to the 'husbandman court'.[40] Typically, the court is run economically, is exemplary in character, and promotes simplicity, a sense of duty and so on. This is based on a religious ideological orientation arising from Protestant Pietism. Bauer shows that the court of Friedrich Wilhelm I of Prussia corresponded most closely to this ideal. In fact, in this point the aforementioned educational ideal and the ideal of economy come together. However, this is not an exclusively German phenomenon. The second half of the eighteenth century saw the publication of a large number of books on the subject of husbandry, both in English and in German, by authors such as Richard Bradley, John Mills and Thomas Hale on the English side, and Wolfgang Helmhard von Hohberg and Otto von Münchhausen among the Germans.[41] They are reformers harking back to ancient models such as Palladius, Columella and Varro. In this context one should also mention the political iconography, developed before 1750, of gardens such as Stowe, which gave the Hanoverian monarchy a place in this classical environment. Only when George III began to imitate this model directly in the way he lived his life were these references to disappear and, even, to be replaced by criticism, albeit criticism expressed by a society oriented towards fashionable consumption. This is an area in which several possible approaches need to be followed up.

Der Hausvater by Otto von Münchhausen, a gentleman farmer from Lower Saxony, was admired by the Empress of Russia as well as by George III. Anyone who reads it will find instructions on new farming and horticultural methods, botany as used in forestry, animal husbandry and so on, as well as recommendations on how the husbandman should behave. These correspond in detail to the many descriptions of the family life and the public appearances of the royal family. So, for his people in Hanover, the King adopted a model which anyone could follow and which is linked to the Enlightenment in Germany. The education and enlightenment of the people was something George III always promoted.

At the same time as *Der Hausvater* was being published, Münchhausen and Jobst Anton von Hinüber (1718–84) oversaw the foundation of Agricultural Societies in Harburg (1764) and Celle (1766). These in turn provided important stimuli for the agricultural scientists Albrecht Thaer (1752–1828) and Johann Beckmann (1720–94).[42] Hinüber himself visited the King twice, and George also issued an invitation to abbey bailiff Christian Friedrich Gebhard Westfeld from Weende (1746–1823). Hinüber put the inspiration he had received into practice in his landscape garden in Marienwerder as well as at the post house in Hanover.[43] Although Justus Möser (1720–94), Advocatus Patriae of the Osnabrück diocese, criticised Hinüber for an excess of garden furnishings, an interest in the new gardens, which combined usefulness with pleasure, had been established.[44] Kew represented an exception in English horticulture, and yet that may have been one of the reasons why, on the European Continent, the gardens made the greatest impression and were the most frequently visited. Kew's success is probably due to the fact that it is laid out as an Enlightenment educational garden promoting architecture, horticulture and agriculture. It served as a model.[45]

Against this background it also becomes evident that, in his eulogistic sermon of 1786, Syndic Georg Friedrich Dinglinger was in fact thanking the King for the new roads, the tree nursery in Hanover-Herrenhausen and a teacher training college.[46] We might add further examples: surveying of the land, the botanical garden at Hanover (1774), the veterinary (1778) and artillery (1782) colleges, the mining college in Clausthal, moorland drainage and settlement, destruction of the antiquated fortifications, and the system of canal locks.[47]

It is hoped that these insights into the background may go some way to explaining the specific characteristics of George III and Queen Charlotte's German families. What becomes obvious is that, when you explore both the English and German backgrounds, a new picture appears. This is no simple matter, as legal experts such as Justus Möser and Johann Stephan Pütter (1725–1807) noted long ago.[48] Their attempts to compare and amend English and German state history was bogged down very early on. It falls to us to continue the work in this area.

NOTES

1. Hanover, Niedersächsisches Staatsarchiv Hannover, Dep. 84B, 1191. Cited by kind permission of HRH Ernst August, Prince of Hanover. The contacts seem to have been made by the family of the influential Hanoverian minister Gerlach Adolf von Münchhausen (1688–1770), whose brother, Philipp Adolf (1694–1762), was in charge of the King's German interests in London. See also E. Boll, *Geschichte Mecklenburgs*, Neubrandenburg, 1856, vol. II, pp. 303–7.

2. Charlotte's living siblings were Christiane, canoness of Herford Abbey (1735–94), Adolf Friedrich IV (1738–94), Carl (1741–1816), Ernst, governor of Celle (1742–1804), and Georg August, general (1748–85).

3. T. Nugent, *Reisen durch Deutschland und vorzüglich durch Mecklenburg*, Berlin/Stettin, 1781, reprint ed. S. Bock, Schwerin, 1998, p. 331 (hereafter Nugent, *Reisen*). This is not an exact translation

of Nugent's *Travels through Germany . . . in a series of letters to a friend*, 2 vols., London, 1768 (hereafter Nugent, *Travels*).

4. Schwerin, Landeshauptarchiv Schwerin 2.12–1/7. Diary entitled *Voyage de Son Altesse Sérénissime Monseigneur le Prince Frédéric François Duc de Meclenbourg-Schwerin, Aout-Dec. 1782.*

5. Hanover, Niedersächsisches Staatsarchiv Hannover, Dep. 84B, 1191: 'qui c'est donné les soins les plus grandes pour bien élever ses enfans.'

6. Quoted in H. Borth, *Belvedere und andere schöne Aussichten*, Friedland, 2002, pp. 35–6 [author's translation].

7. Schwerin, Landeshauptarchiv Schwerin 4, 3–2, 1019 (1730) and 1211.

8. H.M. Doughty, *Our Wherry in Wendish Lands: From Friesland through the Mecklenburg Lakes to Bohemia*, London, 1892, p. 249, describes a birch where 'Princess Charlotte . . . used as a girl to come from the dull old Schloss at Mirow to drink milk under it.'

9. BL, Maps K. Top. 101.22.d and e.

10. K. Schrader, *Der Bildnismaler Johann Georg Ziesenis (1716–1776)*, Münster, 1995, pp. 207–8, no. 149.

11. Schwerin, Landeshauptarchiv Schwerin 4.11–5, 130.

12. *George III & Queen Charlotte*, nos. 8 and 9.

13. C. Lerche, 'Die Herrenhausener Bildnisse von Johann Zoffany – Georg III. und die Darstellung des "Patriot King"', *Niederdeutsche Beiträge zur Kunstgeschichte*, XXXV, Munich, 1996, pp. 99–136.

14. Schwerin, Landeshauptarchiv Schwerin, 2.26–1 Großherzogliches Kabinett I, 213–220, 225, and 4.3–2 Hausarchiv des Mecklenburg-Strelitzschen Fürstenhauses, Briefsammlung, 5/4, 116, 867–882, 993, 1198–1201, 1266–1268; letters of George III to the Dukes of Mecklenburg-Strelitz, 768–770. In 5/4 she reports (*c.*1810) 'Tasse de Porcelain avec le vue de Neu Brandenbourg' under Carl's portrait in Frogmore.

15. *George III & Queen Charlotte*, no. 309.

16. D. Wogen and A.G. Masch, *Die gottesdienstlichen Alterthümer der Obotriten*, Berlin, 1771.

17. Nugent, *Reisen*, p. 279. See also Nugent, *Travels*, vol. I, p. 323; vol. II, pp. 156–9.

18. Nugent, *Reisen*, p. 116. He calls Frederike 'the German Sappho' (p. 144) because she published *Freie Betrachtungen über die Psalme*

Davids (Lübeck, 1772). See also Nugent, *Travels*, vol. I, pp. 273–82.

19. Much the same views can be found in the entries on children and education ('Kind', 'Schul-', and 'Erziehungswesen') in J.G. Krünitz's *Ökonomische Encyclopedie*, vol. XXXVII, 1786.

20. For instance in Thomasius's *Entwurff der politischen Klugheit*, or Wolff's *Gedanken vom gesellschaftlichen Leben derer Menschen*.

21. C. Campbell Orr, *Queenship in Europe 1660–1815: The Role of Consort*, Cambridge, 2004, chapter 14.

22. J.H. Zedler, *Grosses vollständiges Universal-Lexikon*, vol. XV, Leipzig/Halle, 1737, column 659f [author's translation].

23. 'The first feeling of ambition that I felt within me was kindled by Mr Bolhagen, my father's vice-governor and adviser. In the year 1736, being in my room, he read a report of the wedding of Princess Auguste of Saxe-Gotha, my second-degree cousin, with the Prince of Wales. Meanwhile he said to Mlle Cardel: "You know, this princess truly has been much more badly brought up than ours, she is also not beautiful, and nonetheless she is now foreseen to become Queen of England. Who knows what will yet become of ours?" He began to preach to me about wisdom, all the Christian virtues and moral rigour so that I might become worthy of carrying a crown, in case I were ever to be in that position.' Catherine II, *Memoiren*, ed. E. Boehme, Leipzig, 1917, p. 15 [author's translation].

24. G. Frühsorge, 'Die Einheit aller Geschäfte: Tradition und Veränderung des "Hausmutter"-Bildes in der deutschen Ökonomie-Literatur des 18. Jahrhunderts', *Wolfenbütteler Studien zur Aufklärung*, III (1976), pp. 137–57. The state of current scholarship in this field is reflected upon in this work. These subjects – mother and child at home – were also popular in French contemporary paintings.

25. M. Weinland, 'Friedrich II. Der erste Kronprinz und seine Erziehung durch Friedrich Wilhelm I', in *Im Dienste Preußens: Wer erzog Prinzen zu Königen*, Berlin, 2001, pp. 73–81.

26. The first German biography of George III contains several examples of the confrontation of old and modern ideas in the person of the King, both in his actual behaviour and in public expectations. See F. von Bibra, *Georg der Dritte*, Leipzig, 1820, pp. 169, 174, 222, 236–7.

27. A. Klausa, *Friedrich Karl von Hardenberg (1696–1763)*, Hildesheim, 1990, pp. 122–45.

28. Hanover, Niedersächsisches Staatsarchiv Hannover, Dep. 103 IV, 324, 325. Cited by the gracious permission of HRH Ernst August, Prince of Hanover.

29. J. Lampe, *Aristokratie, Hofadel und Staatspatriziat in Kurhannover*, 2 vols., Göttingen, 1963, gives a social history of the Hanoverian nobility and court. A more contemporary description is given in C.E. von Malortie, *Beiträge zur Geschichte des Braunschweigisch-Lüneburgischen Hauses und Hofes*, 7 vols., Hanover, 1860–84, vol. 7, 1884, pp. 115–44.

30. Carl lived from 1768 to 1786 in the Altes Palais von dem Bussche, which was then bought by Frederick, Duke of York. In 1802 Adolphus, Duke of Cambridge moved in. See B. Adam, 'Hannoversche Adelspalais des Barock und Rokoko', in *Stand und Repräsentation*, ed. S. Lesemann and A. von Stieglitz, Hanover, 2004, pp. 30–33.

31. M. Köhler, 'The German Legacy: Richmond in Braunschweig', *Garden History*, 29/I, 2001, pp. 29–35; M. Köhler, ed., *Historische Gärten um Neubrandenburg*, Berlin, 2002, pp. 25–30.

32. Ernst later moved to Neustrelitz, where he died in 1814; see also K. Hustaedt, 'Das ehemalige Prinz Ernst Palais in Neustrelitz', *Sonderdruck der Mecklenburgischen Landeszeitung*, 1916, nos. 221–224. Regarding Celle, see R. Kirsch, *Frühe Landschaftsgärten im niedersächsischen Raum*, PhD thesis, Göttingen, 1988, pp. 43ff.

33. An extensive array of documents concerning Caroline's stay in Celle is found in Hanover, Niedersächsisches Staatsarchiv Hannover, Dep. 84, 866–889.

34. Hanover, Niedersächsisches Staatsarchiv Hannover, Dep. 103 IV, 324.

35. Hanover, Niedersächsisches Staatsarchiv Hannover, Dep. 103 IV, 176. Parts of old services from Schloss Ahlden, Osnabrück, Celle and England ("englisches Service") were melted down. For the purchase of this service in Paris by Friedrich Karl von Hardenberg in 1779, see *ibid.*, Dep. 103 XX, 228. Orders for services and coaches clearly show that the King intended to visit Hanover.

36. B. Crome, 'Die englischen Prinzen in Göttingen', *Zeitschrift des Historischen Vereins für Niedersachsen*, 1905, pp. 421–81. Edward

was ordered back to England because of his debts, just like Frederick in 1747. See Hanover, Niedersächsisches Staatsarchiv Hannover, Hannover 92 IV-F-100. For the princely sojourns see W.R. Röhrbein and A. von Rohr, eds., *Hannover im Glanz und Schatten des britischen Weltreichs*, Hanover, 1977, pp. 53–7.

37. See T. Dann, *Die Königlichen Prunkappartements im hannoverschen Leineschloß*, Hanover, 2000; alterations of Montbrillant by G.L.F. Laves (approved by the King; Hanover, Niedersächsisches Staatsarchiv Hannover 13c Herrenhausen 6 pm). The only classical design shows L.C. Ziegler's unexecuted *Justizkanzlei* from 1778 (Hanover, Niedersächsisches Staatsarchiv Hannover 13c Hannover 63, 1 bpm). In 1796–7 the wing of the Leineschloss, built in 1742–6 after a design by J.F. Blondel, was renovated. See G. Schnath, *Das Leineschloß*, Hanover, 1962, p. 100. Between 1766 and the mid-1770s austerity measures were put in place; apparently the palace at Herrenhausen was to be destroyed in 1775. See also *Architect King*, pp. 21ff.

38. O. Brunner, 'Vom Gottesgnadentum zum monarchistischen Prinzip', in H. Hofmann, ed., *Die Entstehung des modernen souveränen Staates*, Köln, 1967, pp. 115–36. In 1743 Justus Möser wrote an panegyric *Ode* on George II's siege at Dettingen. For George III he once used the expression *primus familiarum* (Akademie der Wissenschaften, Göttingen, *Justus Möser. Sämtliche Werke*, IX, part II, *Patriotische Phantasien*, Oldenburg, 1957–8, p. 245).

39. See O. von Münchhausen, *Der Hausvater*, part I, 2nd edn, Hanover, 1766, pp. 53–6.

40. V. Bauer, 'Die höfische Gesellschaft in Deutschland von der Mitte des 17. Bis zum Ausgang des 18. Jahrhunderts – Versuch einer Typologie', *Frühe Neuzeit*, 12, Tübingen, 1993. Although he refers to very small German courts, in the 1780s this ideal became so widespread that it was embraced even by formerly absolute rulers such as Carl Eugen of Württemberg.

41. K.F. von Dacheröden, *Magazin der Regierungskunst, der Staats- und Landwirtschaft*, 3 parts, Leipzig, 1775–9.

42. L. Deicke, 'Die Celler Sozietät und Landwirtschaftsgesellschaft von 1764', in *Deutsche patriotische und gemeinnützige Gesellschaften, Wolfenbütteler Forschungen*, ed. R. Vierhaus, vol. 8, Munich, 1980, pp. 161–94.

43. O. Ulbricht, '"Im Ealinger Feld habe ich Turnips gesehen . . .": Landwirtschaftliche Aufzeichnungen Jobst Anton von Hinübers

während seines England-Aufenthaltes 1766/67', *19 Jahresheft der Albrecht-Thaer-Gesellschaft*, Hanover, 1979, S. 67–109. Lichtenberg writes, 28 January 1775: 'It is unbelievable how much the King thinks of him' ('Es ist unbeschreiblich wieviel der König auf ihn hält.') (*Georg Christoph Lichtenberg: Schriften und Briefe*, ed. F.H. Mautner, vol. 4.1, Frankfurt-am-Main, 1983, p. 167). A contemporary description is given by C.C.L. Hirschfeld, *Theorie der Gartenkunst*, vol. 5, Leipzig, 1785, pp. 204–31.

44. Akademie der Wissenschaften, Göttingen, *Justus Möser: Sämtliche Werke*, V, part II, *Patriotische Phantasien*, pp. 281–3 ('Das englische Gärten').

45. *Architect King*, p. 60.

46. G.F. Dinglinger, *Gott, der besonders gnädige Schutz guter Regenten: eine Predigt am Dankfeste für die Erhaltung des Königs am 12ten Sontage nach Trinit.*, Göttingen, 1786. Dinglinger was a vicar in Hanover at the time of the sermon, moving later to Brunswick.

47. S. Conrady, 'Die Wirksamkeit König Georgs III. für die hannoverschen Kurlande', *Niedersächsisches Jahrbuch für Landesgeschichte*, vol. 39, 1967, pp. 150–90. Poetic tributes were paid regularly, for example by the Göttingen professors Christian Gottlieb Heyne (1763), Johann Philipp Murray and Johann Adolf Schlegel, or musically by Johann Georg Jacobi (1771) and Karl Ditters von Dittersdorff (1786).

48. For instance, see J. Möser, *Briefwechsel*, Hanover, 1992, pp. 316–18.

II

'THE PATRON OF ARTS'

31. Benjamin West, *The Departure of Regulus*, 1769. RCIN 405416

5

George III and his painters

CHRISTOPHER LLOYD

Of all the painters patronised by George III and Queen Charlotte, the one who most closely matches the King's outlook is the American Benjamin West. As it happens, the King and the artist were exact contemporaries, both being born in 1738 and dying in 1820. Apart from this coincidence, the course of their lives was understandably rather different, although there were several points of convergence. What is certain is that both men had a bad press, with West, for example, being described by Lord Byron as 'Europe's worst dauber, and poor Britain's best'.[1]

From a political point of view, George III's relationship with West was clearly ambivalent owing to circumstances, but, nonetheless, the artist held a number of important posts both at court and in the establishment at large – Historical Painter to the King (1772), Surveyor of the King's Pictures (1791) and ultimately, in 1792, second President of the Royal Academy in succession to Sir Joshua Reynolds. No other painter was so generously employed by George III. West supplied some 60 paintings in many different categories at a cost of £34,187 and from 1780 received an annual stipend of £1,000 while working at Windsor Castle.[2] In short, George III and Queen Charlotte virtually monopolised West. They may have preferred other painters, such as Johann Zoffany or Thomas Gainsborough, for particular, more pleasing types of painting, but for grander, imaginative subjects of 'public' significance West dominated the court.

If George III's contribution to the art of this country was to be the proud founding patron of the Royal Academy, it was West who gave full visual expression to the policy of that Academy in forwarding the cause of British art in general and specifically the treatment of history painting. This claim can be made on the basis of West's skill in expressing George III's political, religious and social ambitions in a clear, direct visual form that was immediately comprehensible to viewers. The successful fusion of form and content makes West a remarkably articulate painter. It is his misfortune, but hardly his fault, that the content of his pictures has so little appeal for us today, except in so far as in the present context they are illustrative of George III's monarchical ideals.

Of all the painted schemes devised by West for George III and Queen Charlotte, the one most pertinent for a discussion of their patronage was once in the Queen's Lodge, a separate building on the south side of Windsor Castle enlarged by Sir William Chambers for the accommodation of the royal family, but pulled down by George IV in 1823.[3] The project for the ceiling decoration of the Drawing Room was begun in 1788 and for its arrangement and iconography the principal source is the 1792 *Guide* to Windsor.[4] The designated material used for this scheme was coloured marble dust (*marmortinto*); it was applied by a German specialist in this medium, to designs by West. A certain amount of the preparatory material survives. The centre of the ceiling (plate IX) was dominated by an oval – *Genius calling forth Arts and Sciences* – and in the four corners were four further oval allegories representing *Agriculture, Manufactory, Commerce* and *Riches.*[5] Four intermediary sections painted in imitation bas-relief depicted eight further subjects: astronomy, navigation, electricity, geography, fortification, gunnery, chemistry and botany. It says a great deal for West's visual imagination – not to say visual ingenuity – that he could devise compositions incorporating such subject matter, but that was precisely his strength as an artist. In the sense that the scheme celebrates the benefits of the reign and the widespread patronage of the King, West was acting like a Renaissance artist.[6]

A Renaissance comparison is also valid for the other all-important series that George III commissioned from West. The artist's reputation had been made in England by the viewing of the *Landing of Agrippina at Brundisium with the Ashes of Germanicus* (1768) painted for Robert Hay Drummond, Archbishop of York.[7] So impressed was the King on seeing this picture that he immediately commissioned *The Departure of Regulus* (fig. 31) and, according to John Galt, West's earliest biographer, proceeded to read aloud the relevant passage from Livy's *Ab urbe condita* – another Renaissance topos.[8] This picture, too, won plaudits, and comparisons with Nicolas Poussin were duly made. A pair to this large painting was then commissioned – *The Oath of Hannibal* – and both were hung in the Warm Room of Buckingham House in the King's Apartments (fig. 32).[9] Three other pictures were then added: *The Death of Epaminondas, The Death of the Chevalier Bayard* and *The Death of Wolfe*, all on one wall.[10] As is well known, *The Death of Wolfe* (fig. 33) was a replica of the painting done in 1770 for Richard, Lord Grosvenor (later 1st Earl Grosvenor), which had been shown in the Royal Academy to great acclaim and is now in the National Gallery of Canada in Ottawa.[11] The composition had been the subject of much comment because it was a picture that depicted an almost contemporary event, with figures accurately portrayed in modern dress. Sir Joshua Reynolds famously remarked, 'I foresee that this picture will not only become one of the most popular, but occasion a revolution',[12] and, indeed, its popularity was such that it did not escape the attention of James Gillray. The Warm Room was completed by two overdoors: *The Family of the King of Armenia before Cyrus* and *Segestes and his Daughter before Germanicus*.[13]

The paintings in the Warm Room treat the themes of heroism on the field of battle and magnanimity by victorious commanders. The cycle revealed that West was a painter who could tackle the traditional themes of history painting based

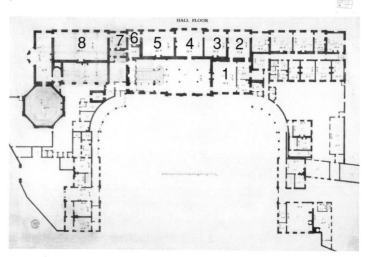

32. Buckingham House in 1776. Westminster Public Library, London.
The rooms of the King's Apartments on the ground floor have been
re-numbered 1–8: 1. Dining Room; 2. Dressing Room; 3. Warm Room;
4. Passage Room; 5. Drawing Room; 6. Closet; 7. King's Bed Chamber;
8. Library.

on erudite sources, but who could at the same time, as in *The
Death of Wolfe,* challenge the conventions. George III, as he
contemplated these pictures, would have been stirred intel-
lectually by the portrayal of valiant deeds and heroic sacrifices,
but he would no doubt also have hoped that his own
commanders would continue to display equal courage in the
turbulent times of his own reign.

The King now needed no further persuasion of West's
abilities to translate cerebral thematic material into striking
visual images. Accordingly, between 1786 and 1789 West was
asked to paint eight pictures for the Audience Room in
Windsor Castle illustrating scenes from the life of Edward III.
This monarch's association with Windsor Castle and the
institution of the Order of the Garter was sufficient motiv-
ation for a second decorative scheme of this subject in
addition to the murals painted by Antonio Verrio in St

33. Benjamin West, *The Death of Wolfe*, 1771. RCIN 407297

George's Hall for Charles II. The principal scenes are representations of Edward III, his son the Black Prince, and his wife Queen Philippa, battling against the French and the Scots and showing magnanimity in victory (fig. 34).[14] This is straightforward history painting based on sources such as David Hume's *History of England* (1754–62) for the narrative flow, but also on the antiquarian research of Joseph Strutt and Francis Grose for details of costume, setting, and arms and armour.[15] The scene of the Order of the Garter would no doubt have been painted with knowledge of Elias Ashmole's *History of the Garter* (1672), but what all these various sources serve to indicate is the renewal of interest in medieval history.

The purpose of the Edward III cycle was ostensibly to underscore the monarchical connections between Edward III and George III. As in the typological framework of many early fresco cycles, there is an implied parallel between Edward III and George III. The fact that during the eighteenth century France was the national enemy and that intimations of republicanism across the Channel were beginning to surface should also be borne in mind. There is, however, nothing complicated about the Edward III cycle, and it is a landmark in the tradition of history painting in

89

34. Benjamin West, *The Burghers of Calais*, 1789. RCIN 404927

Britain. These scenes are the most ambitious representations of subjects from the Middle Ages undertaken during the late eighteenth century.[16]

West was not finished yet and his last commissions for George III extended his repertoire even further. During the 1790s plans were drawn up for a new Royal Chapel at Windsor Castle. This was in fact never built and so it can only be reconstructed from preparatory schematic drawings, payments and lists. It was conceived on a considerable scale, but at a time when West's relationship with the royal family was becoming strained. His annual stipend was stopped in 1801 and work on the paintings for the Royal Chapel was suspended, although the artist persevered on and off with the project at his own expense until his death.

The number of scenes in the Chapel of Revealed Religion, as the project was eventually called, amounted to 36 – all from the Old and New Testaments, extending literally from the Book of Genesis to the Book of Revelation. The scheme was meant to be read in the typological sense, with Old Testament theology echoed and resolved in the context of the New Testament – the working of God's word from its first articulation to its grand finale. Prototypes could be easily found on the Continent, but religious images of this kind were not readily to hand in Protestant Britain and the project was criticised as a retrograde step. West almost certainly had to rely on theologians for advice and there was no shortage of literature on the subject of revealed religion written by divines such as Bishop William Warburton (*The Divine Legation of Moses Demonstrated*) and Bishop Thomas Newton (*Dissertations on the Prophecies*). Guiding minds within the Royal Household were Richard Hurd, Bishop of Worcester (Clerk of the Closet), and the Sub-Dean of the Chapel Royal, the Revd Anselm Bayly. These scholars defended the Anglican position against the Deists who accepted belief in God only on grounds of reason and rejected the biblical testimony of divine revelation. The purpose of the Chapel, therefore, was to answer the rationalists, and West threw himself into the extended project with formidable commitment.[17] The scenes with an established iconography are perhaps slightly pedestrian, but when it came to the Book of Revelation West was inspired. *The Destruction of the Beast and the False Prophet* and *Death on a Pale Horse* (fig. 35) are conceived on a grand scale reminiscent of Michelangelo and Rubens. It is too easy to dismiss such paintings as empty and rhetorical when in fact the visual imagination and technical dexterity needed for work of this kind are exceptional by the standards of any time.[18]

George III and Benjamin West had similar casts of mind. They entertained grand, ennobling thoughts that demanded clear exposition on a suitably dramatic scale. Taken together the Warm Room, the Audience Chamber, and the Chapel of Revealed Religion combine to uphold the basic tenets of George III's concept of kingship – the secular and the religious conjoined by a sense of history inducing a feeling of patriotism. In West George III found a painter with the perfect qualifications for depicting his ideals; similarly, in

35. Benjamin West, Sketch for *Death on a Pale Horse*, 1796.
The Detroit Institute of Arts

George III, West found a patron who needed the services of an artist prepared to make a public statement in visual terms expressing such ideals.

West may have been the most significant artist working for George III and Queen Charlotte, but he was not, by today's standards, the most illustrious. Sir Joshua Reynolds had the support of the King as the first President of the Royal Academy, but that was as far as it went. The dislike was mutual and was duly acknowledged. Essentially, Reynolds found himself blocked by George III's preference for Allan Ramsay in the field of portrait painting and for West in the field of history painting. Also, it is clear that Reynolds's theoretical approach to art in general, as expounded in the *Discourses*, was not favoured by the King: it was too intellectual, too grandiose, too heuristic. Furthermore, on a personal basis there was also some rancour. Reynolds was aloof and inflexible, a bachelor and politically suspect. No doubt normal civilities were politely exchanged when George III and his family visited the Royal Academy's exhibitions and when the artist was made Principal Painter in 1784 following the death of Ramsay, but it was left to George IV to show a proper appreciation for Reynolds's work.[19]

Gainsborough, however, was liked by father and son, and his work was acquired by both of them. George III's admiration was surely based on his sympathy for the man. Where Reynolds was stiff and snobbish, Gainsborough was relaxed and informal. Recognised as 'the Apollo of the Palace', Gainsborough clearly relished his success, 'talking bawdy to the king & morality to the Prince of Wales'.[20] In this spirit Gainsborough from 1780 produced some of his finest work for George III and Queen Charlotte while at the height of his powers.[21]

George III also expressed an interest in the projected composition known as *The Richmond Water Walk* that was comparable with *The Mall*, now in the Frick Collection, New York, and he asked to see *The Woodman*, now only known through a stipple engraving. Queen Charlotte owned the *Portrait of Carl Friedrich Abel*, now in the Huntington Library and Art Gallery, San Marino, as well as a number of drawings in coloured chalks that were sold at Christie's in 1819.

It is perhaps puzzling that Gainsborough should have been so generously supported by the court, for in many ways he was everything that the King disliked about people: he was inclined to be foul-mouthed, dissolute, irresponsible, irascible and lacking any sense of real time even though contemporaries described him as 'a natural gentleman'. The truth might be that Gainsborough, being somewhat chameleon in character, knew how to behave in the presence of the royal family and could turn on the charm.[22] But the question of his personality is compounded by Gainsborough's style of painting which was distinctly modern. This is what Reynolds in the famous Discourse XIV referred to as the 'peculiarity of his manner' and in describing the style itself employed such phrases as 'those odd scratches and marks', 'the effect of accident', 'chaos', 'uncouth and shapeless appearance', 'a kind of mag-ick', which 'at a certain distance assumes form', when 'all the parts seem to drop into their proper places, so that we can hardly refuse acknowledging the full effect of diligence, under the appearance of chance and hasty negligence'.[23]

The hallmarks of modernity can be recognised in Reynolds's careful choice of words in describing Gainsborough's technique. So why was Gainsborough so successful at court? The answer must surely be that in artistic terms he was seen as the heir to Van Dyck. It is significant that when he was at Windsor Castle the artist was transfixed by the beauty of Van Dyck's three-quarters-length portrait of Queen Henrietta Maria, and indicative of his admiration for Van Dyck are the words reputedly spoken on his deathbed: 'We are all going to Heaven, and Vandyke is of the party.'[24]

All the evidence suggests that George III was conscious of his visual heritage. A great deal of emphasis is placed on how he extended the Royal Collection by new acquisitions, but some of the items acquired reveal interesting overlaps. For instance, the iconographical link between Annibale Carracci's *Il Silenzio* (acquired in 1760) and the portrait by Francis Cotes of *Queen Charlotte and the Princess Royal* (of 1767) is suggestive: in both canvases a mother entreats us to silence for the sake of her sleeping infant.[25] At Buckingham House, the pictures were hung in adjoining rooms, namely the King's Bedchamber and Closet. Similarly, given his interest in architecture the King would surely personally have been delighted by the series of eight English, chiefly Palladian, architectural subjects painted for Consul Smith by Antonio Visentini and Francesco Zuccarelli (fig. 36).[26] It seems, in fact, that George III much appreciated the poetic idiom of Zuccarelli's landscapes, and his support of the artist was facilitated by the latter's presence in England for several years (1752–62 and *c*.1764/5–71) and by his position as a founding member of the Royal Academy. In turn, Zuccarelli exerted a considerable influence on British landscape painting.[27]

The interior views of the royal residences in W.H. Pyne's publication of 1819 are notable for the intermingling of the old and the new elements in the Royal Collection (fig. 37).[28] The harmonious arrangement in the rooms at Windsor Castle denotes a careful, purposeful ordering of the displays of paintings. This historical projection is also apparent in the

36. Antonio Visentini and Francesco Zuccarelli, *Capriccio with a view of Mereworth Castle, Kent*, 1746. RCIN 400687

paintings done by Johann Zoffany, who was, for better or worse, the most dependable painter working for George III and Queen Charlotte. If Benjamin West could match the King's intellectual aspirations in paint, Zoffany was there to record the more mundane, quotidian aspect of royal life. It is to the artist's real credit that in doing this he successfully expanded royal iconography, particularly as regards the royal conversation piece in which the emphasis is more on informality – the private world as opposed to the public one. The advantage of Zoffany was that he was a very literal painter and it is the conviction and coherence that he brings to his work, rather than his imagination, that the viewer responds to. A clue to Zoffany's success is provided by his rendering of the Prince of Wales and Prince Frederick at play in the Queen's Apartments in Buckingham House, where there are portraits by Van Dyck hanging on the walls.[29] Such terms of reference become a veritable *omaggio* in *George III, Queen Charlotte and their six eldest children*, where the fashionable Van Dyck costumes, some of the poses, and other elements of the composition bespeak the plentiful influence of

37. Charles Wild, *Windsor Castle: The Queen's Audience Chamber*, 1818.
Watercolour. RL 22100

Van Dyck's portraiture as represented in the Royal Collection.[30] Zoffany's credit began to fall when he committed
lèse-majesté in *The Tribuna of the Uffizi* and upset Queen
Charlotte's sense of decorum,[31] and it was that vacuum which
Gainsborough and Sir William Beechey filled.

George III's acquisition of *The five eldest children of
Charles I* in 1765 was, therefore, a significant and poignant
addition to the Royal Collection,[32] at once honouring his
Stuart predecessors and reflecting his own personal taste. One
should not be too concerned that the King failed to secure
Van Dyck's *Charles I in the hunting field* (Paris, Musée du
Louvre) when it was available five years later as, after all, there
were two other paintings of Charles I by the artist on that
grand scale still in the Collection, both of which were moved
to Buckingham House by George III.[33] But, if any picture by
Van Dyck was to appeal to the King, it would be *The five*

eldest children by virtue of its subject matter and its association with family life.[34]

In sum, George III could have seen painters such as Ramsay, Zoffany and Gainsborough as extending the tradition of Van Dyck, perhaps with himself in the role of Charles I. Historians might stress the political significance of this, namely the link between the Hanoverians and the Stuarts, but there is surely also the hint of an aesthetic continuity that George III and Queen Charlotte sensed in the symbolic arrangement of the paintings in the principal royal residences. To that extent, the King's taste was finely tuned: it was not at all superficial or negative, nor was it devoid of purpose. Gainsborough described the King as 'a good connoisseur, and conversant in the works of the old masters; much more so, indeed, than many of his courtiers, who hold their heads so high upon the advantages of foreign travel; lordlings, who, for all their prate about contour, carnations, and gusto, prefer a racer to a Raffael, and a stud to the studio of Michael Angelo himself'.[35]

NOTES

1. Meantime, the flattering, feeble dotard, West,
    Europe's worst dauber, and poor Britain's best,
    With palsied hand shall turn each model o'er,
    And own himself an infant of fourscore.
    (*The Curse of Minerva*, 1811, lines 175–8; Lord Byron, *The Complete Works*, ed. J.J. McGann, Oxford, 1980, vol. I, no. 151, pp. 320–30.)

2. Calculations given in H. Von Erffa and A. Staley, *The Paintings of Benjamin West*, New Haven and London, 1986, p. 51; based on J. Galt, *The Life, Studies, and Works of Benjamin West Esq.*, London, 1820, part II, pp. 207–15.

3. See *George III & Queen Charlotte*, pp. 133–4.

4. *The Windsor Guide; Containing a Description of the Town and Castle; the Present State of the Paintings and Curiosities in the Royal Apartments; an Account of the Monuments, Painted Windows, etc. in St. George's Chapel . . .*, Windsor, 1792, on which the account

given by Von Erffa and Staley 1986, pp. 90–93, is based. For the individual catalogue entries see Von Erffa and Staley 1986, nos. 435–9.

5. The oil sketches for these compositions are Von Erffa and Staley 1986, nos. 435, 436, 437, 438 and 439 respectively.

6. Consider, for example, the role of Andrea Mantegna at the Gonzaga court in Mantua. Another parallel might be the Studiolo of Francesco I de' Medici in the Palazzo Ducale, Florence.

7. Von Erffa and Staley 1986, no. 33.

8. Galt 1820, part II, pp. 25–6; but on the classical sources see Von Erffa and Staley 1986, no. 10.

9. Von Erffa and Staley 1986, no. 17.

10. *ibid.*, nos. 5, 77 and 94 respectively.

11. *ibid.*, no. 93.

12. Reynolds's remark is given by Galt 1820, part II, pp. 49–50.

13. The overdoors are Von Erffa and Staley 1986, nos. 2 and 32. For the layout of the Warm Room see F. Russell, 'King George III's Picture Hang at Buckingham House', *Burlington Magazine*, CXXIX, p. 528, fig. 49.

14. Von Erffa and Staley 1986, pp. 93–7 and nos. 56, 58–61, 64, 67, 72 and 74.

15. For the series as a whole and its sources see R. Strong, *And when did you last see your father? The Victorian Painter and British History*, London, 1978, pp. 78–85.

16. See Strong 1978, p. 81.

17. A detailed account of these paintings is given by Von Erffa and Staley 1986, pp. 577–81. Biographies of the advisers for the project (Warburton, Newton, Hurd and Bayly) can be found in the *Oxford Dictionary of National Biography*. West also conceived a similar series of paintings at the same time for William Beckford's Revelation Chamber at Fonthill Abbey in Wiltshire.

18. *Death on a Pale Horse*, for example, was an easy target for an illustrator such as George Cruikshank.

19. Reynolds described the post as 'a place of not so much profit and of near equal dignity with His Majestys Rat-catcher' (*The Letters of Sir Joshua Reynolds*, ed. J. Ingamells and J. Edgcumbe, New Haven and London, 2000, p. 129, no. 124), and a former pupil, James Northcote, recorded that 'The King and Queen could not endure the presence of him; he was poison to their sight' (W.T. Whitley, *Artists and their Friends in England, 1700–1799*, London

and Boston, 1928, I, p. 256). Also see R. Wendorf, *Sir Joshua Reynolds: The Painter in Society*, Boston and London, 1996, pp. 173–6.

20. The quotations are from W.T. Whitley, *Gainsborough*, London, 1915, p. 177, and *Farington Diary*, IV, p. 1130 (Sunday, 6 January 1799).

21. Millar 1969, nos. 774, 778–92, 801–2.

22. On this see M. Rosenthal, *The Art of Thomas Gainsborough*, New Haven and London, 1999, p. 80.

23. Sir Joshua Reynolds, *Discourses*, ed. P. Rogers, London, 1992, pp. 312–13.

24. H. Angelo, *Reminiscences of Henry Angelo with Memoirs of his Late Father and Friends*, London, 1828, vol. I, p. 353, and for the words on Gainsborough's deathbed, J. Northcote, *The Life of Joshua Reynolds*, London, 1819, vol. II, p. 239. The painting so admired by Gainsborough was almost certainly Millar 1963, no. 147.

25. *George III & Queen Charlotte*, nos. 5 and 156 respectively.

26. Levey, nos. 669–76.

27. M. Levey, 'Francesco Zuccarelli in England', *Italian Studies*, XIV, 1959, pp. 1–19.

28. *Royal Residences*; see in particular The Queen's Audience Chamber, The Queen's Ballroom and The King's Dressing Room at Windsor Castle.

29. Millar 1969, no. 1200.

30. *George III & Queen Charlotte*, no. 7.

31. *ibid.*, no. 161.

32. *George III & Queen Charlotte*, no. 155.

33. Millar 1963, nos. 143 (*Charles I with M. de St Antoine*) and 150 ('*The Greate Peece*').

34. *ibid.*, no. 152.

35. Angelo 1828, I, p. 354.

38. Giulio Clovio, *Illuminations from choir books made up to form a page.*
RL 13035 and RL 01328a–c

6

George III's acquisitions on the Continent

JANE ROBERTS

Among the many aspects of the *George III & Queen Charlotte* exhibition at The Queen's Gallery in 2004 that may have struck the viewer was the quality and richness of native, British, production – set alongside the numerous fine paintings and drawings from the Continent. This neatly parallels the apparently contradictory statements made by George III that he 'gloried in the name of Briton', while being equally proud to claim that 'My heart will never forget that it pulses with German blood'.[1] The King's magnificent collection of books, drawings and paintings was largely formed by overseas purchases (chiefly from Italy, however, rather than Germany), the earliest of which were made in the 1750s.

At the start, we may remind ourselves that George III grew up among – and later inherited – a superb collection of paintings and other works of art, particularly from Italy and France, which had been assembled over the previous century or so. The acquisitions from the Continent made by his predecessors – particularly Charles I, Charles II, and his father, Frederick, Prince of Wales, who died in 1751 – were the basis for George III's own purchases. We should also recall that the King's chief acquisitions were made in the 1750s and 1760s, at the time of the Seven Years' War and prior to the surge in Grand Tourism that followed the declaration of peace in February 1763.

The inspiration, pattern and process for George III's collecting was largely set by John Stuart, 3rd Earl of Bute (1713–92), on whose advice the King depended implicitly for ten or more years until the mid-1760s.[2] At this period neither Bute nor the King had travelled far outside the shores of the British Isles; although Bute (who had studied at Groningen and Leiden in the early 1730s) was later to spend some time in Italy, the King never set foot outside England. He therefore knew about the rest of the world only through written descriptions, and through drawn, painted and engraved views.[3]

In 1756, after the future George III reached his majority, Bute was appointed his Groom of the Stole, the most trusted member of the Prince's Household. Over the next seven years Bute oversaw most aspects of his master's life, including the formation of his collection. It is no coincidence that the royal purchases involved the subject areas in which the Earl himself was most interested: books, coins, medals, drawings, engravings and scientific instruments. Many of the King's acquisitions were made – under the direction of the Earl of Bute – by the royal librarian Richard Dalton (?1713–91), who had been known to the Earl since at least 1748. Much of Dalton's early life was spent as a coach-painter in London and a draughtsman and copyist in Rome.[4] There is little to suggest that Dalton, who was appointed Librarian to the Prince of Wales in 1755, was a scholar or bibliophile. However, he evidently had a good 'nose' for collecting, knew his way around Italy, and could persuade impoverished owners to part with their treasures for his principals – Bute, the Prince of Wales, and a small group of other British noblemen. Although Dalton enjoyed the continuing confidence of these men, he clearly aroused a certain amount of envious hostility, particularly from his fellow countrymen who were engaged in similar activity in Italy. In 1756 Robert Adam reported from Rome that 'those of true taste esteem [Dalton] one of the most ignorant of mortals',[5] and in 1761 Dalton was described by Horace Mann as 'very ill-qualified for the post of [royal] librarian, being totally illiterate'.[6]

In 1758 Dalton returned to Italy, visiting Bologna, Florence, Rome, Naples, Ferrara and Venice. Twelve letters from Dalton to Bute survive, dated between June 1758 and May

1759, clearly in response to specific instructions from Bute, acting on behalf of the Prince.[7] The first royal purchases made by Dalton involved a collection of medals that had belonged to the Prussian antiquarian Philip von Stosch (1691–1757). However, the acquisition of drawings appears to have been Dalton's principal charge at this time. In October 1758 he reported from Bologna that 'I've met with a number of very fine drawings in diferent collections here and hope to make up two tolerable Collections, one for HRH and the other for your Lordship', adding that 'as here is at present no one a collecting Drawings but myself the want of money will make y^m part with them as no other opertunity seems likely to happen'.[8] By 17 November Dalton had bought nearly 700 drawings for the Prince, including one by Raphael, 40 by Guercino, 'and several of the Carracci & other eminent Masters'. He informed Bute that 'it has been happy for me that I've ransack'd a part of Italy [i.e. Bologna] where none ever stay, they collect in Rome and Florence that are quite stript'.[9] In May 1759 Dalton wrote to Bute from Venice before embarking on the return journey to England. He had arranged for 'a large Case of very fine things . . . collected for the Prince . . . [to] be sent to England in a Man of War' from Livorno.[10] All the costs involved in these purchases were repaid to Dalton by Bute through his 'Separate Account'. In the course of 1759 over £2,500 was transferred for this purpose.

Dalton was not alone among those in Italy charged with acquisitions for the future King at this time. By February 1759 the young Scottish portrait painter John Thomas Seton had purchased from Hamerani, the pope's medallist, six volumes of drawings by 'all the great Masters, from Albert Durer, down to Carlo Marrat', and a seventh volume of 'academies' (figure studies). The cost to the Prince of Wales was just over £600.[11]

With George III's accession in October 1760, the scale of both Bute's and the King's intentions, and requirements, increased very considerably. In the previous decade Dalton,

39. Album of drawings by Sebastiano Ricci in Consul Smith's original
binding. RCIN 970113

now confirmed in his post of Librarian, had evidently
prepared the ground with a number of Italian collectors who
might be persuaded to become vendors – when the time and
price was right. And in 1762 the King was able to purchase

two of the greatest of those collections: the Smith and the Albani collections. With these acquisitions, George III's collection attained truly international importance.

Joseph Smith, who had moved to Italy from London in around 1700, worked in Venice as a merchant banker, and served from 1744 to 1760 – and again briefly in 1766 – as British Consul in Venice.[12] He moved in musical and artistic circles and was well known to both the native Venetian and the visiting European community. Smith's first love was books, including manuscripts, of which he made several collections.[13] The largest of these was listed in the *Bibliotheca Smithiana*, published (with a probable view to sale) in 1755, at which point a possible royal purchase was being mooted but – according to Smith – 'by reason of the present war breaking out about that time nothing was concluded'.[14] The cost – for the library only – was to have been 20,000 *zecchini*, or £10,000. During his stay in Venice in May 1759, Dalton alluded to the importance of Smith's collection but he resisted making an approach to the Consul, prophesying that 'time will produce many valuable things if desired'.[15]

Negotiations with Smith recommenced very soon after the start of the new reign and were entrusted to Bute's younger brother, James Stuart Mackenzie, extraordinary envoy to Turin from 1758 to 1761. According to James Adam, by 1761 Smith was 'devilishly poor' but so 'eaten up with' vanity that it was considered unlikely that he would ever bring himself to sell his collection.[16] However, in May 1762 Smith supplied Stuart Mackenzie with 'Sundry Lists' of the different parts of his collection, and in early July Smith was informed that, for the sum of £20,000, the King 'has been pleased to think the Collection not to be unworthy of His Possession'.[17] George III's purchase of Smith's collection was particularly opportune for it was made at precisely the same time as the acquisition of Buckingham House as the chief London home for the King and Queen. The empty walls of their new residence could thus be filled with a ready-made group of well-framed paintings, in addition to a superb library.

In the winter of 1762 Stuart Mackenzie and Dalton visited Venice to conclude the purchase, and Dalton checked the books before confirming that they were all present, inscribing the catalogue of the Consul's library accordingly in January 1763.[18] The small sheets of notes – listing, in Smith's hand, but in Italian, the contents of each of the volumes of drawings – were probably checked off at the same time.[19]

Unfortunately no contemporary list survives of the paintings acquired from Consul Smith by the King. However, two early nineteenth-century inventories – the so-called 'Italian' and 'Flemish and Dutch' Lists (consisting respectively of 351 and 149 paintings) – are probably copies of lost originals.[20] The Italian List includes 54 paintings by Canaletto (including plate XII); 36 by Zuccarelli (some of which remain in the 'neat Italian frames' as described in the Italian List); 28 by Sebastiano Ricci; 34 by Sebastiano's nephew, Marco Ricci; and 24 works by Rosalba Carriera (of which only five survive in the Collection). Of the 219 works by eighteenth-century Italian artists, 162 are identifiable in the Royal Collection. Of the remaining 130 or so paintings by earlier Italian masters, under half can now be located.[21] Misleading attributions have meant that only a quarter of the entries on the Flemish and Dutch List can be identified today. Among these are two paintings by Rembrandt, one by Rubens, and one by Vermeer (then attributed to Frans van Mieris).[22]

Many of the drawings acquired from Smith were by the same contemporary artists (a number of whom were personal friends of Smith) as were responsible for the paintings. Apart from the chalk heads by Piazzetta,[23] and the extraordinary composite illuminated sheet by Giulio Clovio (fig. 38),[24] the drawings were housed in albums, listed in the *Bibliotheca Smithiana* alongside the printed books, and then re-listed in George III's early nineteenth-century inventories of drawings. Smith's catalogue mentions volumes of drawings by both Sebastiano and Marco Ricci, by Canaletto, Visentini, and by the sixteenth-century artist Ambrogio Figino. The catalogue was compiled in the early 1750s but omitted the material acquired from Zaccaria Sagredo in 1752: three volumes formerly in the Bonfiglioli family collection containing miscellaneous drawings collected 'in the time of Carracci', and four volumes of drawings by G.B. Castiglione. In a few cases – such as the album of drawings by Sebastiano Ricci (fig. 39) – Smith's volumes have remained largely intact today. But in many other cases the drawings from Smith's collection were soon merged (by the King's librarians) with drawings by the same artists from different sources: thus Smith's choice group of drawings by Raphael from the Bonfiglioli and Sagredo collections joined other studies by the master, some of which had been in the Royal Collection since the seventeenth century while others had been acquired by George III elsewhere.[25]

On the same shipment as the Smith collection, which was transported from Livorno to London in 1763, were the volumes of drawings and prints that had been purchased by the King, also in 1762, from Cardinal Alessandro Albani.[26] In this case the negotiations were entrusted to James Adam, younger brother of the King's architect Robert Adam: Robert had become acquainted with Cardinal Albani during his stay in Rome in the mid-1750s. Late in 1761 instructions to go ahead with the purchase were conveyed to James, then resident in Rome, and the purchase was finalised in May 1762, for the sum of £3,500. According to James Adam, the deal had been worthwhile 'both because of its making me more known to H.M. and of more consequence among my countrymen here'.[27] Remarkably, it was completed without the knowledge of the Cardinal's librarian and curator, Johann Joachim Winckelmann.

The two hundred or so portfolios or volumes which made up the Albani collection consisted of a number of distinct parts: the 'domestic' collection, which included the fifteen volumes of architectural designs, chiefly by the architect Carlo Fontana, mostly relating to work for different members of the Albani family;[28] and the various collections purchased by the Cardinal's uncle, Pope Clement XI. Two of these had been

40. Thomas Patch, *A view of Florence*, c.1763. RCIN 403526

acquired in 1703: that of the artist Carlo Maratti (then in his late seventies), and that of the seventeenth-century collector Cassiano dal Pozzo. At the heart of the Maratti collection were the contents of the studio of Domenichino's pupil and heir, Raspantino, including over 1,500 drawings by Domenichino, and many thousands of others especially of the seventeenth-century Roman school. Cassiano's 'paper museum' was a visual record of all that was known of the ancient and the natural world in early seventeenth-century Rome. This was one of the most extraordinary of George III's purchases on the Continent. Over half of the surviving 6,000 drawings from the Dal Pozzo collection remain in the Royal Collection.[29]

The Smith and Albani collections were the major acquisitions of the new reign. However, Richard Dalton, who served as Royal Librarian until 1773 (and was later appointed Antiquarian and Keeper of Medals and Drawings, and Surveyor of the King's Pictures), continued to pay regular visits to Italy throughout the 1760s.[30] In the course of one such visit he returned to the Casa Gennari in Bologna to acquire many hundreds of additional drawings by Guercino, which were now reunited with the 40 from the same source purchased in

41. Giuseppe Bottani, *The return from Egypt*, 1763–4. RCIN 403556

1758.[31] Guercino's painting of the *Libyan Sibyl* was almost certainly acquired from the Gennari family on the same occasion, in the early 1760s.[32] A small group of other paintings by Guercino and members of his family, and drawings by the contemporary Bolognese masters Gaetano Gandolfi (1734–1802) and Jacopo Alessandro Calvi (1740–1815), may have been acquired at the same time.[33] And in 1764 Dalton was repaid by the King for three views of Florence (including fig. 40) by his friend Thomas Patch.[34]

Dalton made other purchases in Rome. Some are listed in an account submitted to the King at some stage in the 1760s.[35] This includes a harpsichord, 'A Curious Cabinet with Drawers, enrich'd with hard stones in Rilievo represent^g Fruit',[36] drawings by Sassoferrato (presumably the 60 still at Windsor),[37] and a number of paintings. In addition to several works by seventeenth-century Italian artists – Simone Cantarini, Ghisolfi, Maratti and others – there were paintings by living artists such as the Cremonese Giuseppe Bottani (including fig. 41).[38] In 1766 the King reimbursed Dalton with £262 for Annibale Carracci's fine painting known as *'Il Silenzio'*.[39] Although the source of this acquisition is not specified, it was probably the Farnese family. Some of the drawings by Michelangelo now in the Royal Collection are known to have belonged to Cardinal Alessandro Farnese in the late sixteenth century; these may also have been purchased from the Farnese family at this time.[40] Two of Raphael's drawings were stated in George III's Drawings Inventory to have been purchased in Rome.[41] As in the case of the Roman caprice views by Panini (see fig. 42),[42] further details of acquisition are not known, but Dalton is likely to have been involved.

Since the signing of the Treaty of Paris in 1763, Italy had been increasingly overrun with Grand Tourists who were both willing and able to pay large sums for paintings, antiquities and other treasures. From around 1770 – by which time Dalton was in his late fifties, with a wealthy wife in London[43] – the length and frequency of his continental travels diminished. In addition, the task of adapting, extending and furnishing Buckingham House was virtually complete, and its walls were full.[44] But although the flow of new royal acquisitions diminished, it did not cease altogether. This was partly because those striving for personal advancement realised that they might achieve this through gifts (or offers) of works of art for the King.

The 'Milordi' in Florence, many of whom were included in Zoffany's *Tribuna*, painted for Queen Charlotte in the 1770s,[45] were particularly well placed to supply the King: within a week of George III's accession Horace Walpole had informed Horace Mann (1706–86), the British representative in Florence between 1740 and his death: 'I will tell you something; the King loves medals; if you ever meet with anything very curious in that way, I should think you would make your court agreeably by sending it to him. I imagine his taste goes to antiques too, perhaps to pictures, but that I have not heard'.[46] Mann was promoted from Resident to Envoy in 1765, but no royal gifts emanating from him are recorded today.

George Cowper (1728–89), who succeeded as 3rd Earl in 1777 and lived in Florence (without any official responsibility)

42. Giovanni Paolo Panini, *Capriccio with a view of Trajan's Column and Roman ruins*, 1735. RCIN 402911

from 1760 until his death, attempted to ingratiate himself with the King through a number of gifts, including the copies (still at Windsor) by Giuseppe Macpherson of artists' self-portraits in the Grand Ducal collection.[47] In April 1780 Cowper wrote to the King:

43. Artist unknown, previously thought to be a self-portrait by Raphael, c.1505. Oil on panel. RCIN 405760

May I once more presume to intreat your Majesty for one of the three vacant Blue Ribbons? [i.e., knighthoods of the Garter] . . . Be assured, Sire, that your Majesty cannot confer it upon any body, that has your Majesty's measures more at heart than myself. Permit me, Sire, to inform your Majesty that I have two Raphaels, one his own portrait done by himself . . . the other a Madonna and child in the highest preservation, which I was offered £2000 for, but refused it, as I was resolved it should go to England: If Your Majesty chooses to purchase them, I will give them both for £2500.[48]

The Niccolini-Cowper Madonna – prominently featured as 'for sale' in the *Tribuna* – was not acquired and is now in the National Gallery of Art, Washington DC. And although in

1781 the supposed self-portrait by Raphael (fig. 43)[49] was given (rather than sold) to the King by Cowper, by 1785 it was hanging at Kensington – its authenticity already doubted, perhaps – and Cowper's Garter was not forthcoming.

Sir William Hamilton (1730–1803), the British envoy in Naples, was also in close touch with those around George III. In June 1766 he received a request from Thomas Worsley (1710–78; Surveyor-General of the Office of Works from 1760), for good painted views of Naples; these were presumably required for one of the King's new apartments at Buckingham House.[50] Three months later Hamilton sent the King a small volume of 'Plans of all the Fortified Places in the Kingdom of the Two Sicilies',[51] for the King's growing topographical collection. Hamilton's connections with Ferdinand IV, King of the Two Sicilies, almost certainly led to the gift in 1787 of the 'Etruscan Service', made at the Naples porcelain factory.[52]

By now Britain was the most powerful country in Europe, and foreign ministers and heads of state – as well as Britons abroad – would ply the King and his fellow countrymen with gifts and privileges. Cardinal Albani, who had recently sold his drawings collection to George III, was placed in charge of redrafting papal foreign policy – to welcome British visitors to Italy, to deprive the exiled Stuarts of their earlier position as respected royals-in-exile, and to begin the issuing of excavation licences which would benefit – and delight – a growing stream of British visitors.[53]

In his letter (quoted above) about the young George III in 1760, Horace Walpole wrote, 'I imagine his taste goes to antiques too'. Although this assumption appears to have been erroneous, two members of the King's immediate family did indeed show an interest in classical antiquities. In 1776 his brother, William, Duke of Gloucester, collaborated in one of Prince Barberini's excavation campaigns, while in 1792 his sixth son, Prince Augustus, took part in an excavation between Ostia and Anzio during which the 'Campo Iemini Venus' was discovered.[54] The figure subsequently entered the collection of Augustus's elder brother, the future George IV; in 1834 another brother, William IV, presented it to the British Museum. Prince Augustus also supplied chimneypieces – made in Rome, but generally by British craftsmen – both to his mother (for Frogmore) and to his brother (for Carlton House).[55] But there is no evidence that George III had any particular interest in such activity and no antique statuary appears to have entered the collection in the course of his long reign. George III's lack of interest in antiquities is unusual in the context of contemporary British collectors and foreign rulers, notably Gustavus III of Sweden and Catherine the Great of Russia.

So much for Italy. Where Germany was concerned, George III's family links could hardly have been stronger. Both the King's parents and his wife had grown up there; his second son, Frederick, held the office of Prince Bishop of Osnabrück (and in 1791 married a Prussian princess), and three of his other sons (Ernest, Augustus and Adolphus) were educated at Göttingen University. But although many of the German princely and noble residences were well furnished, in some cases with treasuries or *Schatzkammern*, and fine libraries, after decades of warfare few of them could boast art collections on the scale or of the importance of those that had been accumulating in England since the early seventeenth century. Germany was not therefore an obvious place to look for 'high art', although the King and Queen received numerous family gifts from their German relations. One acquisition – or rather presentation – from Germany was the Fürstenberg Service,[56] a porcelain dinner and dessert service presented to George III in around 1773 by Duke Charles I of Brunswick, whose son (the future Duke Charles William Ferdinand) had married the King's eldest sister Augusta in 1764.

Other acquisitions may have been made in the Netherlands. In October 1759 sixty Netherlandish drawings now at Windsor – including a number by Avercamp and Battem – appeared in the Abraham van Broyel sale in Amsterdam, where they were purchased by the dealer Pieter Yver before subsequently entering George III's collection.[57] Although details of the royal purchase are not recorded, it could well have involved Captain William Baillie, who was making major purchases of Dutch paintings for Lord Bute at this time.[58]

The King's acquisitions in France are no easier to pin down. It is evident that Simon, 1st Earl Harcourt (1714–77), was in close touch with both the King and the Queen throughout his time as British Ambassador to Paris from 1769 to 1772. Harcourt had been Governor to the King as Prince of Wales and served as the Queen's Master of Horse and Lord Chamberlain after accompanying her from Mecklenburg to England in 1761. In March and October 1770 the Queen wrote to thank Harcourt for 'sending . . . the different things I wished for', and 'for having taken so much trouble in executing your Commissions so well in France'.[59] The many fine pieces of Sèvres porcelain recorded in the Queen's collection were probably among the results of these commissions.[60] At the same period the King received (via the jeweller John Duval) an ivory-turning lathe from Paris, with which he made at least two gold-mounted ivory boxes.[61]

But these were trifles compared with the treasures that the King had already acquired in Italy. He no longer had Bute by his side. Buckingham House was fully furnished. There was no practical need for more. So in January 1770 George III informed Harcourt: 'I have, at least for the present, given up collecting pictures: Therefore shall not trouble you with any commission for the Vandyke.'[62] Unfortunately the painting concerned was the splendid portrait of Charles I – *Charles I in the hunting field* – which remains to this day in France (Paris, Musée du Louvre).

I will end where I might have begun: for (like Smith) the King's first love (encouraged no doubt by Bute) was books. In May 1768 Dr Samuel Johnson wrote to offer advice to Frederick Augusta Barnard – at the time a young assistant in the Royal Library, but later Royal Librarian – who was on the point of setting out for the Continent. In addition to acquiring locally examples of national literature, scientific writings, and so on, Dr Johnson advised that 'It will be of great use to collect in every place maps of the adjacent country and plans of towns, buildings and gardens.'[63] Barnard had at his disposal the not inconsiderable annual sum of £2,000 from the King, with which he developed and continued the work begun by Dalton. Over the next three years he visited Paris, Vienna, Rome, Strasbourg, Dresden, Berlin, Amsterdam, Brussels and Spa, despatching books and booksellers' catalogues to London as he went.[64] Barnard thus helped to form George III's remarkable collection of both books and topographical prints and drawings, the majority of which were presented to the nation in the 1820s. He was in charge of the library while it grew from approximately 10,000 volumes in 1769 to over 65,000 in the 1820s, together with over 50,000 images in the topographical collection (plate XXIV). It became a truly 'universal' library, evidently gathered – in a methodical and scholarly manner – from many of the cities of Europe.

George III's acquisitions on the Continent thus provided him with a first-rate library and cabinet of coins, medals and engraved gems, with a vast collection of drawings and prints, and paintings fit for hanging in any of the royal residences. In spite of the magnificent additions – particularly in the decorative arts – made by his son and heir, these acquisitions still lie at the very heart of the Royal Collection today.

NOTES

1. E. Paintin, *The King's Library*, London, 1989, p. 4 and n. 9; Brooke, p. 314.
2. See *Bute*.
3. For George III as an 'armchair traveller' see Peter Barber's contribution to this volume.
4. On Dalton see J. Ingamells, *A Dictionary of British and Irish Travellers in Italy 1701–1800, compiled from the Brinsley Ford Archive,*

New Haven and London, 1997, pp. 267–70, and D. Mahon and N. Turner, *The Drawings of Guercino in the Collection of Her Majesty The Queen at Windsor Castle*, Cambridge, 1989, pp. xxii ff.

5. J. Fleming, *Robert Adam and his circle in Edinburgh and Rome*, London, 1962, p. 223.

6. *Walpole Correspondence*, XXI, p. 478: Horace Mann to Horace Walpole, 17 February 1761.

7. The letters are transcribed in *Bute*, pp. 217–27.

8. *Bute*, p. 218.

9. Dalton made additional purchases of drawings for the Prince in Rome in December 1758; *Bute*, pp. 220–21.

10. Bute MSS, James Stuart Mackenzie to Bute, by 30 June 1759.

11. Ingamells 1997, p. 847; *Bute*, pp. 34–5.

12. On Smith see F. Vivian, *Il Console Smith, mercante e collezionista*, Vicenza, 1971, and F. Vivian, exh. cat., *The Consul Smith Collection. Masterpieces of Italian Drawing from the Royal Library, Windsor Castle. Raphael to Canaletto*, Munich, 1989.

13. S.L. Morrison, 'Records of a bibliophile. The catalogues of Consul Joseph Smith and some aspects of his collecting', *Book Collector*, XLIII, no. 1, 1993/4, pp. 27–58.

14. From Smith's will of 1761, transcribed in K.T. Parker, *The Drawings of Antonio Canaletto in the Collection of His Majesty The King at Windsor Castle*, Oxford and London, 1948, p. 60.

15. *Bute*, p. 227.

16. Fleming 1962, p. 270.

17. Parker 1948, p. 61, Smith to Stuart Mackenzie, 13 July 1762.

18. Two receipted copies of the *Bibliotheca Smithiana* survive in the British Library. The wording of Dalton's inscription in 123.e.10 (from the King's Library) is transcribed in Parker 1948, p. 62.

19. Several of these lists survive, bound up either with the volumes of drawings to which they relate or with Inventory A. For the contents list of the caricatures volume see A. Blunt and E. Croft-Murray, *The Venetian Drawings of the XVII and XVIII Centuries in the Collection of Her Majesty The Queen at Windsor Castle*, London, 1957, p. 137, fig. 2.

20. The Italian, and Flemish & Dutch, Lists are both included in RCIN 1112568. The Lists were first discussed (in Italian translation) in Vivian 1971, pp. 173–211.

21. See indexes of previous owners in J. Shearman, *The Early Italian Pictures in the Collection of Her Majesty The Queen*, Cambridge, 1983, pp. 425–6, and Levey, pp. 387–8.

22. See index to C. White, *The Dutch Pictures in the Collection of Her Majesty The Queen*, Cambridge, 1982, and *King's Purchase*, p. 46.

23. Although there is no positive evidence that the Piazzetta drawings came from Smith, this would seem the most likely route.

24. A.E. Popham and J. Wilde, *The Italian Drawings of the XV and XVI Centuries in the Collection of His Majesty The King at Windsor Castle*, London, 1949, reprinted, with an appendix by R. Wood, New York and London, 1984, nos. 40–43. The fragments (nos. 40–42) have been reunited within the larger page (no. 43).

25. For the early history of the Windsor Raphael drawings see M. Clayton, exh. cat., *Raphael and his Circle: Drawings from Windsor Castle*, London, The Queen's Gallery, 1999, pp. 211–12.

26. J. Fleming, 'Cardinal Albani's drawings at Windsor: their purchase by James Adam for George III,' *Connoisseur*, CXLII, 1958, pp. 164–9.

27. Fleming 1962, p. 298.

28. Fully discussed in A. Braham and H. Hager, *Carlo Fontana. The Drawings at Windsor Castle*, London, 1977.

29. The collection is in the process of being catalogued; to date, nine volumes have been published.

30. For his caricature portrait, made by Thomas Patch in Rome in 1769, see *George III & Queen Charlotte*, p. 156, fig. 19.

31. Mahon and Turner 1989.

32. *George III & Queen Charlotte*, no. 154.

33. O. Kurz, *The Bolognese Drawings of the XVII and XVIII Centuries in the Collection of Her Majesty The Queen at Windsor Castle*, London, 1955, reprinted, with an appendix by H. McBurney, Bologna, 1988, nos. 271–9 and 21–6.

34. Millar 1969, nos. 977–9.

35. RA GEO/15602–3.

36. *George III & Queen Charlotte*, no. 261.

37. A. Blunt and H.L. Cooke, *The Roman Drawings of the XVII and XVIII Centuries in the Collection of Her Majesty The Queen at Windsor Castle*, London, 1960, pp. 102–10.

38. Levey, nos. 362–3; the two other paintings are untraced.

39. *George III & Queen Charlotte*, no. 156; by the early 1770s the painting was hanging in the King's Closet at Buckingham House (F. Russell, 'King George III's Picture Hang at Buckingham House', *Burlington Magazine*, CXXIX, 1987, p. 529).

40. See M. Clayton, 'The provenance of the drawings by Michelangelo at Windsor Castle', in P. Joannides, *Michelangelo and His Influence. Drawings from Windsor Castle*, exh. cat., London, The Queen's Gallery, 1996, pp. 205–9.

41. Clayton 1999, p. 211.

42. Levey, nos. 558–9.

43. Dalton married in 1764, aged around 50. Zoffany's portrait of Mr and Mrs Dalton with their adopted niece, Mary, painted *c*.1765–8, is in the Tate Gallery. See exh. cat., *Johann Zoffany, 1733–1810*, London, National Portrait Gallery, 1976, no. 32.

44. For the hanging plans for the Royal Apartments made in the early 1770s, see Russell 1987.

45. As discussed *in extenso* in O. Millar, *Zoffany and his Tribuna*, London, 1967.

46. *Walpole Correspondence*, XXI, p. 449.

47. Walker, nos. 484–707; these were presented in two batches, in 1773 and 1786.

48. *The Correspondence of George III (1760–1783)*, ed. J. Fortescue, London, 1927–8, V, pp. 49–50.

49. Shearman 1983, no. 217. The attribution to Raphael is now generally thought to be wrong.

50. The paintings by Fabris are RCIN 401091–2. They are reproduced and discussed in exh. cat., *Vases and Volcanoes: Sir William Hamilton and his collection*, London, British Museum, 1996, pp. 28–9 and 246–7.

51. Now BL, 118.d.1, formerly BL K. Top. 83.76.

52. *George III & Queen Charlotte*, no. 329.

53. Exh. cat., *Grand Tour: The Lure of Italy in the Eighteenth Century*, London, Tate Gallery, 1996, pp. 33–4.

54. The King's brothers Edward (Duke of York) and William (Duke of Gloucester) were in Italy respectively in 1763–4 and in the 1770s and 1780s. The King's son, Prince Augustus, was there for much of the period 1789–99 (Ingamells 1997, pp. 1033–5; 402–4; 35–8). For the 'Campo Iemini Venus' see I. Bignamini, 'The "Campo Iemini Venus" rediscovered', *Burlington Magazine*, CXXXVI, 1994, pp. 548–52.

55. P. Fusco, P. Fogelmann and S. Stock, 'John Deare (1759–1798): A British Neo-classical sculptor in Rome', *Sculpture Journal*, IV, 2000, p. 104.
56. *George III & Queen Charlotte*, no. 325.
57. See M. Plomp, 'Acquisitions for the English Royal Collection from the 1759 Abraham van Broyel sale', forthcoming.
58. *Bute*, pp. 183–90.
59. At the same time, the Queen asked Harcourt the price of 'a compleat Table Service of White China' (*The Harcourt Papers*, ed. W.F. Harcourt, 14 vols., 1880–1905, VI, pp. 4–5).
60. See *George III & Queen Charlotte*, nos. 326 and 327.
61. See *George III & Queen Charlotte*, no. 58.
62. *Harcourt Papers*, III, p. 102.
63. *Bibliothecae Regis Catalogus*, I, pp. v–vi.
64. See J. Brooke, 'The Library of King George III', *Yale University Library Gazette*, LII, no. 1, 1977, pp. 33–45, and Paintin 1989. See also exh. cat., *Royal Treasures*, London, The Queen's Gallery, 2002, no. 325, for George III's purchase of the Mainz Psalter from the University of Göttingen in 1800.

7

Furnishing George III's palaces

HUGH ROBERTS

When George III succeeded his grandfather George II, he inherited responsibility for a widely scattered and extraordinarily motley string of official and semi-official royal residences and public buildings. On the semi-official side, these included the late seventeenth-century Savile House, on the north side of Leicester Square, which George III had shared since 1751 with his younger brother Edward, Duke of York; Leicester House next door (fig. 44), which his widowed mother retained until her removal to Carlton House in 1764; and nos. 28 and 29 on the east side of the square, the home of her third and fourth sons, William, Duke of Gloucester and Henry, Duke of Cumberland.[1] Outside London, George III had Richmond Lodge, a modest red brick building which he used until 1772 when, on the death of his mother, the White House at Kew became available. This last was regularly occupied in conjunction with the neighbouring Dutch House at Kew, at least until the late 1770s when Windsor claimed the King's attention.[2]

The list of official residences which passed with the Crown included the architecturally undistinguished palace of St James's; Kensington Palace, greatly favoured by George II; the vast and unwieldy palace of Hampton Court, virtually abandoned since Queen Caroline's death in 1737; and the ancient but antiquated stronghold of Windsor, little used by the Royal Family since the days of Queen Anne.[3] Of the public buildings, the most important was the Palace of Westminster, which periodically attracted considerable royal attention and

44. After George Vertue, *Leicester Square* (north side), 1748, showing Leicester House (right of centre) and Savile House (left of centre). Engraving.
RCIN 1077886

expenditure. Other governmental buildings in the sovereign's remit included the Whitehall Treasury, the Queen's Treasury and the Secretary of State's offices in Cleveland Row.[4]

This was broadly the position in 1760. What changed the picture entirely was the King's acquisition of Buckingham House.[5] The moment this splendid early eighteenth-century building came into royal possession in 1762, it became the King and Queen's principal metropolitan residence, leaving St James's Palace as the home of the court for official purposes only for the rest of the reign.

Many of the changes at the beginning of the new reign were supervised by the ancient Office of the Great Wardrobe, the Household department which traditionally controlled and directed all matters connected with furniture and interior decoration. The Master, a senior courtier, was responsible for the appointment of suitable artificers to supply the Royal Household. While the Mastership of the Wardrobe changed with the sovereign,[6] the actual suppliers mostly continued in post from the previous reign. Thus the pre-eminent cabinet-maker of the early Georgian period, Benjamin Goodison, appointed to succeed his master, James Moore, at the Great Wardrobe in 1727, remained in office until his death seven years into the new reign.[7]

The first new official appointment was that of Catherine Naish.[8] In 1760 she became joiner (meaning, principally, bed- and chair-maker) in succession to her late father Henry Williams, who had held the post since 1729. In 1761 the pre-eminent maker of the early part of George III's reign, William Vile, and his partner John Cobb were appointed cabinet-makers and upholsterers to the Great Wardrobe. That this was certainly an appointment with the King's imprimatur is clear from the fact that in a letter of 1759 to Lord Bute,[9] whose advice on furniture makers was evidently as important to George III as on most other subjects, the Prince indicated his wish to employ Vile in preference to John Trotter, a regular supplier to the Wardrobe since 1754. By mid-1760 the Prince had run up a bill of some £700 to Vile.

Vile and Cobb were discharged in 1763,[10] to be succeeded a year later by John Bradburn and William France. Bradburn[11] had trained with Vile and Cobb, and France had worked for the partners from 1759. Coincidentally 1764 was the year in which the first royal payments to Thomas Chippendale are recorded, not in the Great Wardrobe accounts but in the private account of William, Duke of Gloucester, to whom Chippendale had dedicated the third edition of the *Director* two years previously. In the aftermath of Vile and Cobb's discharge, Chippendale may have been angling for an appoint-ment to the Great Wardrobe. If so, this was something that in the end eluded him, though he appears to have continued into the 1770s to supply the Duke with furniture, probably for Gloucester House in Park Lane.[12]

The partnership of France and Bradburn ended with France's death in 1773, though Bradburn continued to supply furniture for another four years. 1773 was also the year in which John Russell[13] succeeded Catherine Naish (who had died in 1772) as joiner, and – perhaps coincidentally – John Mayhew and William Ince, Chippendale's principal rivals at the top end of the furniture trade, supplied their only documented (although not now identifiable) work to Queen Charlotte, for which she paid privately.[14] While Mayhew and Ince would almost certainly have wished to obtain an official appointment to the Wardrobe, this goal eluded them as it had Chippendale.

In 1777, the year of Bradburn's discharge, William Gates[15] was appointed cabinet-maker, a post he held with distinction until the abolition of the Wardrobe five years later. The final part of the reign was dominated by Samuel Beckwith and Edward France,[16] appointed around 1784, and by Charles Elliott,[17] cabinet-maker, who was appointed at the same time: these makers continued supplying furniture into the first decade of the nineteenth century.

Outside the official structure of the Great Wardrobe – and subsequently the Lord Chamberlain's Office – there were clearly frequent opportunities for individual patronage by the Royal Family. In the cases of the King and Queen, such activity was funded through the Privy Purse, that is the private and personal funds of the sovereign from which, in George III's words, 'I pay every act of private benevolence, every improvement in my gardens and many articles of convenience for the Queen as well as myself.'[18] Chippendale and Mayhew and Ince have already been mentioned, and there were of course other instances of the King or Queen – and more particularly other members of their family once set up in independent establishments – making private purchases from cabinet-makers with no official standing. It seems likely, for example, that when established at Gunnersbury House, Princess Amelia, the King's independent-minded aunt, commissioned a unique set of four commodes from the immigrant

French cabinet-maker Pierre Langlois in 1763.[19] Langlois, though a successful and innovative maker, was never an official supplier – indeed it is doubtful whether his highly ornamented French-inspired style would have appealed to the King. Similarly, the King and Queen employed privately a range of cabinet-makers – some reasonably well known, others fairly obscure – to undertake particular tasks not thought appropriate, for one reason or another, to be channelled through the official machinery of the Great Wardrobe or Lord Chamberlain's Office.[20]

So much for the structures that George III inherited; what of the actual furniture? Clearly, the palaces came with an accumulation of old pieces, probably including a certain amount of French furniture, formed in the century since the Restoration,[21] together with a great quantity of furniture supplied by Benjamin Goodison for the State Apartments at Kensington, Hampton Court and St James's. Much of this, which included a long run of marble-topped gilt pier tables, stands and pier glasses, would have been familiar to George III from boyhood. Goodison is thus a key figure in the forming of the King's taste for furniture and it comes as little surprise to find pieces of this character brought from disused residences figuring prominently in the early years of the reign in the King's rooms at Buckingham House.

The change to a young, newly married sovereign and the major shift in architectural focus that came with the acquisition of Buckingham House diminished Goodison's role considerably. He continued to provide plain mahogany furniture to the Household, mainly for Buckingham House and St James's Palace, though noticeably it was now for the upper servants' rooms and backstairs areas rather than the principal state apartments.[22]

By contrast the newcomers on the scene, the King's appointees William Vile and John Cobb, were immediately commissioned to work in virtually all the main rooms at St James's and later Buckingham House. Looking first at St James's Palace, we find the start of a programme lasting about five years to refurbish the State Apartments in a traditional manner and to provide appropriate private apartments for the King and Queen.

Wherever hangings or upholstery were renewed, the pre-eminently traditional royal colour, crimson, was chosen, and in 1762 this was the automatic colour for the immensely elaborate carved and gilt mahogany State Bed made for Queen Charlotte to display the newly born Heir to the Throne – the first male heir to be born in England to a reigning monarch since the seventeenth century. Presumably for this precise dynastic reason, Queen Charlotte's Sitting-up bed marks a departure from the careful and economical approach to St James's seen hitherto, and suggests the great importance the King and Queen attached to the proper performance of traditional court ceremonial. Carved by Naish, the bed was provided with five mattresses and seven pillows and upholstered by Vile and Cobb with rich crimson velvet, trimmed with gold lace and lined with best white satin, and cost £1,291 10s 5d.[23] Large as this figure was, it was entirely eclipsed by the cost of the suite of superfine Flanders Point lace for the counterpane and trimming of the pillows, supplied by the lacewoman Priscilla MacEune for the sum of £2,699. Elsewhere in the State Apartments old tapestries and old hangings were carefully cleaned, repaired and rehung by Vile and Cobb, but little else in the way of new furniture was supplied.

Since almost nothing from this programme of refurbishment is identifiable today, some idea of the quality and style of carved and upholstered furniture that the Naish/Vile and Cobb team provided can be gained by looking at the pieces supplied at exactly the same period for the coronation in September 1761 and for the refurbished House of Lords at the Palace of Westminster.[24] The outstanding pieces (in every sense) were the magnificent Homage Thrones for the Abbey. Carved and gilded by Naish and upholstered by Vile and Cobb with gold brocade supplied by Hinchliff, these ostentatiously theatrical pieces were designed to project boldly in the highly theatrical setting of the Abbey. Closer in style to the King's domestic commissions for St James's was the more modest ensemble of parcel-gilt walnut, upholstered in crimson flowered velvet, provided by the same team for the Prince's Chamber in the House of Lords.[25]

In the Private Apartments at St James's (of which once again there is no visual record), Naish provided new mahogany four-post beds and seat furniture, while Vile and Cobb repaired old furniture and brought other pieces from Hampton Court and elsewhere. In a distinctive break with tradition, which can also be seen as a response by the Queen to the prevailing taste for lighter, brighter colours, rich blue damask hangings, curtains of sky blue lustring and fitted Wilton carpets were supplied throughout her rooms.[26] Vile and Cobb also provided an array of furnishings of a more personal character, which included such things as stands for birdcages and for goldfish bowls, a mahogany-handled fishnet, houses for a Turkey monkey and brackets for china. The more costly furnishings for the Queen's rooms, all provided at the end of 1761, included two 'fine and large' mahogany commode chests of drawers with 'Neat Wrot Brass feet and Ornaments up the Corners finished with Gold Lacquer' at £25 each. Although none of these pieces is now identifiable, the description of the last-mentioned pieces suggests comparison with a sumptuous padouk commode[27] which, though lacking in precise documentation, probably belongs to this phase of furnishing the Queen's rooms at St James's. In its restrained rococo lines it reflects just the degree of fashionable Frenchness that suited the Queen's taste, and which we shall see Vile developing for the Queen over the next few years.

Of the documented pieces supplied for the Queen at this date, the most outstanding was without question her superb inlaid jewel cabinet (plate VIII).[28] The Queen's jewels were spectacular, and it was certainly appropriate that the most expensive single piece Vile supplied, costing £138 10s, was destined to contain them. The lavish and virtually unparalleled use of ivory inlay (which must have been executed by a specialist marqueteur of continental – perhaps German – origin), the variety of exotic woods used and the elegantly controlled rococo curves of cabinet and stand, all suggest further progress by Vile in refining a distinctive vocabulary suited to the Queen's taste. And in a more monochrome way, so does the Queen's sumptuous secretaire,[29] with its elegantly curvaceous base, finely figured veneers and crisply carved scrolls at cresting and foot, supplied for her Dressing Room at St James's.

Rather less seems to have been done to the private apartments of the King, for whom Naish and Vile provided a relatively modest amount of plain mahogany furniture and upholstery. Among the few recognisably personal touches, we find the King ordering from Vile a mahogany Ionic column on which he placed a revolving wax model of the infant Prince of Wales under a glass cover;[30] and the King evidently had in his rooms a large ebony cabinet for which Bradburn supplied twelve new ball feet in 1765.[31] This was later moved to the King's rooms at Buckingham House. In the Library, the real focus of the King's interest (on the ground floor of St James's Palace), Vile was heavily engaged in the provision of new furniture in 1761–2 at a cost of well over £800.

Buckingham House had been purchased by the King for £28,000 in 1762. Almost immediately, William Chambers was employed to undertake alterations and additions. These mainly involved the creation of new library rooms in the south-west corner, while leaving the principal rooms much as they had been in the time of the Buckinghams, with the King in the Duke's rooms on the ground floor and the Queen in the Duchess's on the first floor.

Useful insights into the appearance of Buckingham House in this early period come from a number of royal conversation pieces set in the interiors of Buckingham House, as well as from a group of hanging plans of c.1774[32] and the descriptions of the few who gained admittance to this essentially private house. That of Mrs Philip Lybbe Powys in 1767 is among the most revealing of the difference between the King's and the Queen's apartments. The King's were characterised as 'rather neatly elegant than profusely ornamental' whereas the Queen's were 'ornamented . . . with curiosities from every nation that can deserve notice . . . full of roses, carnations, hyacinths, &c., dispersed in the prettiest manner imaginable' and by her bed 'an elegant case with twenty-five watches, all highly adorn'd with jewels.'[33]

The 'neatly elegant' – or, as W.H. Pyne had it, remarkably plain[34] – quality of the King's rooms, on the west front of the house overlooking the garden, is probably best seen in the famous image of Queen Charlotte and her two eldest sons by Zoffany of *c.*1765 (plate III).[35] The Queen is portrayed in the King's rooms on the ground floor of the house because her own rooms on the first floor were being altered at this date. Her own furniture, imported for the occasion, included the richly ornamented French clock, still in the Royal Collection,[36] the toilet table made by Vile and dressed with more Flanders lace from Mrs MacEune costing just over £1,000, probably the mandarin figures and the flowered carpet. Reflecting the King's taste are the plain, drab-painted walls, unlined silk festoon curtains, old-fashioned giltwood furniture and uncarpeted floors, the King apparently believing carpets unhealthy.

Looking at the old furniture in these rooms we see a pier table and glass which could be among the numerous examples supplied by Goodison for St James's, Hampton Court or Kew in the 1730s. The elaborate chairs might have been the pair of 'State Chairs' made by Goodison for Leicester House in 1743 at a cost of £25 10s,[37] and the table in the room beyond could be the 'carved & gilt Table Frame for a Marble Top, Festoons & Ornaments burnish'd' which, with the marble, Goodison supplied for Kensington Palace in 1756 at a cost of £17 12s 7d.[38] The King himself, in the arresting image of 1771, also by Zoffany (plate X), sits on a plain mahogany armchair next to the table shown in the background of the earlier painting.

The furnishing accounts for these rooms in the 1760s confirm this restrained picture: relatively little new upholstery, the repair and regilding of old furniture undertaken by Vile, and the supply of a modest amount of new furniture. As at St James's, far and away the most significant expenditure was on furniture for the library. On first occupying the house, the King evidently used rooms on the west front, one of which was then known as the Blue Library. In 1762–4, following the purchase of Consul Smith's extensive collection of books, drawings, prints and manuscripts, the Great or West Library was built, to be followed by the South and Octagon Libraries in 1766–7 (fig. 45) and finally the East Library in 1772–3. Eight of the bookcases supplied for St James's in 1761–2 were moved by Vile in 1762 to the Blue Library, four being simply altered and the other four made into six.[39] A year later Vile altered a further bookcase from St James's[40] for the King's Dressing Room, which opened via his bedroom directly into the West Library. Bradburn continued the extensive work of fitting out the new library rooms in 1766, first providing a drawing for the King's approval of major alterations.[41] Characteristically, the words 'neat' and 'plain' recur in almost every one of Bradburn's accounts for the King; and the same theme is echoed by John Adams, the future American President, on his visit in 1783 when he noted 'In every apartment of the whole house, the same taste, the same judgement, the same elegance, the same simplicity, without the smallest affectation, ostentation, profusion or meanness.'[42]

What then of Queen Charlotte's rooms on the first floor? Mrs Lybbe Powys's evocative account mirrors the image we have from the Zoffany portrait of c.1765, and this is reinforced by the portrait of the Queen he painted in 1771 (plate XI).[43] The contrast with the companion portrait of the King could hardly be more marked. Here she is seen very much *à la Française*, exquisitely dressed and seated in an elegant fauteuil in the Louis XV style, leaning lightly on a rich velvet cushion placed on a marble-topped giltwood console table next to a vase brimming with summer flowers. The accounts for the

45. James Stephanoff, *Buckingham House: The Octagon Library*, 1818. Watercolour. RL 22147

Queen's furniture mention the words 'French' and 'inlaid' reasonably often, and while such pieces are now for the most part difficult or impossible to identify, indications of her taste for continental furniture survive in the form of a pair of elaborately inlaid pewter and tortoiseshell cabinets[44] (for which Bradburn made new and rather severe stands in 1766; fig. 46), which were selected by the Queen for the royal bedroom at Richmond, and a cabinet set with pietra dura plaques,[45] purchased by Richard Dalton in Rome in the late 1760s, which she used at Frogmore.

Looking at the accounts for 1762–3, we see the mercer Robert Carr supplying the Queen with crimson lustring for the curtains and crimson damask for the walls and bed hangings in her Bedchamber, and the same colour scheme in the adjoining Dressing Room and Private Closet.[46] The effect of this scheme is vividly shown in Zoffany's portrait of the young Prince of Wales and Duke of York in the Dressing Room, painted in 1764 (fig. 47).[47] The seat furniture is almost certainly by Naish and the exotically figured carpet is perhaps one of the series of bordered Brussels carpets laid by Vile and Cobb in 1762. Green lustring was selected for the Ante Room and Closet in the south-west corner, and in the largest and grandest room of the house, the Saloon, green damask was used for the festoon curtains and upholstery.[48] Most rooms had fitted and bordered carpets, generally Wilton or Brussels, though some were replaced by Kidderminster or Axminster carpets in the later 1760s.

The retention and refitting in 1763 of the Duke of Buckingham's lacquer panelling in the New Japan or Organ Room,[49] suggests another strand of the Queen's interests, hinted at in the earlier Zoffany, where two Chinese painted figures appear on the gilt table. This interest in the exotic percolated into other areas including the new furniture supplied for Richmond Lodge. For example, Naish's new bed for the King and Queen was upholstered in Decker work[50] (embroidered Indian silk from Dacca); and this bedroom also contained Chinese porcelain and ivory boxes. The Orient was allowed considerably fuller rein in the 1790s when the Queen was furnishing Frogmore House, her 'Petit Trianon' at Windsor, with her considerable collection of Indian and Chinese furniture.[51]

Reverting to Buckingham House, Vile continued to provide the Queen in her new Apartment with furniture broadly in the style he had used at St James's. Furniture of particular personal interest was transferred immediately to Buckingham House. This included pieces such as the jewel cabinet, for which Vile provided a marbled leather cover following its move.[52] In a substantially different vein, Vile made a splendid mahogany bookcase for her Bedroom.[53] While it is markedly

46. German(?) and John Bradburn, *Cabinet-on-stand*, late seventeenth century, and 1766. Tortoiseshell, pewter, ebony, oak, gilt and silvered bronze. RCIN 2587.2

more architectural in character than other pieces of the Queen's furniture, and in that sense closer to the King's taste, the exceptional decoration of minutely rendered flower-swags

47. Johan Zoffany, *George, Prince of Wales and Prince Frederick, later Duke of York*, 1765. RCIN 404709

and drops, wreaths, scrolls and masks, 'the whole very handsomely carv'd' (in Vile's words), perhaps carried out by the specialist carver Sefferin Alken, contrasts vividly with the neat and plain work the King preferred.

As in the private rooms at St James's, one can sense throughout Buckingham House a highly personal, if sometimes ephemeral, aspect to a great deal of the furniture and decoration in the 1760s and 1770s. Bradburn and France provided the Queen and her growing family with an all-embracing service, ranging from hanging miniatures and watches in the New Dressing Room and Bedroom, to the provision of dog cushions, china brackets, and cases for a gondola, a Chinese barge and a silver ship for the 3-year-old Prince of Wales. For the 7-year-old Princess Royal, Bradburn made a mahogany table with steps and a pair of foot directors on the top so that she could get on the table to view maps and have her feet straightened at the same time.[54] Less ephemeral and wholly representative of the plainer but fine quality work for the children's rooms was the 'Neat mahogany Secretary' (fig. 48) made for the same Princess a year later, in 1774, at a cost of £20.[55]

When the focus of the King and Queen's interests moved to Windsor in the later 1770s, the pace of change slackened considerably in London. Some updating inevitably took place, and the rooms occupied by the older children continued to require new and – in the case of the Prince of Wales – extremely expensive furniture, much of it supplied by John Russell and William Gates.[56] Meanwhile at Windsor a number of schemes were undertaken to modernise both the State and the Private Apartments. Of particular significance was the new furnishing of the Queen's State Bedroom. While the function of the room demanded a formal and traditional ensemble, the theme of the decoration, in response to Queen Charlotte's passionate interest in botany, was to be entirely floral. In 1778 the Queen took delivery of a new State Bed in the neo-classical style, perhaps designed by John Yenn, Sir William Chambers's assistant.[57] The hangings were decorated with richly coloured and botanically accurate floral needle-work embroidered by the pupils of Mrs Phoebe Wright's 'Royal School for Embroidering Females', an establishment actively supported by the Queen. A little later came two armchairs and a set of ten stools, upholstered en suite.[58] The seat furniture and bed were probably made by Robert Campbell, whose premises in Great Newport Street adjoined those of Mrs Wright. Accompanying this seat furniture was an even more remarkable and distinctive suite of three pieces, a chest of drawers and pair of corner-cupboards, elaborately

48. John Bradburn, *Secretaire cabinet*, 1774. Mahogany, mirror glass, gilt bronze. RCIN 725

mounted and richly decorated with flowers.[59] It is likely that the unknown maker of this suite, almost certainly of continental origin, was in some way connected to the former royal cabinet-maker John Cobb. How and where Queen Charlotte acquired these pieces is unknown: the whole project, including the seat furniture and bed, was evidently financed by the Privy Purse, and no record survives.

This paper concludes with a brief glance at the King's use of the Gothic style, to which he eventually became a complete convert under James Wyatt's influence at the end of the century. That he recognised the national and symbolic importance of the Gothic is clear from his privately funded commission to the carver Henry Emlyn in 1782 to repair and embellish the interior of St George's Chapel, one of the finest Perpendicular Gothic buildings in the country as well as the religious centre of the Order of the Garter.[60] Later on, under Wyatt's direction, much further gothicising took place in the Upper Ward of the Castle and an antiquarian spirit evidently guided the King when it came to the choice of furnishings. In the Queen's Ballroom for example, surviving pieces of seventeenth-century silver furniture were used for the great housewarming party to celebrate the completion of Wyatt's work in 1805.[61] And as a coda to this conservative and traditional approach to furnishing and decoration, we see the King at the very end of his active reign ordering an extraordinary virtuoso limewood carving from Edward Wyatt, in which the British Lion is shown defending Freedom, Justice and Commerce, flanked by the insignia of the Orders of the Garter and the Bath.[62] It was placed in the Queen's Audience Chamber at Windsor where it was doubtless intended to stand comparison with the work of Grinling Gibbons and in its rich blend of modernity, tradition, fine craftsmanship and Britishness to underline and exemplify many of the King's abiding interests.

NOTES

1. The unofficial royal residences around Leicester Square at this date are described in *Survey of London*, XXXIV, pp. 459–64 (Savile House), pp. 441–55 (Leicester House) and pp. 500–01 (28 and 29 Leicester Square).

2. *George III & Queen Charlotte*, nos. 120, 121 and 123.

3. *ibid.*, nos. 102, 103, 105, 106 and 125–35.

4. Furnishing payments for the official residences are mostly contained in TNA, PRO LC9.

5. *George III & Queen Charlotte*, nos 108–18.

6. George II's last Master, Sir Thomas Robinson, Lord Grantham was replaced in 1760 by the 2nd Earl Gower. He was followed by three further Masters until the abolition of the office as part of Edmund Burke's Economical Reforms in 1782.

7. G. Beard and C. Gilbert, eds., *Dictionary of English Furniture Makers, 1660–1840*, Leeds, 1986 (hereafter *DOEFM*), pp. 351–4.

8. *ibid.*, p. 638.

9. *Bute*, p. 38.

10. Vile was probably already ailing (he died aged 52 in 1767); and Cobb's notoriously high-handed manner no doubt alienated the King. See R. Edwards and M. Jourdain, *Georgian Cabinet-Makers*, rev. edn, London, 1950, p. 55.

11. *DOEFM*, pp. 95–6 and 316–17.

12. *George III & Queen Charlotte*, no. 281.

13. *DOEFM*, p. 772.

14. BL, Add. MS 17870, f. 84.

15. *George III & Queen Charlotte*, no. 284.

16. *DOEFM*, pp. 57–8.

17. *ibid.*, pp. 273–4, and *George III & Queen Charlotte*, no. 290.

18. Quoted in *King's Works*, VI, p. 5.

19. *George III & Queen Charlotte*, no. 263.

20. e.g. *ibid.*, nos. 280, 282, 283, 285 and 289.

21. e.g. *ibid.*, no. 260.

22. e.g. TNA, PRO LC9/293–294.

23. TNA, PRO LC9/307, qtr to Christmas 1762: no. 82 (Catherine Naish, carver and joiner); no. 80 (Vile and Cobb, upholsterers); no. 77 (Robert Carr, mercer); no. 79 (Thomas Hinchliff, mercer); no. 87 (Francis Plummer, gold laceman); no. 91 (Priscilla

MacEune, lacewoman); no. 96 (William Gwillim, feather dresser).

24. These pieces were taken as perquisites of the Lord Chamberlain and the Lord Great Chamberlain. See H. Roberts, 'Royal Thrones', *Furniture History*, XXV, 1989, pp. 61–85.
25. *ibid.*, fig. 7.
26. TNA, PRO LC9/306, qtr to Michaelmas 1761.
27. *George III & Queen Charlotte*, no. 266.
28. *ibid.*, no. 269.
29. *ibid.*, no. 268.
30. TNA, PRO LC9/308, qtr to Christmas 1762, no. 8.
31. TNA, PRO LC9/313, qtr to Christmas 1765, no. 8.
32. *George III & Queen Charlotte*, no. 115.
33. The full description is contained in BL, Add. MS 42160, ff. 19–22.
34. *Royal Residences*, II, London, 1819, Buckingham House, p. 8.
35. *George III & Queen Charlotte*, no. 4.
36. *ibid.*, no. 298.
37. Duchy of Cornwall Archives, Household Accounts of Frederick, Prince of Wales, vol. XV, 1742–3, ff. 351–9.
38. TNA, PRO LC9/291, October 1756, no. 32.
39. TNA, PRO LC9/307, qtr to Midsummer 1762, no. 56, and qtr to Christmas, no. 84.
40. TNA, PRO LC9/308, qtr to Lady Day 1763, no. 22.
41. TNA, PRO LC9/313, qtr to Christmas 1766, no. 93.
42. Quoted in Brooke, p. 306.
43. *George III & Queen Charlotte*, no. 9.
44. *ibid.*, no. 272.
45. *ibid.*, no. 261.
46. TNA, PRO LC9/307, qtr to Midsummer 1762, no. 49.
47. Millar 1969, no. 1200.
48. TNA, PRO LC9/310, qtr to Christmas 1763, no. 6 (the gilt seat furniture and window cornices by Naish) and no. 4 (the upholstery by Vile and Cobb).
49. *George III & Queen Charlotte*, no. 113.
50. TNA, PRO LC9/310, qtr to Midsummer 1764, no. 60 (France) and no. 62 (Naish).
51. *George III & Queen Charlotte*, nos. 141, 477 and 478.
52. TNA, PRO LC9/309, qtr to Michaelmas, no. 54.
53. *George III & Queen Charlotte*, no. 267.

54. TNA, PRO LC9/320, qtr to Lady Day 1773, no. 25.
55. *George III & Queen Charlotte*, no. 273.
56. See, for example, *ibid.*, no. 284.
57. Now at Hampton Court Palace (RCIN 1470).
58. *George III & Queen Charlotte*, no. 282.
59. *ibid.*, no. 280.
60. *ibid.*, no. 287.
61. *ibid.*, no. 132.
62. *ibid.*, no. 291.

8

Music at the court of George III and Queen Charlotte[1]

STEPHEN ROE

When Princess Charlotte of Mecklenburg-Strelitz set sail from Cuxhaven for England at the end of August 1761 to marry George III, she had a harpsichord in her quarters on the ship and played English tunes on it, in order, it was said, 'to encourage her companions in their misery'.[2] Fifty years later, when the lonely, lost and mad King was shut away, he, too, consoled himself by playing the harpsichord. He also played the flute; she enjoyed singing. Music was highly important to the King and Queen and to their family. They both collected music, printed and manuscript.[3] A large part of their music library, including the exceptional collection of Handel autographs, was deposited in the British Museum during the reign of King George V and formally presented by The Queen in 1957. It is, with the remainder of the Royal Library, now the centrepiece of the new British Library. George III and his consort were certainly the most musical king and queen since Charles II, perhaps even since Elizabeth I; they were equalled afterwards only by Queen Victoria and Prince Albert, and by George IV, of whom it was later said anonymously that he was 'not only a musician among princes, but a prince among musicians'; this says much for the musical training instigated by his parents. Both George III and Queen Charlotte had their own musical establishments; both enjoyed going frequently to the opera; both had regular concerts of orchestral and chamber music at their various residences, and both participated in performances at court with members of their family – once a week at St James's in the early years of their marriage.

On George III's accession, London was one of the two or three major centres of music in Europe. With Paris, it dominated European music. Vienna did not rise to prominence until the 1780s and Berlin was too much under the thumb of Frederick the Great to display the liveliness and diversity of London, whose more open society, new middle class and enlightened aristocracy were eager for entertainment and intellectual satisfaction. The 'rage for music' in the second half of the eighteenth century resulted in the rise of the public concert, such as the Bach-Abel concerts from 1765, the erection of concert halls, such as the Hanover Square Rooms in 1775, and the proliferation of music publishers, engravers and music sellers. London was also a major centre of musical instrument manufacturing and pioneered the new square piano, a handy, simple, portable and expressive instrument which made its first public appearance in the 1760s, and later the grand piano or fortepiano. For the first time music and musical instruments were produced in sufficient quantities for any moderately well-off person to have in their home. A large number of instruments were purchased by the King and Queen, particularly early in their reign. In February 1764, for example, the King bought three harpsichords, including two by Kirkman. His residences were certainly well stocked, and some instruments were modified to fit the rooms. For example, a very large claviorgan, whose cabinet is attributed to Benjamin Goodison,[4] seems to have been altered in 1763 to fit the Japan Room at Buckingham House, where much music was played. An organ by Snetzler in a case by John Bradburn, supplied in 1766/7, can be seen in the Japan Room in James Stephanoff's view for Pyne's *Royal Residences* (fig. 50). The organ survives in the Queen's Chapel, St James's Palace.

Musical life in George III's capital was dominated by foreigners, mostly Italians, Germans, Bohemians and French. No English composers' music was heard at the King's Theatre, where the Italian opera was performed, and many of the

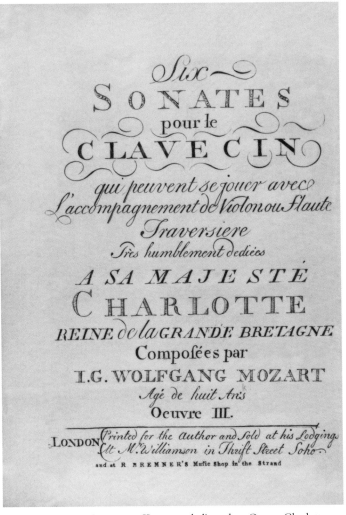

49. W.A. Mozart, *Six sonatas*, K.10–15, dedicated to Queen Charlotte. British Library, London

singers were foreign imports. Although the King and Queen frequently attended, the opera house in the Haymarket was independent and not, by and large, subject to royal whim.

50. James Stephanoff, *Buckingham House: The Queen's Breakfast Room*, 1817. Watercolour. RL 22145

Composers flooded in: C.F. Abel, J.C., J.C.F. and W.F.E. Bach, Vento, Giordani, Sacchini, Rauzzini, Kammel, the young Mozart with his father and sister in 1764–5, Clementi, the oboist Fischer (plate XIII), Schroeter, the Duports, Dussek, Salamon, and Haydn on two notable visits in the 1790s. Mozart was invited to come again in 1792, a move that might have restored his depleted finances and resurrected his international career, but death intervened. Beethoven, whose music was published in London as early as the first decade of the nineteenth century, was invited on several occasions, but never left Germany or Austria.

Some of these composers had connections with George III's court, but despite the evident enthusiasm of the royal couple for music, royal patronage was in decline. The court was no longer the main focus of the musical life of London, whose real diversity and liveliness lay elsewhere. The court reflected what was going on in the city, but it was no longer the propulsive force it had been a hundred years before, at the time of the Restoration. The court of Charles II, emulating that of France, was the most ambitious musical household we have ever had. Charles II founded the King's Band with its twenty-four players, mirroring the *Vingt-Quatre Violons du Roi*. George I was the last monarch personally to audition musicians for his orchestra. They had a lot to live up to: George I's Hanover *Kapellmeister* Georg Frideric Händel was now the leading musician in London. He changed his name, and British musical life, for ever.

Handel was the dominating figure during the reigns of the first three Georges, even though he died in 1759, just before the accession of George III. His music was especially beloved of the new King, who played it at every opportunity. In his youth, he had met the composer and expressed such enthusiasm that Handel apparently remarked: 'While that boy lives, my music will never want a protector.' This oft-quoted remark was repeated by the King himself to Fanny Burney during one of his illnesses.[5] Handel was right: under George III he became effectively posthumous court composer in perpetuity. The King acquired a large collection of the composer's autograph manuscripts, as well as the famous Roubiliac bust (fig. 51),[6] which had been made for Handel himself, and he was proud to own a harpsichord that had belonged to Handel.[7] The King patronised and was the prime mover behind the Handel centenary celebrations, which took place a year early in 1784. He apparently read in manuscript Charles Burney's *Account of the Musical Performances in Westminster Abbey and at the Pantheon in Commemoration of Handel* (1785), offering suggestions for its improvement, though these were not always deemed helpful by the author.[8] In the *Account* Burney supplied the first catalogue of all the autographs of Handel (or what were then deemed thus) in the King's Library. This centenary celebration was the first time any

51. Louis-François Roubiliac, *George Frederick Handel*, 1739. Marble.
RCIN 35255

composer's birthday had been marked ceremonially, and it represents a new interest in music of the past, even though it was only the recent past. The King took an interest in the subsequent annual Handel celebrations, and there is no doubt that Handel's posthumous reputation was enhanced during George III's reign thanks largely to the King's own great enthusiasm and support.

In George III's day the King's Band was an orchestra still of roughly twenty-four musicians. As foreigners were excluded, it did not contain the cream of London music life. It was presided over by the Master of the King's Music. The deaf, conservative Handelian William Boyce lasted until 1779, followed by the blind, conservative Handelian John Stanley, until 1786. After him no musician of great standing held the post until Edward Elgar in the twentieth century. The King's Band accompanied the court odes, performed at the New Year and at the time of the King's Birthday (4 June). These were performed in the midday drawing room at St James's Palace. Boyce churned out these odes with mechanical regularity from 1761 until 1779. When the King was at Windsor, the King's Band played every night. The King devised the programmes, as he did, incidentally, for the Concerts of Ancient Music from 1785, which were decidedly Handelocentric. These Handelian evenings were clearly of great importance to the King, to judge from his insistence on a concert on the very evening of an attempt on his life, as Fanny Burney relates, in 1786.[9] Some of the King's programmes have survived and these mix overtures, choruses and arias from oratorios by Handel, with perhaps one of his concertos. A typical example was performed on 25 April 1793:

Ouverture Admetus [Handel]
Concerto Oboe
Chorus no. 7 Deborah [Handel]
5th Concert from Corelli Solos
Concerto Flauto
Concerto French Horn
Chorus no. 8 Deborah [Handel]
Overture Scipio [Handel]
Concerto Violino
Chorus no. 9 Deborah [Handel][10]

Composers in the surviving programmes are rarely mentioned. Whether some of the unidentified concertos are also by Handel, it is not possible to say. Corelli, whose music was published in England throughout the eighteenth century, is one of the few other identifiable masters. He died in 1713. All in all, George's taste was conservative and favoured the Baroque masters. Even though in February 1795, at the instigation of the Prince of Wales, he did attend performances of more modern music, hearing some London symphonies of Haydn, he did not return for subsequent performances.[11] George III's passion for Handel was all embracing.

Queen Charlotte was much more progressive. She was perhaps a more able, intuitive and sensitive musician than the King and she valued music highly. In 1779 James Harris, then private secretary to the Queen, records her disappointment with her progress at music, especially when she came to England, noting pointedly that all she heard on her arrival was 'Handel, Corelli and Geminiani, very different from that to which she had been accustomed.'[12]

Queen Charlotte had two ensembles. The Queen's Band was formed on her arrival in 1761 and consisted of around nine Britons by 1770. In 1783 this was augmented by the deliberate importation of twelve Germans, 'to put the natives of poor old England out of countenance as much as possible,' as one commentator ruefully put it.[13] The Queen's sympathies were undoubtedly German and it can be no accident that her private chamber ensemble, a small group of virtuosi, was centred round J.C. Bach and Abel, and was almost entirely German. We are fortunate in having several accounts of musical performances by this ensemble and also of larger groups, from Mrs Delany,[14] Mrs Papendiek,[15] and James Harris.[16] There were quartet concerts twice a week on Tuesdays and Thursdays, except in the summer, when they were once a fortnight. These took place at Buckingham House, and in the summer at Kew or Windsor.

From the surviving descriptions, the music performed by the Queen's bands was contemporary, much of it written by the performers, though occasionally this would be leavened with older music by Handel and the like. A chamber concert in 1779 was described by Mrs Delany: 'I had two hours most

52. Charles Jean Robineau, *Carl Friedrich Abel*, 1780. RCIN 403540

delightful entertainment: the musick, tho' modern, was excellent *in its kind* and well performed; particularly the first fiddle by Cramer, Abel on the *Viol da Gambo* (tho' I don't like that instrument) and a new hautboy, just come in from Germany.'[17]

Carl Friedrich Abel (fig. 52) had come to England around 1759 and with Johann Christian Bach, a fellow pupil of Johann Sebastian Bach, was a pillar of London musical life.

149

Like Christian Bach, Abel was a member of an important musical dynasty: his musician father had been a friend of J.S. Bach in Cöthen. Abel was a great friend of the painter and fellow gamba player Thomas Gainsborough, who painted several memorable portraits of him, one holding his instrument (now in the Huntington Library Art Collections, San Marino, California). The viol da gamba was an instrument then somewhat out of fashion in England – indeed it virtually disappeared with the death of Abel in 1787. Abel transfixed his audiences, particularly for the refinement of taste and depth of feeling in the adagios. A notable bon viveur and wine importer, in his last years he had to be propped in his seat to perform, but apparently did so magnificently.

Abel was described as chamber musician to the Queen. Johann Christian Bach, whose portrait was also painted by Gainsborough (fig. 53), was also her chamber musician. From as early as 1763 he was 'Music Master to the Queen' and later 'to the Queen and the royal family'. In addition to his duties as a performer at court, he also taught Queen Charlotte singing and accompanied her, and later assisted in instrumental lessons with the children as they became old enough.

Born in 1735 in Leipzig, Johann Christian's earliest musical education was supervised by his father Johann Sebastian. In addition to being a keyboard player of the first rank, he helped his father as amanuensis, particularly after the latter went blind. (One of the few connections between Johann Sebastian Bach and Handel is that they were both effectively rendered blind by the same English oculist, John Taylor.) On his father's death in 1750, Johann Christian went to Berlin for five years. There he studied with his half-brother Carl Philipp Emanuel, composed his first major works and established a reputation as a keyboard performer. In 1755 he travelled to Italy, reputedly with an Italian female dancer; he settled, became a Catholic, was appointed second organist at the Cathedral in Milan and wrote Italian operas. The contact with Italy and Italian musical life transformed Bach's style. Gone was the severe manner of his brother's music; gone was the

53. Thomas Gainsborough, *Johann Christian Bach*, *c.*1776. National Portrait Gallery, London

stricter style of his Lutheran ancestors. It was replaced by a more easygoing, genial, truly modern manner, with an Italianate grace, underpinned by German rigour. It was this that must have attracted the Queen, as it would the young Mozart.

When Bach moved to London in 1762 it was to compose Italian operas for the King's Theatre.[18] He was also intending to return to Italy after one year, but the affection that he was held in at the court bound him to England and he settled in London, remaining until his death on 1 January 1782. He was the principal composer in the country during that time, founding the Bach-Abel concerts and establishing its finest concert hall in Hanover Square. He espoused the pianoforte and promoted it, wrote music for it, and sent pianos to friends and acquaintances around Europe, including the daughter of the philosopher Diderot. J.C. Bach's address book must have been one of the most glittering of any musician in Europe, with friends and acquaintances ranging from the British, Prussian and French courts, to Gainsborough, his Bach brothers, and probably even Casanova. Benjamin Franklin could well have been an acquaintance in Paris through their mutual friend Madame Brillon.[19]

Bach's publishing career effectively began in London and many of his works are dedicated to members of the royal family. With the exception of Princess Augusta, the dedicatees are mostly on the Queen's side, indicating his closeness to her. His keyboard concertos Opus 1 were dedicated to her and the last movement of the last concerto is a set of variations on a theme which, even after only two years in London, might have been all too familiar to her, 'God save the King'.

James Harris provides a charming account, in a diary entry dated 3 May 1774, of a concert given by Bach and Abel at Buckingham House, at which Bach's new cantata *Amor vincitore* was performed. It reveals the etiquette of perform-ances in the eighteenth century and how the royal children were involved. The performance took place in the Japan Room, where a plaster copy of Roubiliac's bust of Handel held pride of place. One of the singers was Cecilia Grassi, Bach's wife:

> I had a message from the queen to attend her – it came after dinner & was for me to attend her a little after seven. I went, imagining it was a message that I should carry in the last quarterly bill. When I came into the Japan-wainscot room, I found it to my surprize filled with all the capital musicians –

Bach, Abel, Cramer, the celebrated violin, five or six opera violins, Gordon[,] & another violoncello, 2 opera double bases, hautboys, horns, tenors, Beir the clarionet, Richter the bassoon, Weiss the german flute, Fisher the hautboy, Millico, Grassi, & the chorus singers.

I past by them into the room, where the Guidos hung. There I first saw the Queen; then the King, the Prince of Wales, & three of his brothers, & four of his sisters. The Prince & his brothers were attended by their proper governors & nursery people: the company were the Duchess of Argyle, Lady Effingham, Lord Delawar and my self. The King stood & walked the whole time, the Queen & ladys sometimes sate.

When the concert began, the royal children (the younger part) stood arranged in the same room with the music – the King sometimes came out, & the Queen also – a song of Handels in Otho was sung admirably by Millico, & a duett by him & Grassi from Rodelinda – this & some solo concerto's & other peices made the first act. Bach's new cantata (in it were choruses) made the second. During this the Queen came into the music room, & sate.

When the music was finished, & dismissed about half past ten[,] the door of the music room was shut, & the royal children withdrew. There remained only the King & Queen, together with the Duchess of Argyle, Lady Effingham, Lord Delawar, and myself. All stood & formed a circle, and a very chearful and easy conversation ensued, till about a quarter past eleven, when the King & Queen withdrew, & we all departing, Lord Delawar in his coach bringing me home. The King & Queen honoured me with much of their conversation during and after the concert.[20]

This description seems to suggest that while the royal children were in the room where the music was performed, the King and Queen moved backwards and forwards, though the Queen evidently gave full attention to Bach's music in the second half.

Bach did provide one birthday ode for the King, 'Happy Morn, auspicious rise', the autograph of which is in the Royal Music Library in the British Library (RM 22 a.16). This must date from the early 1770s and is especially interesting in that one movement was probably sung by two of the royal children. The musical content is relatively unchallenging and the text suggests that the Prince of Wales participated with one of his siblings:

Blest to our Parents rise
Each minute steal a care away
And drop a Blessing as it flies
Blest to our Country be this day
Peace smile beneath a George's sway
While factious discord dropping dies.

What of the Queen's own musical accomplishments? Recently, while examining some eighteenth-century printed music in a private collection, I found a volume which once had royal provenance.[21] It contained an unknown autograph manuscript of J.C. Bach, which had been bound in a volume of otherwise printed music, probably in the late 1770s. Though Bach's name is not on the manuscript, it is entirely autograph and bears the title: 'Aria nell'Oratorio Gioas re di Giuda'. *Gioas* was composed by Bach in 1770 for the King's Theatre. The aria is called: 'Te adoro te solo'. Comparing this manuscript with the other sources, notably the first edition (London, 1770) and the incomplete autograph full score (London, Royal College of Music, MS 24), we find that the aria in the manuscript is much shorter and considerably altered. It is effectively a new composition making use of older material. The vocal line is simpler and less florid: it is a scaled-down version in every respect and is scored, not for voice and orchestra, but for voice and keyboard. This is almost certainly teaching material. Bach, as we know, was the Queen's singing teacher. Given the royal provenance of the manuscript and the reduced forces and simplified musical text, it seems likely that this aria was probably used by Queen Charlotte and Bach when he accompanied her in her singing lessons. It has a low range, which suggests that, unlike the young Queen Victoria, she did not have a high voice. Perhaps the Queen was taken with the aria when she attended performances of the oratorio in the King's Theatre and Bach made this modified version for her. It is certainly a charming arrangement and one that reflects on the special affection that the Queen had for Bach. After his death on 1 January 1782, the Queen paid for Bach's funeral and later gave £100 to his widow, who had sung in *Gioas*, to enable her to return home to Italy. Several of Bach's autograph scores remained in the Queen's music library.

A number of Bach's friends, pupils and protégés were also involved with music at court, the most notable being the young Mozart. The Mozart family – father, wife, daughter Nannerl and 8-year-old son Wolfgang Amadeus – appeared in London in 1764/5. Both Bach and Abel befriended the family and both were great and important early influences on the young musician. Mozart copied out a symphony of Abel, which was subsequently believed to be his own work. The Mozarts appeared at court and made a great impression on the King and Queen. Within four days of their arrival in London, Wolfgang and his sister met George III and Queen Charlotte on 27 April and were presented with 24 guineas, as they were also on their second appearance on 19 May. A third presentation took place in October. Within a few days of their first appearance at court, the Mozarts were walking in St James's Park and the King and Queen came driving by. Leopold Mozart, writing to his friend Lorenz Hagenauer in Salzburg, on 28 May 1764, continued the story: 'although we all had on different clothes, they recognised us nevertheless; but the King opened the window, leaned out and saluted us and especially our Master Wolfgang, nodding to us and waving his hand'.[22]

The King was greatly impressed by the proficiency of the young genius, as Leopold relates:

The King placed before him not only works by Wagenseil, but those of Bach, Abel and Handel, and he played off everything *prima vista*. He played so splendidly on the king's organ that they all value his organ-playing more highly than his clavier-playing. Then he accompanied the Queen in an aria which she sang, and also a flautist who played a solo. Finally, he took the bass part of some airs of Handel (which happened to be lying there) and played the most beautiful melody on it and in such a manner that everyone was amazed. In short, what he knew when we left Salzburg is a mere shadow compared with what he knows now. It exceeds all that one can imagine.[23]

The young Mozart composed six sonatas in London written for keyboard with the accompaniment of violin or flute and bass (fig. 49). These were published by Leopold as 'composed by I.G.Wolfgang Mozart, Agé de huit Ans' as Opus III, 'Printed for the Author and sold at his Lodgings At Mr Williamson in Thrift Street, Soho'. They are humbly dedicated to 'Sa Majesté Charlotte Reine de la Grande Bretagne' and contain a florid dedication, no doubt drafted by someone else, but bearing Wolfgang's signature.

As in other areas of the Queen's interests, her level of appreciation of more modern music waned as she got older. After the 1770s, perhaps after the death of J.C. Bach, she rarely played the harpsichord, and, though she continued to sing, her appreciation of music became ossified. The King and Queen did meet Haydn, listened to his music, and were friendly and courteous to him on his visits in the 1790s. George III even presented a Handel manuscript to him. But Haydn's new and popular style was rather beyond the King and Queen. It was the Prince of Wales who was more sympathetic to the music of Haydn, Cherubini, and Beethoven and the other composers who survived into the nineteenth century.

Nevertheless, the King and Queen still acquired a large amount of music and made some skilful purchases. By the 1780s the collection was so large as to require a librarian, Frederick Nicolay, friend and amanuensis of Johann Christian Bach, member of the Queen's Quartet Band and former Page of the Back Stairs. His inscription, 'This Volume belongs to The Queen 1788', is found in a large number of volumes in the Royal Music Library. He looked after the Handel autographs meticulously, noting where leaves were mixed up or missing, and prepared them for binding. That the Handel autographs survived so well for so long is thanks to him, though they have been less well served by their twentieth-century guardians in their efforts in conservation. He also acquired music for the Library. Eschewing the autographs of Boyce's odes at his sale at Christie's in 1779, Nicolay nevertheless acquired the celebrated Cosyn Virginal Book, twelve symphonies and the opera *Tigrane* by Scarlatti, and a number of other antiquarian volumes.[24] Musical antiquarianism received its first real impetus in the reign of George III, as is evidenced not only in the Concert of Ancient Music, and the publication of sixteenth-century manuscripts of madrigals, and the music of Purcell and other earlier composers, but also in the preparation of the music histories of Sir John Hawkins and Charles Burney,[25] dedicated respectively to the King and Queen. They mapped the development of music, as Samuel Johnson traced the development of the English language in his dictionary.

George III and Queen Charlotte's real achievements in music are the Royal Music Library, the preservation of the Handel autographs, and their fostering and encouragement of musicians such as J.C. Bach, Abel, Mozart and others, and music historians such as Burney and Hawkins. Their taste may well have mirrored the lively musical life of the capital. But George III's passion for Handel and his strenuous and successful efforts to revive his music played a major part in keeping the composer's name in front of the public eye. Thanks to the King's active encouragement, Handel's reputation has never diminished.

George III presided over a court that resounded with music. We must think of the unnatural silence that Fanny Burney noted so poignantly when, in George III's first illness at Kew, all music ceased in order not to excite the King.

NOTES

1. This is a revised version of what was originally a lecture with music, performed by *Charivari agréable*, directed by Kah-Min Ng, on George III's birthday, 4 June 2004, in The Queen's Gallery at Buckingham Palace. The works performed were: Handel, *Passacaille*, from the Trio Sonata, op. 5 no. 4; Abel, 3 pieces for viol da gamba; J.C. Bach, Harpsichord Concerto, op. 1 no. 6, last movement, Variations on 'God save the King'; W.A. Mozart, Sonata for Keyboard, Flute and Cello in F, K.13, first movement; J.C. Bach aria, 'Te adoro', from *Gioas, re di Giuda* in the newly discovered version; and Handel, aria 'Mio caro bene' from *Rodelinda*.

2. Quoted (without earlier reference) in J. van der Kiste, *George III's Children*, London, 2004, p. 4.

3. See P. Scholes, 'George the Third as Music Lover', *Musical Quarterly*, XXVIII, 1942, pp. 78–92, and S. McVeigh, *Concert Life in London from Mozart to Haydn*, Cambridge, 1993, esp. pp. 49–52.

4. *George III & Queen Charlotte*, no. 264. See also RA GEO/ 55510ff.

5. *Burney Diary*, IV, p. 248.

6. *George III & Queen Charlotte*, no. 252.

7. The harpsichord is probably the Ruckers of 1612 on loan from the Royal Collection to the National Trust at Fenton House, Hampstead. The instrument by Shudi (*George III & Queen Charlotte*, no. 262) has also been suggested as Handel's instrument. Handel left all of these items to his amanuensis J.C. Smith, whose son, J.C. Smith the younger, left them in turn to George III. For details of the manuscripts see D. Burrows and M. Ronish, *A Catalogue of Handel's Musical Autographs*, Oxford, 1994, especially pp. xv–xx.

8. R. Lonsdale, *Dr Charles Burney*, Oxford, 1965, pp. 299ff.

9. *Burney Diary*, II, p. 417, entry for 2 August 1786.

10. Royal Library, Windsor Castle, RCIN 1140992. Other programmes for 1794 in the King's hand are RCIN 1140980. Further examples have appeared at auctions over the years.

11. H.C. Robbins Landon, *Haydn in England, 1791–1795*, London, 1976, pp. 283–5.

12. D. Burrows and R. Dunhill, eds., *Music and Theatre in Handel's World: The Family Papers of James Harris (1732–1780)*, Oxford, 2002, p. 1007.

13. *The London Magazine*, IV, 1785, p. 141. See also McVeigh 1993, p. 50.

14. Lady Llanover, ed., *The Autobiography and Correspondence of Mary Granville, Mrs Delany*, 6 vols., London, 1861–2.

15. *Papendiek.*

16. Burrows and Dunhill 2002.

17. Llanover 1861–2, V, pp. 478–9, letter of 29 October 1779.

18. There is no evidence that Bach visited Strelitz on the way, as has often been written.

19. See S. Roe, 'The Paris Bach', in *Bunte Blätter Klaus Mecklenburg zum 23 Februar 2000*, ed. A. Moirandat, Basel, 2000, pp. 247–54.

20. Burrows and Dunhill 2002, pp. 765–7.

21. I am very grateful to the owner for allowing me to mention this here.

22. E. Anderson, ed., *The Letters of Mozart and his Family*, London, 1986, p. 46.

23. *ibid.*, p. 47.

24. See A. Hyatt King, *Some British Collectors of Music*, Cambridge, 1963, pp.115–29.

25. J. Hawkins, *A General History of the Science and Practice of Music*, London, 1776; C. Burney, *A General History of Music*, London, 1776–89.

III

QUEEN CHARLOTTE

54. Allan Ramsay, *Queen Charlotte and her two eldest sons*, c.1764–9. RCIN 404922

9

Queen Charlotte and her circle

CLARISSA CAMPBELL ORR

The exhibition *George III & Queen Charlotte: Patronage, Collecting and Court Taste* showed that George III was not the only bibliophile and reader in the royal family. Queen Charlotte amassed her own collection of approximately 4,500 volumes, and once she had purchased Frogmore and had it rebuilt as her own personal retreat in 1790, she was able to put her own books there.[1] She also had a printing press, duly licensed. However, as her books were sold at her death we have only the 1819 Charles Wild watercolour (fig. 55) to represent the importance of books in her life. This indicates a typical country house library complete with busts of literary and moral worthies atop the shelves. It is harder still to discover what the books might have meant to the Queen: why she chose them, whether she read them all, which books she liked best. The Royal Archives have a few of Queen Charlotte's diaries, but frustratingly for the intellectual historian these do not include a list of or comments on what she was reading.

We do know, however, that reading was not a solitary and purely private activity for the Queen. It was supported by a number of household appointments: a Librarian, Edward Harding, who had been a specialist book-dealer and print-seller, and three Readers: Jean-André DeLuc, who read to her in French; Marie-Elisabeth de La Fite, German-born but of Huguenot stock; and Fanny Burney, who surmised that her position as Second Keeper of the Robes was supposed to include a literary dimension as adviser on contemporary

55. Charles Wild, *Frogmore House: The Queen's Library*, 1817. Watercolour.
RL 22120

English literature. As well as the social and recreational reading enjoyed at Windsor in the evenings, described in Fanny Burney's diaries, the Queen had books read to her while she was having her hair dressed for formal occasions, as she hated to waste time. Charlotte had no taste for riding or hunting, so her recreational interests tended to the sedentary. There is little sign that quiet reading played a larger part in her life when she was awaiting or recovering from one of her fifteen confinements, as she was fortunate in giving birth easily and sometimes remarkably quickly.[2] These three Readers were also authors who, along with other writers and translators, dedicated books to the Queen and effected introductions of visiting literary celebrities to her. We can therefore see Queen Charlotte as a figurehead in the international 'Republic of Letters', and a 'Patroness of the Enlightenment', like other

German princesses with a learned circle, who might also receive regular newsletters from literary figures or have books dedicated to them.[3]

The Queen's library was also part and parcel of the education she helped to provide for her children, especially her daughters, and it therefore links her to a network of cultured women and specialist advisers who assisted in this, such as Lady Charlotte Finch, the much loved Royal Governess who had many connections to the 'Bluestocking Circle'.[4] She appears in two of Zoffany's family group portraits (plates III and XIV).[5] Through the Queen's correspondence with her brother Carl, and with some of the aristocratic women who held court positions and became close personal friends, we can also catch glimpses of what books were to the Queen's taste and which ones she recommended enthusiastically to them. We can trace, too, a certain nostalgia for the small-scale court life of the princely courts in Germany where she was born[6] and to which Carl, the only one of her brothers to marry, was connected through the two daughters of Landgrave George of Hesse-Darmstadt whom he married, one after the other. The German dimension to a court whose rulers were also Elector and Electress of Hanover, and the Anglophilia of many of the smaller German courts in an age of Sensibility, which was nourished by English authors such as Samuel Richardson, need to be borne in mind.[7]

A tea party described by the German novelist Sophie von la Roche when she visited Mme de La Fite in 1786 helps evoke the literary circles and educational personnel of the court. The party comprised the French Reader DeLuc and his English wife, formerly a member of the Duke of Marlborough's household, and Mme de La Fite. 'I looked around me blissfully,' she wrote, 'and rejoiced in the thought: That the bonds of a common respect for all that is virtuous, good and knowledgeable had brought four people together from such different quarters of Europe. Mme La Fite born in Altona and married in Holland; de Luc from Geneva and myself a Swabian . . .'.[8] After her visit to Windsor, she declared: 'my spirit was moved, and with tears in my eyes I besought Providence always to provide this country with a king as fatherly as George III, and a queen with as great a learning and virtue as Charlotte of Mecklenburg.'[9]

Sophie von la Roche's most famous book was *The History of Lady Sophia Sternheim* (1771),[10] a portrait of female, rational sensibility under siege. It presents a critique of court culture that owes something to Rousseau, highlighting it as a source of corruption: the heroine is under pressure to become the prince's mistress and help influence policy to favour her relatives. Despite many setbacks, Lady Sophia devotes herself to the welfare of others and to the education of the lower orders wherever she lives, and is rewarded with marriage to a Scottish benevolent aristocrat. But the novel does not altogether reject courts, implying that they can be a source of cultural refinement and set the moral tone for society – which was surely the King and Queen's goal.

Von la Roche's cousin was Christoph Wieland, tutor to the two sons of the widowed Anna Amalia, Duchess of Saxe-Weimar, the eldest of whom was the future patron of Goethe and Schiller. Wieland's arrival in Weimar inaugurated the extraordinary efflorescence of this small court as a centre of German letters. The Duchess's mother was Frederick the Great's sister Philippine Charlotte, Duchess of Brunswick-Wolfenbüttel, another bibliophile princess.[11] Queen Charlotte was an enthusiastic reader of Wieland's philosophical novel *Der Goldene Spiegel* (*The Golden Mirror*, 1773), written just prior to his appointment as the Weimar tutor, and she had it read to her daughters.[12]

The novel was in the tradition of Bishop Fénelon's famous moral fable *Telemachus* (1699), which depicted Odysseus's son travelling the Mediterranean world in the company of his tutor, the original Mentor, and discovering wise and unwise ways to rule. Written for Louis XIV's grandson the Duke of Burgundy, the fable was construed at the time as a veiled critique of the aggressive foreign policy and absolutist style of rule of the great French monarch. Similarly, the political message endorsed by Wieland's tale was the need for constant vigilance lest absolute monarchy degenerate through corruption, showing the role of constitutional structures in mitigating this tendency.[13] In the Zoffany portrait of *Queen Charlotte with her two eldest sons* (plate III) the Prince of Wales is wearing a Telemachus costume. Amateur theatricals were a tool to help teach posture, confident performance and speech-making, but the message of the story is surely also important. In 1773 Bishop Markham of Chester, who had taught these two sons, showed a letter to his friend the Scottish poet James Beattie, another royal protégé, which he had received from Frederick, Duke of York and Prince-Bishop of Osnabrück in the Holy Roman Empire. The letter described a walk with his father in Kew Gardens: 'The King gave us many instructions in regard to the duties of princes: told us that princes not being obliged to labour with their hands, were to labour with their heads, for the good of their people.' The buildings at Kew, including a mosque, a pagoda and a ruined arch, representative of world architecture (fig. 7), must have helped the children imagine themselves to be Telemachus in search of good government.[14]

Although the Queen learnt English rapidly and fluently, she remained fond of German and kept up with German books. She liked the Scottish painter and man of Enlightenment Allan Ramsay, who spoke German with her while she was still mastering English and obtained German books for her. His early portrait of her (fig. 54), showing John Locke's *Treatise on Education*, identified a key interest of the Queen. She was keen that her daughters should be well versed in German language and literature, and therefore when Jean André DeLuc introduced to her his friend Mme de La Fite, she gave her an appointment as a Reader with a particular brief to teach German to the Princesses. A German Protestant, possibly of Huguenot extraction, Mme de La Fite was bilingual, and it is not clear whether French or German was her native tongue. While married to a Dutch Huguenot pastor, Jean-Daniel La Fite, who had also been a Royal Chaplain to the House of Orange in The Hague, Mme de La Fite had collaborated with him in producing a literary journal which was explicitly anti-Deistic, the *Bibliothèque des Sciences et des Beaux-Arts*. Once appointed to Queen Charlotte, Mme de La Fite wrote various French books with the royal Princesses in mind, such as *Eugénie et ses élèves* (1787), dedicated to Princess Elizabeth, and *Entretiens, Drames, et Contes Moraux à l'usage des femmes* (1801), dedicated to Queen Charlotte. She translated Sophie von la Roche's *History of Lady Sophia Sternheim* into French, and later Hannah More's critique of aristocratic morality, *Thoughts of the Manners of the Great*.[15]

Another of Mme de La Fite's translations was a biography of the Saxon moralist Christian Fürchtegott Gellert, the Saxon Professor of Poetry, Rhetoric and Ethics at Leipzig from 1744 to 1769 and an extremely influential teacher. He is a good example of the cross-fertilisation between English and German letters in the mid-century, being influenced by the style of the English divine John Tillotson.[16] Queen Charlotte could not esteem Gellert too highly. In 1774 her brother had sent her one of Gellert's books and she wrote enthusiastically: 'a thousand, thousand thanks for M. Gellert's book ... if ever there was a saint on earth, he is one. The greatest libertine could not read him without becoming good.'[17] Years later she was still recommending him to her friends: in 1787 she sent his *Works* to her Lady in Waiting Lady Elizabeth Pembroke, saying 'I myself read them with avidity as the matter is so good & Instructive that I have always been benefited by its precepts.'[18] The Princess Royal similarly urged her brother Augustus to read him as he was a favourite author.[19]

Gellert's critique of French libertinism in his novel *The History of the Swedish Countess of Guildenstern*,[20] extolling the role of reason and moral sentiment over unregulated passion, is a reminder that the francophone character of the European elite presented religious and moral challenges. French was the language of polite society as well as a common currency in the Republic of Letters, yet France was a Catholic and absolutist culture. A key factor in the formation of the European Enlightenment was the reaction to Louis XIV's expulsion of the Huguenots in 1685, crystallising for Protestant princes such as William of Orange and the Great Elector of Brandenburg the desirability of succouring Protestant refugees as well as resisting French Catholic bigotry. Later Voltaire initiated a crusade in favour of toleration. Yet the Deist and free-thinking character of the Voltairean Enlightenment was unacceptable to devout Protestant German princely cultures such as Queen Charlotte's native Mecklenberg or George III's Electorate of Hanover. The Electoral University at Göttingen encouraged theological liberalism but still expected Christianity to be upheld.[21] It is in this context that we need to consider the appointment of the Geneva *savant* Jean-André DeLuc as Queen Charlotte's French Reader. Geneva was safely Protestant as well as usefully francophone; young gentlemen on the Grand Tour could safely spend time at the Académie there and avoid contamination from either Catholicism or French moral laxity. The Queen's brother Carl studied in Geneva, undoubtedly for these reasons, and several courtiers, including the 10th Earl and Countess of Pembroke, the Duchess of Hamilton, and Lord Bute, sent their sons there.[22] By 1787, Edward, Duke of Kent, Queen Charlotte's fourth son, was spending some time there.[23]

Lord Bute's son Lord Mountstuart was accompanied by the Genevan Paul-Henri Mallet; after his duties were over he acted as a literary correspondent to the new Queen of Denmark, George III's sister Caroline Matilda. Prior to this he had tutored the Danish crown prince, whose mother Louisa was an aunt of George III. While he was at the Danish court Mallet wrote several works on Danish prehistory and antiquities, including *Histoire de Dannemarc* (1758), the first volume in a sequence on Danish history. From her letters in 1772 to her brother Carl we can see that Charlotte read these histories and recommended them to her brother.[24] Other readers of Mallet were noble literati and savants in courtier circles, such as the Duke of Northumberland and his chaplain Louis Dutens.[25] We can also infer from later letters to her brother Carl that the Queen was interested in Mallet's histories of the Hesse, Brunswick and Mecklenburg dynasties, all of whom had multiple family ties with the British court, and from all of whom he received pensions.

Perhaps the Queen's acquaintance with Mallet as a figure representative of Genevan culture predisposed her to appoint Jean-André DeLuc her Reader in 1773 when he came to England; he had the recommendation of Lord Holdernesse, the Governor of the Royal princes. If Mme de La Fite nourished the Queen's literary interests, DeLuc helped her with her scientific ones, especially botany and geology. Through his friendship with James Watt he was also an additional link to the Birmingham-based Lunar Society, the circle of entrepreneurs and inventors which included Matthew Boulton and Josiah Wedgwood, 'Potter to Her Majesty'. Both King and Queen were fascinated by the technological advances of the age.[26]

As the Queen's Reader, DeLuc's main duties were to read French books out loud to her, and to discuss the ideas they expressed. He was a retired watchmaker with a special interest in scientific instruments; now that he had given up business, he was writing up his geological theories. He dedicated the first sketch of his theory of the earth's development to Queen Charlotte.[27] His later correspondence with the Göttingen philologist J.D. Michaelis and the anthropologist J. Blumenbach on the interpretation of Genesis and its geological implications, illustrates the link between the British court and the Electoral University.[28]

DeLuc's geological and philosophical letters to Queen Charlotte reflect the dilemma visited on many of Rousseau's admirers by his paradoxical religious views. DeLuc and his father had made friends with Rousseau when he had resumed his Genevan citizenship in 1754. On the one hand he seemed to provide them with a religiosity, a spiritual conviction determinedly opposed to the materialist view that man was just a mechanistic bundle of sensations. In the contemplation of natural beauty in the Swiss mountains, amidst people with simple customs and manners, both DeLuc and Rousseau were convinced that man's soul was a palpable entity. DeLuc rhapsodised over this simplicity of living in the Swiss valleys, believing it held the key to happiness, and wrote to Charlotte that she was well placed, even in her elevated rank, to appreciate the blessings of domestic contentment.[29] On the other hand, it could not be denied that Rousseau fell short in his Christian convictions, even though he had set himself against the atheism of his Parisian associates in the *Encyclopédie*. However, DeLuc wrote to Charlotte,[30] Rousseau really did respect Christianity from the bottom of his heart. Thus Rousseau – the reluctant, then paranoid, pensionary of George III – was not in tune with the court's religious outlook, but his attempt to refute materialism was entirely in accord with royal religious convictions.[31]

Other women in Queen Charlotte's circle shared an interest in gardens and botany, which made them hospitable to Rousseau on his visit to England in 1766, while also sharing an ambivalence about his problematical Christianity. The Duchess of Portland, who had an extensive number of natural history collections, gave him rare plants and he described himself as the Duchess's 'herboriste'. The Duchess's house at Bulstrode was so close to Windsor that the King was able to ride over one morning and announce the birth of Princess Amelia. The King and Queen's kindness to the Duchess's friend Mrs Delany (fig. 56) is well known.[32] She was famous for her botanically accurate paper cut-outs. She warned her niece about Rousseau's orthodoxy, though: 'I always take an alarm, however, when virtue in general terms is the idol, without the support of religion, the only foundation that can be our security to build upon . . .'.[33] Probably the warmest aristocratic supporter of Rousseau at this time was the young Lord Nuneham. He and his wife were designing a 'garden of sensibility' at their home in Nuneham Courtenay which had a bust of Rousseau in homage. But twenty years later this Rousseauist republican ardour had cooled, and the couple, now the 2nd Earl and Countess Harcourt, became close friends of the King and

56. John Opie, *Mary Granville, Mrs Delany*, 1782. RCIN 400965

Queen and joined their respective households as Master of the Horse and Lady in Waiting.[34]

Botany also links Charlotte more specifically to the Blue-stocking Circle. Hannah More wrote her poem *Bas Bleu* in homage to these serious-minded gatherings and George III requested she make him a personal copy of it.[35] Later, in 1805, she wrote the *Hints for a Princess* as a moral guide in the upbringing of Princess Charlotte, the Queen's granddaughter

57. Edward Francis Burney, *Mrs Frances d'Arblay (Fanny Burney)*, c.1784–5.
National Portrait Gallery, London

and heiress apparent after her father, the Prince of Wales.
Fanny Burney (fig. 57), who became a protégée of the
Bluestockings after publishing her first novel, was introduced
to the Queen by Mrs Delany. The decision to make her
Second Keeper of the Robes was partly a recognition of the

place held by her father, Charles Burney, in English letters. His comprehensive *History of Music*, dedicated to the Queen in words chosen by Samuel Johnson, is probably the most important English example of Enlightened encyclopaedism.

Fanny Burney rightly realised her position was also to be a kind of English Reader and literary adviser: 'From the time that the Queen condescended to desire to place me in immediate attendance upon her own person, I had always secretly concluded she meant me for her English reader.'[36] Burney liked discussing books with the Queen: 'the excellence of her understanding and acuteness of her observation never fail to make all discourse with her lively and informing'; and sometimes the Queen read to Burney.[37] This mutual reading was especially consoling to the Queen during the first weeks of the King's frightening illness of 1788. The Queen also consulted Burney on the suitability of reading material for the Princesses. The Bluestocking Cornelia Knight, a protégée of Johnson, wanted to dedicate her novel *Dinarbas* – a continuation of Johnson's oriental fable *Rasselas*, written a little in the manner of *Telemachus* – to the Queen; Burney was able to say it was suitable for the Princesses to read. Later Miss Knight became a companion to the Queen and Princesses; some of her poems were printed on the Frogmore printing press.[38]

Another young woman who frequented the Bluestocking assemblies was William Hamilton's niece Mary, who for a while was preceptress to the princesses.[39] And the Queen lent German books to the famous scholar and classicist Elizabeth Carter. The Queen also sent her remedies for her headaches; the connection was furthered by the fact that the son of Lady Charlotte Finch, George, 9th Earl of Winchilsea, was Governor of the Cinque Ports, and thus resident in Deal, Carter's home town.[40]

It would not be an exaggeration to describe Charlotte as a Bluestocking Queen, who shared books and intellectual interests with her Readers, her children's governesses and tutors, and also with aristocratic women in her circle such as

Lady Pembroke and Lady Harcourt. It is also significant that in their affectionate marriage, which, though arranged, was in many respects what historians of the family would describe as companionate, the circles of the King and Queen were not separate; they included several couples where the husband and wife had appointments respectively in both households, or – in the husband's case – as a government minister. As well as Lord and Lady Pembroke, who entertained the King and Queen at Wilton House when they travelled to Weymouth, and Lord and Lady Harcourt, who lodged them at Nuneham Courtenay when they visited Oxford, another example would be Lord and Lady Weymouth, subsequently 1st Marquess and Marchioness of Bath. Louisa, Lady Weymouth, who served as a Lady of the Bedchamber and then Mistress of the Robes, was a daughter of the learned Duchess of Portland; her husband shared the King's interest in astronomy as well as in hunting.[41] He was Master of the Horse to Queen Charlotte from 1763 to 1765 and then held government office as Lord Lieutenant of Ireland and Secretary of State for the Southern Department.

Queen Charlotte was a consort who was also, at least until the first frightening bout of porphyria, her husband's friend; with him she shared many overlapping interests in theology, science, literature, music, and above all the education of their children. As Flora Fraser's new study shows, it would be these adult daughters who became central to the Queen's circle after their father's recurrent illnesses began.

NOTES

1. See *George III & Queen Charlotte*, no. 140.
2. Princess Sophia, for example, was born within fifteen minutes of labour commencing (*Princesses*, p. 49).
3. For a fuller attempt to explore the continental dimension, see C. Campbell Orr, 'Charlotte of Mecklenburg-Strelitz, Queen of Great Britain and Electress of Hanover: Northern Dynasties and the Northern Republic of Letters', in *Queenship in Europe: The Role of the Consort, 1660–1815*, ed. C. Campbell Orr, Cambridge, 2004.

4. So called because the botanist Benjamin Stillingfleet wore blue worsted stockings, not evening silk ones, to the soirées arranged by the famous Mrs Montagu, Queen of the Blues; see S. Harckstock Myers, *The Bluestocking Circle*, Oxford, 1990.

5. *George III & Queen Charlotte*, nos. 4 and 10. See also no. 78, and J. Shefrin, *Such Constant Affectionate Care: Lady Charlotte Finch, Royal Governess, and the Children of George III*, Los Angeles, 2003.

6. See Marcus Köhler's paper in this volume.

7. See Campbell Orr 2004.

8. *Sophie in London*, p. 187.

9. *ibid.*, p. 293.

10. *Der Geschichte des Fräuleins von Sternheim.*

11. A. Johns, 'Books as Cosmopolitan Objects', unpublished paper given at the conference on *Women and Material Culture, 1660–1830*, Chawton House Library, Alton, Hampshire, 14–15 July, 2004. Professor Johns's work on Philippine Charlotte will be published as part of a forthcoming study on female cosmopolitanism.

12. Schwerin, Landeshauptarchiv Schwerin, Hausarchiv des Mecklenburg-Strelitzschen Fürstenhauses/Briefsammlung 4. 3–2, 869, 22 June 1773, letter from Queen Charlotte to Carl, Duke of Mecklenburg-Strelitz.

13. For further discussion of this genre of oriental tales written for eighteenth-century courts see C. Campbell Orr, 'Aristocratic Feminism, the Learned Governess, and the Republic of Letters', in *Women and Enlightenment: A Comparative History*, ed. S. Knott and B. Taylor, Basingstoke, 2005. On Wieland's novel see J.A. McNeely, 'Historical Relativism in Wieland's concept of the Ideal State', *Modern Language Quarterly*, 22, 1961, pp. 269–82, and L.E. Kurth-Voight, *Perspectives and Points of View: Early Works of Wieland*, Baltimore, 1974, pp. 171–3.

14. On Chambers's work at Kew see *Sir William Chambers*, chapter 6; on James Beattie and the patronage he received from George III and Queen Charlotte see C. Campbell Orr, 'The Late Hanoverian Court and the Christian Enlightenment', in *Monarchy and Religion*, ed. M. Schaich, German Historical Institute/ Oxford University Press, forthcoming 2006.

15. See C. Campbell Orr, entry on Mme de La Fite, *Oxford Dictionary of National Biography*, electronic update, 2005.

16. N. Hope, *German and Scandinavian Protestantism, 1700–1918*, Oxford, 1995, p. 200.

17. Schwerin, Landeshauptarchiv Schwerin, Hausarchiv des Mecklenburg-Strelitzschen Fürstenhauses mit Briefsammlung, 4. 3–2, 869, 8 November 1774, letter from Queen Charlotte to Carl, Duke of Mecklenburg-Strelitz; the precise book is not specified.

18. Lord Herbert, ed., *Pembroke Papers, 1780–94: Letters and Diaries of Henry, 10th Earl of Pembroke and his Circle*, London, 1950, pp. 342–3.

19. *Princesses*, p. 92.

20. Published in English in 1757.

21. C.E. McClelland, *State, Society, and University in Germany, 1700–1914*, Cambridge, 1980.

22. C. Campbell Orr, 'Geneva in England: Rousseau's disciples at the court of George III and Queen Charlotte', in *Genève Lieu d'Angleterre, 1725–1814*, ed. S. Bahar and V. Cossy, in *Travaux sur la Suisse des Lumières*, Geneva, 2004. For Lady Elizabeth Hamilton's family and court service see H. Bleackley, *The Beautiful Duchess, Elizabeth Gunning, Duchess of Hamilton and Argyll*, 2nd edn, London, 1927.

23. *Princesses*, p. 97; D. Duff, *Edward, Duke of Kent*, London, 1938, chapter 7.

24. Schwerin, Landeshauptarchiv Schwerin, Hausarchiv des Mecklenburg-Strelitzschen Fürstenhauses mit Briefsammlung, 4.3–2. 868/19–22 and 868/73–76, letters of ?(illegible) May 1771 and 6 March 1772, letters from Queen Charlotte to Carl, Duke of Mecklenburg-Strelitz.

25. C. Campbell Orr, 'Queen Charlotte as Patron: Some Intellectual and Social Contexts', *The Court Historian*, VI, no. 3, 2001, pp. 183–212.

26. See discussion in *George III & Queen Charlotte*, pp. 161–5, esp. notes 54–7 and 60, and nos. 314–18.

27. *Lettres Physiques et Morales sur les Montagnes, et sur l'Histoire de la Terre, Adressées à la Reine de la Grande Bretagne*, The Hague, 1778. His views were amplified in a six-volume version a year later, *Lettres Physiques et Morales sur l'Histoire de la Terre et de l'Homme, Adressées à la Reine de la Grande Bretagne*, The Hague, and Paris, 1779.

28. See also C. Campbell Orr, 'Charlotte . . . and the Northern Republic of Letters'; T. Biskup, 'A University for Empire? The University of Göttingen and the Personal Union, 1737–1837', in *The Hanoverian Dimension in British History, 1714–1837*, ed. B. Simms and T. Riotte, Cambridge, forthcoming 2006.

29. *Lettres Physiques*, 1778, p. 131. See also Letter XI, pp. 155–72, on the delights of the simple life. The 1779 edition enlarges on this in Discourse IV.

30. *Lettres sur l'histoire physique de la Terre, adressées à M. Le professeur Blumenbach, renfermant de nouvelles preuves géologiques et historiques de la mission divine de Moyse*, Paris, 1798; cited in *Correspondance Complète de Jean-Jacques Rousseau*, ed. R.A. Leigh, Geneva, 1966, III, Appendix 130, pp. 326–7.

31. For DeLuc's depiction of George III as the Defender of Faith, see Campbell Orr, 2004, and C. Campbell Orr, forthcoming (2006).

32. R. Hayden, *Mrs Delany: her life and her flowers*, London, 1980.

33. *Mrs Delany: a Memoir, 1700–1788*, compiled by George Paston, London, 1900, pp. 189–90.

34. For a fuller discussion see C. Campbell Orr, 'Charlotte: Scientific Queen' in *Queenship in Britain, 1660–1837: Royal Patronage, Court Culture and Dynastic Politics*, ed. C. Campbell Orr, Manchester, 2002.

35. W. Roberts, *Memoirs of the Life and Correspondence of Hannah More*, 4 vols., London, 1834, I, p. 319.

36. *Burney Diary*, III, p. 5.

37. *ibid.*, IV, pp. 100 and 300.

38. R. Fulford, ed., *The Autobiography of Cornelia Knight*, London, 1960.

39. E. and F. Anson, eds., *Mary Hamilton at Court and at Home, 1756–1816*, London, 1925; *Princesses*, pp. 45–8, 51–2, 62.

40. C. Campbell Orr, 'Lost Hanoverian Libraries', in *Lost Libraries*, ed. J. Raven, Basingstoke, 2004.

41. For these interests of the King's, see *George III & Queen Charlotte*, p. 125, fig. 13, and p. 127, and Jane Wess's contribution to this book. The Enlightenment Gallery, British Museum, illustrates George III's scientific and bibliographical interests in the context of eighteenth-century connoisseurs and collectors.

Plate IX. Benjamin West, *Genius Calling Forth Arts and Sciences*, 1789. M.H. de Young Memorial Museum, San Francisco

Plate X. Johan Zoffany, *George III*, 1771. RCIN 405072

Plate XI. Johan Zoffany, *Queen Charlotte*, 1771. RCIN 405071.

Plate XII. Canaletto, *Venice: A Regatta on the Grand Canal*, c.1733. RCIN 404416

Plate XIII. Thomas Gainsborough, *Johann Christian Fischer*, 1779–80.
RCIN 407298

Plate XIV. Johan Zoffany, *Queen Charlotte with members of her family*, 1771–2. RCIN 401004

Plate XV. Thomas Lawrence, *Queen Charlotte*, 1789. National Gallery,
London

Plate XVII. Andrew Robertson, *Princess Sophia*, 1807.
Watercolour on ivory. RCIN 420227

Plate XVI. Andrew Robertson, *Princess Amelia*, 1810.
Watercolour on ivory. RCIN 420224

Queen Charlotte's jewellery: reconstructing a lost collection

JUDY RUDOE

Queen Charlotte owned prodigious quantities of jewellery. Today only a handful of pieces survive or have been identified.[1] Any reconstruction is therefore based on contemporary sources, not on the jewels themselves. Much work has been done by others on the Hanoverian hereditary jewels and this is summarised here.[2] The personal jewels, by contrast, have never been the subject of detailed study and so form the backbone of what follows. In particular, I have attempted an analysis of the jewellery listed in the 1819 sale catalogue of Queen Charlotte's private collection, both for what it reveals of the Queen's taste and scholarly interests, and as a remarkable contemporary record.[3]

In her will Queen Charlotte divided her jewels into three categories: first, the hereditary jewels of George II that were given to her by George III in 1761; second, the Arcot diamonds, given to her by the Nawab of Arcot in 1767; and third her personal collection, 'purchased by Myself at various Periods or being Presents made to Me on Birthdays and other occasions'. These categories will be discussed in the same order.[4]

The Hanoverian hereditary jewels were presented by George III to the Princess Charlotte Sophia on her arrival in September 1761. Coming from two groups that the King had reunited by retrieving those that had gone to Hanover for safe-keeping in 1745 and buying back the rest from his uncle the Duke of Cumberland, for £54,000, the jewels were truly

58. Allan Ramsay, *Queen Charlotte*, 1761. RCIN 405308.

spectacular. She wore them immediately at the wedding and the coronation. Her dazzling costume on both occasions was described by the Duchess of Northumberland. For the wedding:

> The Bride was dressed in a Silver Tissue, stiffen body'd gown, embroidered and trimmed with Silver, on her head a little cap of purple Velvet quite covered with diamonds, a Diamond Aigrette in Form of a Crown, 3 dropt Diamond ear Rings, Diamond Necklace, Diamond Sprigs of Flowers on her Sleeves and to clasp back her Robe, a Diamond Stomacher, her purple Velvet mantle was laced with Gold and lined with Ermine. It was fasten'd on the shoulders with large Tossells of Pearls.[5]

The Duchess had already seen the jewels (except those for the Queen's head) in July; her account given then is the most detailed that survives:

> There are an amazing number of Pearls of a most beautiful Colour & prodigious Size. There are Diamonds for the facings and Robings of her Gown, set in sprigs of Flowers; her Ear Rings are three drops, the Diamonds of an immense Size and fine Water, they are all well set and very light. The Necklace consists of large Brilliants set round; there is a string of the same to hold a Cross. The Stomacher, which is valued at £60,000 is the finest piece of Magnificence & Workmanship I ever saw. The Fond is a network as fine as Cat Gut of Small Diamonds & the rest is a large pattern of natural Flowers, composed of very large Diamonds, one of which is 18, another 16, & a third 10 Thousands pounds price. The middle Drop of the Ear Rings cost £12,000.[6]

'Brilliants' at this date was a standard term for diamonds, but multifaceted rather than the simple rose-cut, and indeed the Duchess uses both terms indiscriminately; 'set round' refers to a simple round box setting or collet. The earrings were an elaborate variant on a common eighteenth-century design comprising three pendant diamond drops, in other words, the '3 dropt diamond ear Rings', but with a huge central pear-shaped stone. They are clearly depicted in the two Frye

59. Thomas Frye, *Queen Charlotte*. Mezzotint, published 1762. RCIN 604596

mezzotints of Queen Charlotte in her wedding attire with
their exceptionally beautiful rendering of the diamonds and
pearls: the pearl 'tossells' are in fact loops of ribbon-tied pearl
strings (fig. 59).

60. Queen Charlotte's nuptial crown. Hanover Collection

Frye's mezzotint busts barely hint at just the top edge of the stomacher, but an inventory of the hereditary jewels compiled by General Sir Herbert Taylor, the Queen's private secretary and executor, notes that it consisted of 'three Brilliant Pieces', lending it some degree of flexibility in wear and enabling the different elements to be worn separately: this was standard practice with such a large ornament.[7] Taylor also lists a necklace of 26 collets, which may be one of the two described by the Duchess of Northumberland, and 'An open pattern brilliant Brooch with solid Drop', which may be the bow-knot jewel with large single drop at her neck in fig. 59.[8]

The Duchess of Northumberland's description of the coronation robes suggests that much was evidently the same as for the wedding, but with the addition of a girdle and a fan.[9] The Duchess makes no mention of the frontlet diadem shown in both mezzotints; the headdress with its mass of lace and plaited tresses is difficult to interpret as the 'purple cap quite covered with diamonds'. The 'Crown Aigrette' is equally puzzling but must surely refer to the small nuptial crown on which Queen Charlotte rests her hand in Ramsay's full-length portrait of the Queen in robes of state (fig. 58).[10] According to Millar, Ramsay had the jewels in his studio with a 24-hour guard, enabling the huge pearl clusters at the ends of the girdle, the floral stomacher and the nuptial crown to be painstakingly depicted.[11] The crown is the only hereditary item that survives to this day in Hanover, where it is still used as the Hanoverian Royal Wedding Crown (fig. 60).[12] Many of the diamonds worn by Queen Charlotte at the coronation had belonged to Caroline of Ansbach, but it seems that Caroline rarely wore them. By 1761 she had been dead for twenty-five years, and this perhaps explains why the arrival of a glamorous young queen who received and wore magnificent jewels that had not been seen for decades should have made such an impression.[13]

The total bill for the coronation robes came to £1,592 and included payments to the pearl-stringer Susannah Berrisford, the jewellers Francis and John Duval, and to Henry Martens for a 'Sett of Coronation Locks'.[14] Those flowing ringlets were not her own. If she was wearing entirely hereditary jewels, does the payment of £438 8s to the various jewellers represent the purchase of new pieces or was it rather the work involved in altering Queen Caroline's jewels and, most likely, the cost of additional stones? One such instance is Queen Caroline's bodice ornament, which contained the £18,000 diamond mentioned by

61. Sir Joshua Reynolds, *Queen Charlotte*, 1789. Royal Academy, London.
The Queen wears a series of gem-set bows on her stomacher.

62. Johan Zoffany, *Queen Charlotte*, 1771–2. Oil on copper. RCIN 402938

the Duchess of Northumberland and was transformed into a new stomacher for Charlotte.[15]

Regular transformation is one aspect of valuable jewels; another was the need to construct them to be worn in different ways. The Duchess of Northumberland describes the Queen's coronation petticoats as adorned with diamonds. At the drawing room for the recovery of the King in 1789, the

Queen wore a bandeau with 'Long Live the King' in diamond letters.[16] In instances like these, the diamonds must have been sewn on, but were they available solely for this purpose or were they taken from other pieces? And if the latter is true, how did this work? A clue is provided by the fully documented jewels made for Augustus the Strong in the Grünes Gewölbe in Dresden. The stones in many of these jewels are removable. The backs of the settings are pierced so that a metal wire can be threaded through and twisted round to hold the stone in place. The stones themselves are set in collets that extend beyond the depth of the stone, providing an extra band of metal that can be pierced to take the thread. A simple twist of the wire releases the stone. For example, the two larger opals in the opal and diamond Order of the Golden Fleece of 1724 are removable.[17] A group of emeralds that entered the Dresden collection in 1737 remain in their collet settings but are not mounted in any jewel, so the construction is absolutely clear. Even coat buttons contain removable central sapphires.[18] The Dresden jewels are a rare survival of convertible settings that enable valuable stones to be worn in different ways. Some of the Hanoverian jewels may have been made in Germany at this time and may well have had settings of this type.

The Taylor inventory of Charlotte's hereditary jewels also included a pair of pearl drop earrings in brilliant frames, and a set of three pearl and brilliant bows, one very large, and two smaller: perhaps those depicted in the portrait painted by Reynolds in 1779 for the Royal Academy (fig. 61).[19] The costume is close to the Ramsay portrait, with the nuptial crown and the pearl girdle. In addition to the pearl and brilliant bows, Taylor also lists two diamond bows; perhaps one of these is shown in Zoffany's oil on copper portrait of 1771–2, which gives us one of the best views of the stomacher, suggesting a row of large diamonds down the centre (fig. 62).[20] The jewels in her hair were probably personal pieces to judge by the number of 'brooches for the hair' in the 1819 sale catalogue. These brooches for the hair were attached to long hinged pins, so that they could be securely placed in padded hair at the desired angle; they rarely survive with the original pins.[21] Of the 'superb brilliant nosegay' in Taylor's inventory we have no image or detailed description. Perhaps it resembled the magnificent diamond and emerald bouquet from the Russian State Treasury, made around 1760 by French jewellers working for the Russian court.[22]

Formal appearances at drawing rooms were occasions for magnificent displays of both state and personal jewels, frequently recorded by and engraved for the newly introduced women's journals, such as the *Lady's Magazine*. One report of a drawing room on 4 June 1792 estimated the total value of the Queen's dress and jewels at £100,000.[23] In 1786 Queen Charlotte had admitted to Fanny Burney that the weight of her jewels fatigued her.[24] The choice was not hers, however. Walpole tells us that early on she begged the King not to have to wear them, but, 'as if diamonds were empire, she was never allowed to appear in public without them.'[25] Such was their importance that on certain occasions, the drawing room of 1787 for instance, their arrangement had to be approved by Benjamin West.[26]

As has been noted, the fate of the jewels of state after Queen Charlotte's death is discussed elsewhere. Suffice it to say here that they passed to George IV, who immediately reset many of the stones for Lady Coningham. Queen Adelaide had stones from the stomacher set first in her coronation crown and then in a new circlet known as the Regal circlet, but she did pass a number of Queen Charlotte's pieces intact to Queen Victoria, including the large diamond earrings, the diamond necklace and cross, the point of the stomacher (the only part still set with stones), and the nuptial crown, worn by Queen Victoria for the opening of the Great Exhibition in 1851.[27] It was returned to Hanover in 1858.

After the Hanoverian jewels in Queen Charlotte's will came the Arcot diamonds, seven large diamonds which belonged to her personal jewels and were part of a gift of gems and jewels from the Nawab of Arcot in 1767.[28] A point worth making here is that they were not the only Indian stones owned by Queen Charlotte. The 1819 sale included two groups of 'lask' diamonds: many Indian stones were cut as flat tablets known as lasques and completely different from Western faceting. One group came from the Shah of Persia, the other comprised a necklace, earrings, three brooches and a 'top and drop for the forehead'.[29] It is tempting to identify this with the jewel worn by the Queen in her hair at the centre of a lace cap in the Meyer miniature of c.1772.[30]

Turning to the personal jewels, Queen Charlotte's will describes them as 'purchased by Myself at various Periods or being Presents made to Me on Birthdays and other occasions', yet it is impossible to work out what the Queen might have purchased herself. The Treasurers' accounts of the Queen's household list the amounts paid annually to the various tradesmen, including jewellers and toymen, or suppliers of small decorative objects. Charlotte made many purchases to support British trade, but without any surviving bills we do not know what the payments were for, and the payments to jewellers are all trivial by comparison with the sums paid to mercers, lacemen and milliners.[31] The accounts of Garrards, the Royal Jewellers, then Parker & Wakelin, are rigid with orders for jewellery, but not from Queen Charlotte: almost all of her purchases, and there were many, were of silver. Identifying the 'Presents made to Me' is equally problematic. There are a few bills for jewellery and other objets d'art ordered in Germany in the summer of 1761 by Colonel Graeme on the King's behalf and delivered to Princess Charlotte in Strelitz; some of these items may have remained in her possession, but many may have been intended as gifts for members of her household who helped her prepare for or who accompanied her on the journey to England.[32] Whatever the case, the Queen possessed fine jewellery of her own before she arrived in England; this is evident from the portrait of her as Princess of Mecklenburg-Strelitz by Ziesenis of c.1761 (plate VII). Here she wears large diamond earrings, two frontlet ornaments (one of pearls, the other of diamonds), a diamond clasp for her cloak and a pearl-strand bracelet with diamond-bordered miniature. There must have been gifts from the Queen's own family too, especially her brothers; further research is needed to identify these.[33]

Apart from the King's wedding-day gifts of pearl bracelets and rings, which are discussed below, specific details for most of the King's many later gifts are sadly lacking. The Privy Purse account books survive for a short period of George III's reign only, from 1763–72; they are not comprehensive and details of items are rarely given. Far more rewarding are the abstracts of bills paid to Messrs Duval & Sons from April 1764 to October 1766. Here we find that the King paid significant sums for jewelled Garter insignia for the Duke of Mecklenburg (the Queen's brother), the Duke of Gloucester, the Hereditary Princess of Brunswick and the Prince of Wales. For the Queen, he purchased on 12 September 1765 a sapphire ensemble comprising a nosegay costing £1,318 10s, a necklace costing £939 2s 6d, earrings at £303 7s 6d and an egret at £239. In January that year he had paid £174 for 'the Queen's ruby solitaire' (a single-stone ring) and in June 1766 he bought her a diamond ring for £550. The occasional bill from Duval survives; one example, dated 7 December 1768, lists the stones for a diamond and emerald bouquet costing a total of £953 including the setting. At such a date the King might easily have been paying for a gift to mark the birth of Princess Augusta in November that year, but the recipient is not recorded.[34] George IV, too, gave her many jewels; however, his accounts, which do survive, specify several pieces ordered for his sisters, but none for the Queen.[35]

The wedding day gifts are well documented, both in Mrs Papendiek's descriptions and in portraits. Prominent in several images is the pair of pearl bracelets. Both had oval clasps attached to 'six rows of picked pearls as large as a full pea'; one clasp contained a miniature of the King, the other his hair and cipher in diamonds. Such bracelets were a standard design from at least the 1750s for the next four decades.[36] Similar

63. Johan Zoffany, *Queen Charlotte*, 1771. RCIN 405071.
Detail showing the Queen's pearl bracelets, a wedding gift from the
King. The bracelet with a miniature of the King by Jeremiah Meyer is
worn on her right arm.

64. One of Queen Charlotte's pearl bracelets, photographed for Queen Mary's *Catalogue of Bibelots* in 1920.

bracelets appear time and again in the Garrard ledgers. The Queen wears both bracelets in Zoffany's painting of 1771 (fig. 63):[37] her right arm rests on the table to display Meyer's profile portrait, while the other bracelet is worn with the hair

65. Thomas Lawrence, *Queen Charlotte*, 1789. National Gallery, London. Detail showing the pearl bracelet with diamond cipher and matching diamond-set ring on the Queen's left hand, together with a plain gold ring with a heart-shaped diamond (see also plate XV).

and cipher facing inwards. Are the earrings perhaps the Hanoverian pearl drops in brilliant frames? The bracelets passed to Queen Victoria and are listed in the 1896 inventory of her jewels. Queen Mary subsequently illustrated one of them in her catalogue of bibelots (fig. 64); the photograph makes the pearl strings look rather long for a bracelet, suggesting that they may have been restrung. The pearls themselves seem very much smaller in real life than those depicted by Zoffany.[38]

As well as the bracelets, the King gave Charlotte a tiny version of the Meyer miniature set into a gold ring, 'to wear on the little finger of her right hand at the marriage

66. Johan Zoffany, *George III, Queen Charlotte and their six eldest children*, 1770. RCIN 400501. Detail showing Queen Charlotte with a diamond-bordered miniature of the King clasped to a triple strand of pearls.

ceremony', in Mrs Papendiek's words. Bordered with diamonds, the miniature itself is protected not by the customary rock-crystal or glass cover but by a flat-cut diamond of wonderful fire.[39] But it is far too big for the little finger of a young slim girl: either Mrs Papendiek is wrong or the ring has been enlarged at a later date. It is significantly larger than the diamond keeper ring given her at the same time, 'of a size not to stand higher than the wedding ring, to which it was to serve as a guard'.[40] Set all round with diamonds, the keeper

194

ring is inscribed with the date of the wedding. Of the wedding ring itself, there is no description, but if Mrs Papendiek is correct that the keeper was smaller, the wedding ring must have been set with sizeable gems. A payment in the Jewel House Accounts made in April 1762 for 'a diamond hoop ring, one gold ring and two small buckles for garters, £17 11s' may perhaps relate to the keeper as a 'diamond hoop ring'.[41]

By the time of Lawrence's sensitive portrait of 1789 (plate XV), the King had suffered his first serious bout of illness and Queen Charlotte's hair had gone grey. She had not recovered her own health when the sittings began, and when the King complained at her lack of head-covering she discontinued the sittings but was persuaded to allow Mrs Papendiek to take her place and to wear the bracelets and the pin that held her scarf.[42] The Queen also wears a tiny fob-seal strung on a black silk cord tucked into her bodice. Here, unusually, the bracelet with diamond cipher is also visible and on the little finger of her left hand is a matching ring, with a diamond ornament – possibly a flower spray – set on deep blue enamel (fig. 65).[43] On the fourth finger is a thin gold ring with a heart-shaped diamond; this might be the wedding ring, rather than a plain gold band, but there is another possibility here: the 'ring with single brilliant' delivered to Charlotte in Strelitz in August 1761 at a cost of 3,800 Louis d'or.[44]

Apart from the miniatures in the bracelets and ring, Queen Charlotte regularly wore the King's portrait as a pendant bordered with pearls or diamonds, even those that seem almost too large to wear. In the Zoffany family portrait of 1770 she wears a diamond-bordered miniature, surmounted by a diamond crown, of the King in three-quarter view, the same image as in the painting itself; the miniature is clasped to her bodice with a triple strand of pearls (fig. 66).[45] These portrait jewels are symbols of allegiance as much as symbols of marriage in that they were worn in the same way by members of the royal family and by courtiers: when the Queen gave her own miniature to the Duchess of Ancaster in 1767, Lady Mary Coke writes of a 'magnificent present ... her Majesty's

67. John Hopkins, *Queen Charlotte*, c.1803. Watercolour on ivory.
RCIN 420192. The Queen wears a miniature of the King after the portrait
by Beechey of 1800.

picture set in a kind of frame of diamonds; the crown in
diamonds at the top; the Duchess wore it on one side as the
Queen wears his Majesty's.'[46] Later, Queen Charlotte wore

the King's miniature on long chains. In the 1803 miniature by Hopkins after a drawing by Edridge, for example, she wears one of many miniature copies of Beechey's portrait of 1800 (fig. 67).[47] As the King's portraits were painted they were copied in miniature and the Queen must have had them all. Significantly, the miniatures increase in size as the King's health deteriorates. Others can interpret better that I how far this was a sentimental habit and how far it indicates the Queen's hope that he would recover and her wish to remind the world that he was still King. Right at the end of her life, at the marriage of Princess Elizabeth in April 1818, she was still wearing conspicuously a large miniature portrait of the King.[48]

The evidence from portraits, however, in no way prepares us for the startling variety of jewels to be found in the 1819 sale catalogue of her personal collection. This extraordinary document repays detailed study, for it enables the appearance of Queen Charlotte's personal jewels to be re-created and serves as a remarkable record of types of jewellery now completely lost. The personal jewels were bequeathed to her four youngest surviving unmarried daughters. The executors decided that after the Princesses had chosen what they wished to keep, the remainder would be sold by public auction. There are no surviving lists of the four equal shares and we have no idea how much the daughters took or what proportion of Charlotte's entire collection the sale items represent. Nor do we know what proportion were acquired by the Queen by gift or by purchase. The Queen's restraint in purchases, 'having a considerable stock of her own', was noted by her contemporaries: when offered a pair of diamond earrings by Thomas Gray in the early 1780s she admired them at length, then laid them down, saying 'very handsome indeed, but – very dear!'[49] The jewels were divided into 324 lots sold over six days in two sessions of three days each. Many lots contained several items, so at a conservative estimate there must have been well over 1,000 pieces. Apart from an arbitrary division into 'diamonds' and 'trinkets' (arbitrary because the latter category is still full of precious stone jewellery), the order is utterly random, making a coherent picture impossible.[50]

The types of jewel represented consist of brooches, earrings, rings, necklaces, chains, buttons, buckles, bracelets (always in pairs), bandeaux and suites.[51] Of these the number of brooches far exceeds any other category. Taking the 57 lots grouped under the heading of diamonds, the total number of individual items comes to 120; within that there were 44 brooches, 10 necklaces, 6 pairs of earrings, 6 lockets, 5 chains, 4 buckles, 4 buttons, 3 pairs of bracelets, 1 bandeau, and a series of miscellaneous items. These included purse runners (17 May, lot 31), 'An S chain border for the top of a stomacher, of brilliants with drops ... with large and fine centre stone' (17 May, lot 51), and a 'set of seven cluster diamond rosette hair pins' (lot 82), perhaps those in the Zoffany portrait of 1771–2.[52] Brooches were pinned all over the dress and in the hair, which may explain their disproportionate numbers compared to other categories. There were also 2 suites of 9 items each, one of chrysoprase and diamond, the other opal and diamond. The suites form a subject of their own: there were a further 28 among the trinkets, plus those jewels that clearly matched although they were not lotted together, presumably because the original boxes no longer survived. A typical composition would be one or more necklaces, a pair of bracelets, earrings, bandeau, sliders (ornaments with loops at the back for attachment to a ribbon), girdle clasps and up to 8 brooches, many for the hair. Still in the diamond section, at least 30 items were made of pearls, including a pearl snake with drop pearl suspended from its mouth, and at least 6 rows of up to 220 pearls each, as well as 58 large unstrung pearls and a quantity of seed pearls. And these were in addition to the Hanoverian pearls.

The jewels classed as 'Trinkets' in the sale catalogue include some spectacular gem-set pieces: 'a magnificent brilliant and emerald bow, the brilliants large and of the purest water, and the emeralds singularly clear', with two smaller bows to match

68. Johan Zoffany, *Queen Charlotte with her two eldest sons* (detail), *c.*1765. RCIN 400146. The Queen's 'sprig and ribbon' aigrette is reflected in the mirror.

(18 May, lot 83). Perhaps this was the vast emerald and diamond knot 'which almost covered her stomacher', singled out by the Duchess of Northumberland among the Queen's jewels at the baptism of the Prince of Wales in 1762.[53] Her emerald and diamond jewels also included six honeysuckle brooches (18 May, lot 82), a cross (18 May, lot 77), a necklace from which hung an emerald in the shape of a bunch of grapes (18 May, lot 75) and a pair of sprig and ribbon brooches (18 May, lot 86), perhaps like that worn in her hair in Zoffany's painting of the Queen with her two eldest sons; the reflection in the mirror shows clearly that it is a

199

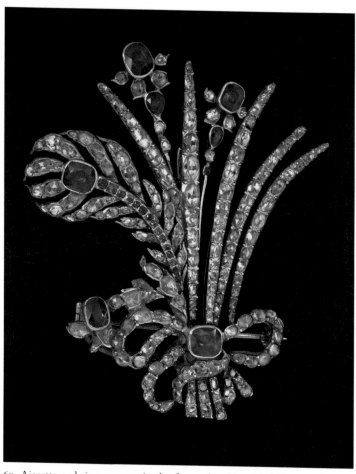

69. Aigrette or hair ornament in the form of a ribbon-tied spray similar
to the 'sprig and ribbon' jewel worn by Queen Charlotte in fig. 68.
Amethysts and colourless zircons, c.1760. Hull Grundy Gift,
British Museum, London

typical mid-eighteenth-century ribbon-tied spray (figs. 68 and
69).[54]

Precious stone jewellery was to be expected. Far more
surprising is the astonishing variety of hard stone jewellery:

necklaces of jasper, cornelian or onyx beads, or whole suites of pale striped agates, mocoa agates (moss agates), bloodstone, lapis lazuli, yellow jasper and malachite. It seems hard to believe that the Queen would have accumulated quite so much as gifts; she must have had a real enthusiasm for the stones themselves. This was no doubt influenced by the King's interests in minerals, but a taste for stones with natural markings and beautiful colours would have followed on easily from her passion for flowers and plants. She had her own specimens of ores and minerals (26 May, lot 84) and 'A box formed of the bark of a tree, the top inlaid with five large specimens of agate, also a small leather case, with sliders containing polished specimens of gems, and catalogue' (17 May, lot 92). It is tempting to suggest that the leather case with sliders was a set of interchangeable ring stones like those to be found in continental princely collections.[55] The interest in hard stones extended to boxes and other small objects. Among the items now in the Royal Collection is a small oval amethyst box with diamond and ruby catch that descended from Charlotte's daughter Princess Sophia to Queen Mary. Queen Mary identified it with an amethyst box in the 1819 sale (18 May, lot 9) that had flowers of diamonds and coloured stones on the lid; the shape of the box is not mentioned and it has been noted rightly that this may be an optimistic association.[56] There is, however, another possibility that goes back to 1761: the group of bills for objects delivered by Colonel Graeme to Princess Charlotte in Strelitz includes a 'tabattiere oval von Amatist mit Diamants bec'. There is no mention of rubies, but the shape and decorated catch fit Queen Mary's box.[57]

Most startling of all is a suite of labradorite jewellery. Labradorite feldspar, known for its flashes of colour over large areas of its grey surface, is found in Labrador, hence its name, and Russia. It was first introduced into Europe in 1770. It is a brittle stone, which makes it difficult to carve, and surviving examples set in jewellery are almost unknown before the Victorian period. Charlotte owned 'a suit of necklace, ear-

70. Necklace, earrings and brooches set with glass micromosaics depicting views of Rome in gold mounts, *c.*1800. Hull Grundy Gift, Kenwood House, London

rings, top and drop ditto, bracelets, girdle, Maltese cross, one large square, four ditto oval and four smaller brooches of Labrador feld spath, gold mounted, and a pendant heart, the latter set with filigree border' (17 May, lot 107). The inclusion of a Maltese cross in Charlotte's suite suggests a date in the early nineteenth century. Maltese crosses were the height of fashion in the years around 1805–10: the Prince of Wales purchased gem-set Maltese crosses from Rundell's for his sister, Princess Mary, in 1807 and for his daughter, Princess Charlotte, in 1811. In 1810 he had purchased 'a necklace composed of monkey's heads in cameo on Labrador spar in gold' for £27 16s.[58]

If the quantity of hard stone jewellery is remarkable, other categories are more typical. Cameos and intaglios appear set in necklaces, crescent brooches and bandeaux, all characteristic ornaments of the late eighteenth to early nineteenth century. The stones used here were the same: red cornelians cut as intaglios in a fairly thin sliver that was translucent when light passed through, and layered agates and onyx cut vertically through the layers to achieve the image in one or more colours, instead of flat polished across the stripes.[59] For much of the eighteenth century the distinction between polished specimens and worked stones did not exist and most collectors had examples of both. Besides jewellery, the sale also listed 'A mahogany cabinet with 5 drawers, containing divisions and numerous pastes of Tassie, from antique gems' (26 May, lot 48). James Tassie's glass casts from ancient gems were a standard means of learning classical history and legend; casts could be arranged according to subject, providing a visual record of the ancient world.[60] Catherine the Great was Tassie's greatest patron; Queen Charlotte's interest was clearly on a much smaller scale, but it is the scholar in her that comes through so often. She had her own 'large assortment of conchology' alongside her many shell cameos, carved coral and coral bead strings (26 May, lot 82). The cameos were most likely to have come from Italy, though it should be remembered that there was a flourishing school of gem engraving in Germany in the eighteenth century. The coral, traditionally gathered off the coast of Naples, was without doubt an Italian import.

Mosaics were another Italian speciality. The sale catalogue descriptions of 'a pair of mosaic brooches in purpurine set in gold filigree', or 'a necklace and clasp composed of twelve mosaics set in lapis lazuli and gold chain, with pendant mosaic from the centre, a pair of ditto earrings and two broaches' leave no doubt that these were micromosaics – miniature mosaics made of tiny pieces of glass cut from thin rods and set into coloured glass grounds imitating purpurine or lapis (26 May, lots 4 and 30). Micromosaics were developed in Rome in the 1770s mostly for box lids and other small-scale items.[61] Surviving jewellery incorporating them dates from around 1790 onwards and Charlotte's may have been some of the earliest examples to be set as jewellery (fig. 70). It was a labour-intensive art and the best examples were highly prized.

The diverse and novel materials also included necklaces, brooches and earrings of jet in gold settings. Empress Josephine had a jet parure and there are references to jet jewellery in the Garrard ledgers in the first two decades of the nineteenth century, but examples of this early date do not survive.[62] One of the more popular forms of black jewellery in the early nineteenth century was Berlin ironwork. Cast or wrought into delicate openwork designs, it was produced from the early nineteenth century, and during the Napoleonic wars became a substitute for gold jewels handed over to finance the war effort. The sale catalogue lists 'two iron Maltese crosses with very fine iron chains' (26 May, lot 6), which date most probably from the years around 1810, when many iron crosses were made as mourning jewels for the much-loved Queen Luise of Prussia, who died in July 1810.[63] Curiously, cut-steel jewellery is completely absent from the catalogue, despite the fact that the Prince of Wales was buying innumerable cut-steel ornaments from the 1780s onwards. Steel nail heads were faceted to imitate diamonds, and hand-pierced steel florets made sparkling chains. If there was any, perhaps the daughters kept it precisely because it was so attractive and wearable. Last but not least were the suites of imitative emeralds, false lapis (26 May, lot 7) and false garnets (26 May, lot 20). These were made of coloured glass or paste, the transparent stones enhanced, like diamonds, with tinted foils.[64]

Many jewels contained messages and can be paralleled exactly in the Prince of Wales's accounts and the Garrard ledgers. For example, the Queen had three hearts' ease or pansy brooches (meaning 'thoughts', from the French 'pen-sée'), accurately depicted in amethysts and topaz to represent the top and bottom petals (24 May, lot 11). Other jewels were in the form of hearts, or hearts and arrows; one is described as 'an arrow of fine large white brilliants, with a festoon, and inscription "Amicitia Aeterna" in diamonds, with two large white brilliant drops' (17 May, lot 86).[65] There were further message jewels in the form of keys or padlocks (17 May, lot

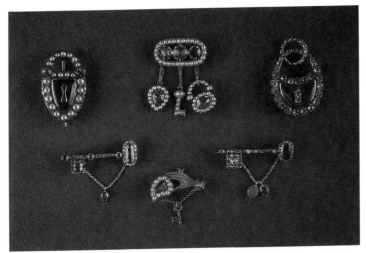

71. Group of jewels in the form of padlocks and keys, some set with hair. Gold, gemstones, pearls and enamel. English, *c*.1800–10. Hull Grundy Gift, British Museum, London

32), almost identical with those purchased by the Prince of Wales from around 1800 (fig. 71). Queen Charlotte herself loved to give modest sentimental jewels of this kind, often set with hair. They were regularly exchanged between members of the family, and to Mrs Delany she gave a small oval locket bordered with seed pearls with a lock of her hair; the letters 'CR' are clearly visible in the portrait by Opie of 1782 (fig. 56).[66]

Other jewels, by contrast, suggest that the dating of types usually given to the Victorian period should be reconsidered. There were two lily of the valley brooches, one with gold and pearls, the other with gold and diamonds (17 May, lots 31, 32); these are generally associated with the language of flowers and the taste for naturalistic jewellery of the 1830s onwards. Signifying 'the return of happiness', lilies of the valley were a popular birthday offering.[67] Queen Charlotte owned brooches in the form of bunches of grapes in garnet and earrings in the form of bunches of currants in cornelian (24 May, lot 8).[68] Currants meant 'You please all' and were typically made in

72. Gold signet ring of Mary, Queen of Scots, the arms cut
in rock-crystal with the colours in enamel beneath.
Formerly owned by Queen Charlotte and the Duke of York.
British Museum, London

cornelian and chalcedony for red and white currants. In only
one instance does the sale catalogue give any indication of
date: lot 26 on 18 May is described as 'A beautiful pair of
modern bracelets formed of amethysts, connected by rosettes
of fillagree set with small rubies and brilliants', suggesting that
these were made in the latest fashion.

Space has not permitted more than a fraction of the sale
catalogue jewels to be considered, but even these few throw
a different light on Queen Charlotte's jewels by adding the
private as opposed to the public dimension. I would like to
end with a piece of historic jewellery: a famous object, but
one whose provenance back to Queen Charlotte is perhaps

not widely realised. In 1792 a paper read to the Society of Antiquaries on the Royal and Baronial Seals of Scotland described the impression of a ring 'from a seal of Mary Queen of Scots, in the Royal collection at the Queen's House; it is set in gold, and has the letters MR in cipher on the back of the seal' (fig. 72).[69] The arms are engraved in a sliver of rock-crystal, enamelled beneath with the correct tinctures, a standard device for achieving the colours so that the signet ring could then be used as a seal without damaging the enamel. No one has yet been able to read satisfactorily the cipher on the reverse, described as MR in 1792; most likely it is intended to be a MARIA monogram. The ring passed from Queen Charlotte to the Duke of York and was included in the sale after his death in March 1827; it was purchased by the antiquary Richard Greene for 14 guineas.[70] Greene subsequently sold it to the British Museum in 1856 for £100.[71] The ring seems to have entered the possession of Queen Charlotte with a group of curiosities that appear to have belonged to Queen Caroline of Ansbach. Whether Queen Charlotte collected other historic royal jewels we do not know. No doubt future research will provide the answer.[72]

Acknowledgements

In what was a new area for me, the above account could not have been written without invaluable help given by many. At the Royal Collection I wish to thank Matthew Winterbottom, Jonathan Marsden, Jane Roberts, Sir Geoffrey de Bellaigue, Pamela Clark and Kathryn Jones. Charlotte Gere has been a constant source of advice, and much useful information has been supplied by Marcia Pointon, Richard Edgcumbe, Simon Jervis, Francis Russell, Nigel Israel and Anne Louise Luthi. My greatest debt is to the late Shirley Bury for her pioneering work on which all subsequent research has relied.

NOTES

1. Most of them are in the Royal Collection; see *George III & Queen Charlotte*, nos. 441–6.

2. The history of Queen Charlotte's state jewels, that is, the Hanoverian jewels, is fully discussed by Shirley Bury in 'Queen Victoria and the Hanoverian claim to the Crown Jewels', *The International Silver and Jewellery Fair and Seminar Handbook*, London, 1988, pp. 9–16. Much of this material is repeated in Bury's later publication, *Jewellery 1789–1910: A Social History*, 2 vols., Woodbridge 1991, but distributed throughout the book under the relevant member of the royal family.

3. The sale took place over several days between January and August 1819. For the jewels see *A Catalogue of a Superb Assemblage of Jewels, Trinkets, A Desert Service of Fillagree Plate ... and useful Table Plate*, Christie's, London, 17–19 and 24–6 May 1819. For the full list, see *George III & Queen Charlotte*, p. 386.

4. I must acknowledge here my debt to Matthew Winterbottom for his account of the dispersal of the Queen's property (*George III & Queen Charlotte*, pp. 385–9) and to Marcia Pointon's articles: 'Intriguing jewellery: royal bodies and luxurious consumption', *Textual Practice*, XI, no. 3, 1997, pp. 493–516; 'Intrigue, jewellery and economics: court culture and display in England and France in the 1780s', in *Art Markets in Europe 1400–1800*, ed. M. North and D. Ormrod, Aldershot, 1999, pp. 201–19; 'Surrounded with brilliants: miniature portraits in eighteenth-century England', *Art Bulletin*, LXXXIII, March 2001, no. 1, pp. 48–71.

5. *Diaries of a Duchess*, p. 31 (8 September 1761).

6. *ibid.*, p. 28 (26 July 1761). How these values were arrived at is unclear; if remotely accurate, they represent enormous sums.

7. The report was kindly drawn to my attention by Jonathan Marsden; RA 50412, with enclosures (50418 and 50419).

8. A smaller version of the bow-knot and drop appears also in the other Frye mezzotint, but the larger, wider bow is absent, suggesting that it was a separate element (*George III & Queen Charlotte*, no. 21).

9. The Queen wore: a '. . . Diamond Stomacher, Purple velvet Sleeves Diamds, Pearls as big as Cherrys, Girdle, Petticoats Diamnds, Purple Velvet Surcoat & Mantle with Ermine and lace, Purple Velvet Cap, only one string of Diamds & Crown Aigrette, Fan Mother of Pearl, Emeralds, Rubys and Diamds' (*Diaries of a Duchess*, p. 36; 22 September 1761).

10. The meaning of 'crown aigrette' here is discussed at length by Shirley Bury in *Crown Jewels*, I, pp. 491–2. The term 'aigrette' is

generally understood to denote a hair ornament often resembling feathers in form, if not used to clasp real feathers, but its use here suggests that it encompassed all hair ornaments, whatever their shape.

11. Millar 1969, no. 97, plate 2. Millar notes that this is the only portrait in which Queen Charlotte's hair is painted in this way: pale and frizzed, with a diamond feather aigrette.

12. Bury 1991, I, plate 14.

13. For Queen Charlotte's coronation jewels see *Crown Jewels*, I, pp. 472 and 494. Bury makes the distinction between the royal regalia, for which stones were traditionally hired (George III and Queen Charlotte were no exception), and the additional personal jewels worn on the costume.

14. The bill for the coronation robes is to be found in the Accounts of the Treasurers of Queen Charlotte 1761–77, BL, Add. MS 17870, f. 6r. (see Pointon 2001, n. 81). Pearl-stringing has traditionally been a female occupation and still is today. For Duval, see Bury 1991, I, p. 15.

15. Bury 1988, p. 10.

16. W.C. Oulton, *Authentic and Impartial Memoirs of her Late Majesty, Charlotte, Queen of Great Britain and Ireland*, London 1819, pp. 286–7.

17. See U. Arnold, *Die Juwelen Augusts des Starken*, Munich, 2001, plate 73. There are several other views of the backs of jewels showing the twisted wires attaching the stones, but no illustrations of the pierced collet settings. I am therefore especially grateful to Ulrike Weinhold for allowing me to examine these jewels closely so that it was possible to understand how the settings functioned.

18. For the unmounted emeralds, see Arnold 2001, plate 93, but the pierced settings are not visible. Although later additions, they are grouped with the emerald garniture of 1719. For the sapphire waistcoat buttons, see *ibid.*, plate 26.

19. See exh. cat., *Reynolds*, London, Royal Academy, 1986, no. 115. See also D. Mannings, *Sir Joshua Reynolds: A Complete Catalogue of his Paintings*, 2 vols., London, 2000, I, no. 718, II, fig. 1301. The bows occur again in a portrait known only from an image in the National Portrait Gallery archive, where it is described as after (?)Nathaniel Dance.

20. See exh. cat., *Johan Zoffany 1733–1810*, London, National Portrait Gallery, 1977, no. 69.

21. For an example of a mid-eighteenth-century diamond hair pin retaining the original hinged pin, see H. Tait, ed., *The Art of the Jeweller: A Catalogue of the Hull Grundy Gift to the British Museum*, 2 vols., London 1984, no. 16.

22. O. Gorewa *et al.*, *Die Schatzkammer der Sowjetunion*, Munich, 1990, pp. 15–16 and 29. The diamonds in the bouquet are colourless, but by placing tinted metal foils into the settings behind the stones, a riot of colour has been achieved. The use of foils to suggest coloured stones must have been a fashionable novelty at this time, to judge by the number of references to 'foilstone' jewellery in the Garrard ledgers for the 1760s.

23. If this was really true, it may explain the merciless satires of the Queen's dress and jewels discussed by Pointon. The account described the Queen in a petticoat of green silk covered with lace drawn up in festoons with six large bouquets of diamonds, each formed of 'one large rosette, from which rise bending sprigs in imitation of snowdrops. From each rosette fall two large diamond chains and tassels; and upon each festoon of the drapery is a chain of large diamonds'. The six bouquets were valued at £8,000 each and incorporated in each rosette a central stone valued at £2,000 each. See exh. cat., *In Royal Fashion: The Clothes of Princess Charlotte of Wales & Queen Victoria, 1796–1901*, London, Museum of London, 1997, pp. 28–9.

24. *Burney Diary*, III, p. 88.

25. H. Walpole, *Memoirs of the Reign of King George III*, ed. D. le Marchant, 4 vols., London, 1845, vol. 2, p. 73.

26. *Burney Diary*, III, p. 254. My thanks to Sir Geoffrey de Bellaigue for drawing my attention to this passage.

27. The earrings are visible in an 1838 print of Queen Victoria in the Royal Box at Drury Lane by Wagstaff after E.T. Parris (Bury 1991, I, plate 157). The necklace, together with the regal circlet, is clearly to be seen in the Winterhalter half-length portrait of Queen Victoria of 1856, in which the Koh-i-Nûr diamond is worn as a brooch (Bury 1991, plate 174). The point of the stomacher was dismantled by Queen Victoria to furnish stones for a diamond and opal tiara in 1853 (Bury 1988, p. 15).

28. See *George III & Queen Charlotte*, p. 385.

29. Christie's, 18 May 1819, lot 20 and lot 3.

30. *George III & Queen Charlotte*, no. 31.

31. To give but one example, in 1769–70 she paid £1,935 to her milliner, £1,476 to her mercer, and just £17 14s to Peter

Wirgman, toyman, and £14 5s 10d to Willerton & Co., jewellers. Treasurers' Accounts, BL, Add. MS 17870, f. 62. The accounts cover the years 1761–1807, Add. MSS 17870–17893. The jewellers listed are as follows: Peter Wirgman, toyman: 1760s–97 (described as jeweller by 1797); Thomas Wirgman, jeweller: 1802–5; Robert Willerton, toyman: 1760s–1804; Willerton & Co., toymen and jewellers: 1793–1801; J. Kirkup, jeweller: 1796–7; Nathaniel Jeffreys, jeweller: 1796–7; John Stedman, jeweller: 1800–18; Horne & Co., jewellers: 1804–7; Thomas Gray, jeweller: 1805–6; Philip Gilbert, jeweller: 1806–7. The name of the Royal Jeweller, Duval, appears once, for the coronation robes.

32. Liverpool Papers, BL, Add. MS 38333, ff. 126–137. Some items from these bills have been discussed by Pointon 1997, 1999 and 2001.

33. The sitter depicted in the bracelet miniature has not yet been identified but it is likely to be a member of her own family.

34. For the abstracts of bills from Duval, see RA 16085–6. For the bill dated December 1768, see RA 16821. My thanks to Francis Russell for alerting me to the existence of Duval bills in the Royal Archives and to Pamela Clark for kindly finding them for me. The 1819 sale of Queen Charlotte's jewels contains many sapphire jewels but nothing resembling the pieces described in the Duval bills.

35. The family regularly gave each other jewels, frequently set with their own hair, such as the carved ivory locket with the Queen's cipher and seven different shades of hair, almost certainly a gift to her from the children (*George III & Queen Charlotte*, no. 416).

36. Mrs Papendiek was given a pair with a portrait of her husband and with hair and cipher at the christening of her daughter in 1783. See *Papendiek*, I, p. 200. Her description of Queen Charlotte's bracelets is in vol. I, pp. 12–13.

37. *George III & Queen Charlotte*, no. 9.

38. *Inventory of jewels &c., the property of Her Majesty The Queen*, 1896 (RCIN 1114856); *Catalogue of Queen Mary's bibelots, miniatures and other valuables, the property of Queen Mary*, 1920 (hereafter QMB), p. 25, no. 112, plate V.

39. *George III & Queen Charlotte*, no. 441.

40. *Papendiek*, pp. 12–13.

41. This reference from the Jewel House Accounts was kindly supplied by Matthew Winterbottom. The keeper passed to the

Princess Royal and subsequently to Queen Victoria, who may possibly have added the inscription and date, since the lettering seems to be in a later style. The ring with miniature was acquired by George V and Queen Mary.

42. *Papendiek*, pp. 141–3. The introduction of these scarves, or handkerchiefs as they were called, can be clearly documented from the Garrard ledgers, where 'handfpins' are among the most common items ordered in the 1780s.

43. For similar use of blue enamel as a background for diamonds, see the chatelaines with watch and locket (*George III & Queen Charlotte*, nos. 404–5).

44. Liverpool Papers, LXLIV, BL, Add. MS 38333, f. 129: 'une bague à un Brillant'.

45. For the painting, see *George III & Queen Charlotte*, no. 7. The diamond crown surmounting the miniature is barely distinguishable, but there seems no reason to doubt that it was intended; the crown is clearly visible on the diamond-set miniature worn in Ströhling's oil on copper portrait of 1807 (Millar 1969, no. 1094, plate 236).

46. *The Letters and Journals of Lady Mary Coke*, II, *1767–68*, Bath, 1970, p. 56.

47. For the Hopkins miniature, see Walker, no. 833; for the Edridge drawing, in which the Queen also wears the pearl bracelet with the King's miniature, see *George III & Queen Charlotte*, no. 15. For the Beechey painting, see Millar 1969, no. 658, plate 157 and for a miniature by Grimaldi after the Beechey, see *George III & Queen Charlotte*, no. 26.

48. D.M. Stuart, *The Daughters of George III*, London, 1939, pp. 183–4.

49. Oulton 1819, pp. 192–3.

50. For this reason the sale catalogue has been understandably but unjustly neglected and even the present account does no more than scratch the surface. To complicate matters further, unsold items were apparently incorporated into a later day's sale and the catalogues printed at the last minute, so one needs to look

carefully for identical descriptions (information kindly supplied by Charlotte Gere).

51. I have not included watches and chatelaines in this survey. Many are listed in the sale catalogue. In addition to the two chatelaines in the Royal Collection (*George III & Queen Charlotte*, nos. 404–5), two watches with enamels by G.M. Moser are recorded in R. Edgcumbe, *The Art of the Gold Chaser in Eighteenth-Century London*, Oxford, 2000: p. 121, Moser no. 42, fig. 110 (in the Clockmakers Company), and p. 123, Moser no. 50, fig. 114 (at Grimsthorpe, having descended in the family from Mary, Duchess of Ancaster, Mistress of the Robes to Queen Charlotte, 1761–93). A design for a watch made for Queen Charlotte is held by the Society of Antiquaries (information kindly supplied by Simon Jervis).

52. A later entry, 18 May, lot 52, was for 'a pair of shoulder straps composed of numerous fine brilliants'.

53. *Diaries of a Duchess*, p. 50.

54. For the amethyst and zircon spray shown in fig. 69, see Tait, 1984, no. 3. The emerald and diamond cross may be the cross sold at Sotheby's, London, 18 June 2002, lot 121.

55. For an illustration of a mineralogical ring set of this kind dated to *c.*1800 see B. Marquardt, *Schmuck. Klassizismus und Biedermeier 1780–1850, Deutschland, Österreich, Schweiz*, Munich, 1983, no. 428, p. 261. Similar ring sets are to be found in the Schatzkammer of the Württembergisches Landesmuseum in Stuttgart, the Maximilianmuseum, Augsburg, and in the Grünes Gewölbe in Dresden.

56. *George III & Queen Charlotte*, no. 394; *QMB* I, no. 283. For Queen Mary's role in reassembling Queen Charlotte's collection, see C. Gere, 'How Queen Mary collected Queen Charlotte', *Apollo*, August 2004, pp. 50–55. For Queen Charlotte and Queen Mary as collectors, see also C. Gere and M. Vaizey, *Great Women Collectors*, London, 1999.

57. BL, Add. MS 38333, f. 134. The amethyst snuff box is part of a large order of boxes, watches, etc., from Crageman & Kroon of Hamburg.

58. RA, George IV Accounts, Goldsmiths & Jewellers: RA 25786, 24 April 1807: 'A fine Bt Maltese cross for HRH the Ps Mary, £148'; RA 25820, 1 January 1811: 'A fine Bt and Ruby Maltese Cross for Pss Charlotte, £155'; RA 25789, 28 February 1808: 'A

Necklace composed of Monkey's heads in cameo on Labrador Spar in gold, £27 16s'. All three purchases were made from Rundell, Bridge & Rundell. The full series of accounts runs from 1783 to 1818 (RA 25640–26328).

59. For cameos cut in layered stones from the collection of George III, see *King's Purchase*, p. 56.

60. For more on gem collecting in the eighteenth century and the significance of gem casts, in plaster or sulphur as well as glass, see J. Rudoe, 'Engraved gems: the lost art of antiquity', in *Enlightenment*, pp. 132–9.

61. For the origins and techniques of micromosaics, see J. Rudoe, 'Mosaico in piccolo: craftsmanship and virtuosity in miniature mosaics', in J.H. Gabriel, *The Gilbert Collection: Micromosaics*, London, 2000, pp. 27–48.

62. For early nineteenth-century references to jet jewellery, see Bury 1991, I, pp. 106 and 152.

63. For an iron 'Luisenkreuz', see Marquardt 1983, no. 477, p. 269. Commemorative iron crosses continued to be made during the Napoleonic wars.

64. With so many contemporary descriptions of court ladies covered in diamonds, one wonders whether some of these might not have been paste.

65. This may perhaps be the brooch given by the Prince of Wales to Queen Charlotte on her birthday in 1805 (Scarisbrick, 1994, p. 357; RA 25756) but with the sapphire centre removed.

66. For the portrait by Opie, see *George III & Queen Charlotte*, no. 165. The locket is illustrated at the front of Lady Llanover, ed., *The Autobiography and Correspondence of Mary Granville, Mrs Delany*, 3 vols., London, 1861, and its reception is described in vol. II, p. 254: 'so precious a gift is indeed inestimable'.

67. For the language of flowers, see Tait 1984, p. 105.

68. For the currant brooches in the British Museum, see Tait 1984, nos. 656–9.

69. *Vetusta Monumenta*, vol. III, p. 12, plate xxvi, fig. 8.

70. *Catalogue of the highly valuable collection of Fire Arms, Oriental and European Weapons, Trinkets and Jewellery of His Royal Highness The Duke of York*, Christie's, 27–30 March 1827, lot 35 (27 March), where it is described as: 'An extremely curious massive gold ring, with the arms of Mary Queen of Scots, having also the monogram of Queen Mary and the crown, engraved on the back of

the gold setting.' For the purchase of the ring by Greene, see *Gentleman's Magazine*, XCVII, part 1, p. 359.

71. Registration number 1856, 10–15, 1. See A. Way, 'The Signet-ring and Silver Bell of Mary Queen of Scots', *Archaeological Journal*, XV, 1858, pp. 253–66. For later accounts, see O.M. Dalton, *Catalogue of the Finger Rings, Early Christian, Byzantine, Medieval & Later, in the British Museum*, London, 1912, no. 316; exh. cat., 'Jewellery through 7000 Years', London, British Museum, 1976, no. 422; C. Gere, in Ward *et al.*, *The Ring from Antiquity to the Twentieth Century*, London, 1981, no. 210.

72. Matthew Winterbottom has kindly passed on his discovery that the ring is included in Walpole's list of 'Other Pictures and curiosities at Kensington', dated 2 June 1763 and written into the back of his own annotated copy of W. Bathoe, *A catalogue of the Collection of Pictures belonging to King James the Second*, London, 1758 (Royal Library). A further annotation records that the curiosities were 'sent to his Majesty at Kensington', presumably for Queen Charlotte, on 22 March 1764.

73. Thomas Gainsborough, *The three eldest daughters of George III*, 1783–4.
RCIN 400206

I I

Princesses: telling the story

FLORA FRASER

For fifteen years my first port of call for biographical information has been the Round Tower at Windsor Castle, stalwart home of the Royal Archives. Among much else to be read up there, at the top of that damnably steep stairway, are thousands of letters in the Georgian and Victorian Papers relating to the six subjects – the Princess Royal, and the Princesses Augusta, Elizabeth, Mary, Sophia and Amelia – of my most recent biography, *Princesses*. These letters intrigued me in the autumn of 1988, on my very first visit to the Archives, when I began researching *The Unruly Queen* (1996), my book about the Princesses' sister-in-law, Queen Caroline. In the autumn of 1996 I returned to make these letters of the Princess Royal, of Princess Augusta, and of their sisters – which were sometimes vivid and witty, and sometimes allusive and enigmatic – the focus of my attention. *Princesses: The Six Daughters of George III*, published in September 2004, was the outcome. And a high proportion of what I read in the Archives in the Round Tower appears in the book, as countless references beginning 'RA GEO' attest in the notes.

One day I shall write about my visits to the Archives over those fifteen years, and about those years wrestling with handwriting high in the sky. But for now I wish to dwell on three other haunts of mine during the writing of *Princesses* – namely, the Print Room, also at Windsor; the atmospheric Charlotte Closet at Frogmore House in the Home Park at Windsor; and, in London, the office of the Surveyor of the Queen's Pictures in Stable Yard House, St James's Palace.

As the *George III & Queen Charlotte* exhibition at The Queen's Gallery showed, the six daughters of George III were not only very artistic, but they were also regularly painted by leading artists of the day over a period of forty years – from the 1760s until the 1800s. So it made perfect sense for me to 'hang out' at the Print Room at Windsor while researching their lives. The Princesses' own drawings and paintings, as well as miniatures of them, are kept there. More of their artistic productions hang at Frogmore, the house acquired by Queen Charlotte at Windsor. And there are family portraits in that feminine retreat too, not to mention – in the Charlotte Closet – almanacs and bibles that the Princesses owned, pieces of their hair, and – most touching of all – unfinished 'work' in workbags. In the Surveyor's office in London, meanwhile, are inventories of the pictures and family portraits among which the Princesses lived in the different royal palaces, as well as files of information relating to their images in the Royal Collection. I became engrossed.

When I researched and wrote *The Unruly Queen*, I was interested by my subject's artistic output – she painted and sculpted and did fancy work. But Queen Caroline, while a skilled politician, was no particular artist. The accomplished work of her sisters-in-law took me by surprise. They copied almost everything that lay around them with accuracy and in an astonishing range of media. Botanical specimens in water-colour, historical manuscripts in ink, mothers and babies in silhouettes, butterflies in rolled paper, and even Roman pavements in needlework – these were only some of their productions.

As for Queen Caroline's own person, she was never a great beauty and the artistic glories associated with her name are political – lavish propaganda portraits by Lawrence, and cartoons commissioned by others from Gillray and Theodore Lane. With the six daughters of George III, who were considered a 'vision of beauty' when they were young, there were not only portraits by Lawrence to examine. There were groups by Zoffany, by Gainsborough, by Benjamin West and by Copley, in which they appeared. There were miniatures by Cosway, and paintings by Hoppner. There were serial sittings to Beechey, to Stroehling, to Andrew Robertson and to Henry Edridge . . .

For a long time I needed no other study aids than Oliver Millar's two volumes of *Later Georgian Pictures in the Royal Collection*, and Richard Walker's *Miniatures in the Collection of Her Majesty the Queen: The Eighteenth and Early Nineteenth Centuries*. Indeed these images, in reproduction, served as background to a hundred trains of thought about the Princesses' early years, about their hopes and fears and dreams. The result was that I felt quite dazed and disoriented when I eventually saw at Windsor and in London the glorious originals of the illustrations over which I had pored so long. All useful biographical thought eluded me, and I had to return to Oliver Millar's and to Richard Walker's publications to remember all those questions and puzzles about the Princesses that dogged me till I answered or, exasperated, abandoned them.

I learnt as much as I could about the Princesses' sittings to these painters as children and as adults – and to lesser known portrait painters, as they grew older. And I was fascinated. In so many of their portraits there is an eighteenth-century Everywoman blankness, a milk-and-water uniformity in the white dresses and pensive expressions that is mirrored in a thousand paintings, drawings and miniatures of now anonymous Englishwomen who lived in the eighteenth century. And yet from their letters I knew the Princesses to be as strong-willed and passionate, and alive to absurdity, as Jane Austen herself or any of her characters. So why this striking dissonance between the public image and their private life? At first I was confused and disappointed. But as I read more of the Princesses' letters, and came to know the extent of what lay hidden, I became instead impressed by the milksop image they projected in their portraits.

I also studied the work that the Princess Royal, Princess Augusta and Princess Elizabeth produced. And I thought long and hard about it all, and asked the curators of the Royal

Collection further questions about the Princesses and art, design, décor and taste. They responded patiently, and never suggested – which was the truth – that I was an ignorant savage, a naïve biographer who had foolishly jumped ship, and was now afloat and rudderless on a sea of art history.

But the truth will out, and the narrative of *Princesses* became cursed and impeded when I tried to write in successive drafts and at length about the Royal sisters' portraits, about their sittings to artists, and even about the Princesses' own artistic productions. Becalmed by art history, I jumped back on the stately ship of biography which was cruising by. Chronological turbines turning, engine power returned to the text, and it was strong narrative drive, full speed ahead. There is a satisfaction in knowing one's limitations as a writer, and the limitations of one's craft. When a curator at the Yale Center for British Art revealed to me that she had difficulty, when mounting a historical show, fitting the chronology in with all that she had to convey artistically, I understood that it cuts both ways. Biography and art history are allied but separate states, and one should respect the frontiers.

In one sense, I suppose the amount of time I loitered in different parts of the Royal Collection cannot be justified by the space devoted to matters artistic in my finished book, *Princesses*. For the narrative is largely concerned with 'hearts and minds', or the responses of these six royal sisters to crushing circumstance, as well as to more cheerful mundanities of family life. The lifeblood of the Princesses' biography – as I see it – is not contained in their drawings or in their portraits. And so the Print Room, and the Charlotte Closet, and the Surveyor's offices were not, as it turns out, rich sources of biographical information. But I am still glad to have pursued the royal sisters into the further reaches of art history, although it is their thought processes that dominate my book. The galaxy of their portraits at Windsor and in Buckingham Palace still shines in my mind.

Indeed, far from regretting my foray into art history during the years of researching *Princesses*, I feel the biography is

infinitely the better for my journey. Above all, I am glad that
I was able to make informed choices about the images – and
they are mostly portraits – that I show in the three sections of
colour plates inserted between the pages of my finished book.
Like the family tree I provide at the front of the book, the
portraits in these inserts are supplementary to the text. But the
family tree is not only useful as a reading aid. It also shows,
for instance, that Queen Mary – who famously secured so
many letters and material belongings of the family of George
III for the Royal Collection – was, like her husband George
V, a great-grandchild of George III. In the same way, the
portraits in the book perform the important task of showing
what the Princesses looked like, but they also provide extra
food for the reader's imagination.

For instance, I quote in my text a vivid letter by Fanny
Burney describing an invalid Princess Amelia, with her hair
streaming over her shoulders, and wearing a riding habit with
pink lapels, lying on a sofa. An attentive reader will, in my
view, look with more interest, having read Fanny Burney's
words, at Andrew Robertson's miniature (plate XVI) of a
healthy Princess Amelia in a hat and blue riding habit.
Another reader, who has had an initial flick through the
colour plates, will be, I think, the more moved by Burney's
image of the invalid Amelia for having seen the glowing
Robertson. If the illustrations in my book can achieve this
level of fertilisation of the imagination, I am a happy
biographer with an interest, where appropriate, in art history.

While I could not hope to reproduce in my book all the
portraits made of the Princesses, many of them, like the three
Hoppners of Princess Mary, of Princess Sophia and of Princess
Amelia as children, interested me, especially in the contribution they made to the serial portraiture of the Princesses.
George III is said to have kept no cellar, but to have sent out
to Kew Green or to the Windsor wine merchant for a bottle
of claret as need arose. He had a different policy, however,
where artists and portraiture were concerned – not to mention
the production of children. More was definitely better, and an

artist called to Windsor to paint the Princesses, as they grew to maturity, was expected to paint all of them.

Gainsborough famously scooped the pool in 1783, positioning the King and Queen and thirteen of their children in a block of gold-edged ovals. But Zoffany before him had shown the elder Princes and Princesses in the 1760s to advantage in numerous famous conversation pieces. Benjamin West, who succeeded as the King's 'Apollo', painted the royal children in the 1770s as well – in pairs, and in groups, and once all together with their mother. Of all that West executed, however, a pencil sketch of some of the Princesses and Princes playing before a sitting stays in the mind most agreeably. A painting of the Queen and the Princess Royal at 'work' together on a piece of embroidery is too fatiguing even to think of. Neither participant appears to be taking any pleasure in the process, and even West's painting of his own Quaker family appears lively by comparison.

'Mediocre' William Beechey succeeded West in the King's favour, following the King's notorious illness in the winter of 1788–9. Beechey was dubbed 'Mediocre' by Thackeray in his lectures on 'The Four Georges', but the artist's series of portraits of George III's daughters commemorates the last time the six were ever together as adults. The Princess Royal (fig. 74) was on the point of marrying the Hereditary Prince of Württemberg in 1797, a prince who caused Beechey every possible difficulty as a sitter, incidentally. His stomach was so large that he appeared deformed. Furthermore Beechey was 'three days at Windsor waiting for the Prince of Wurttemberg to sit', his fellow-artist Joseph Farington reported. When the Prince did appear, he sat 'so unsteadily that the King seeing Beechey's distress endeavoured to fix the Prince's attention by going into a part of the room to which in conversing with His Majesty the Prince must look in the right direction.'

Beechey's portraits of the Princess Royal and her sisters – commissioned by the Princesses' brother, the Prince of Wales – are not outstanding. Indeed, they could serve as examples of

74. Sir William Beechey, *Charlotte, Princess Royal*, c.1795–7.
RCIN 403413

anodyne eighteenth-century female portraiture. And yet
Princess Augusta said later of sitting to Beechey, as the artist
and diarist Joseph Farington reported in 1809, that, 'when he
thought he had succeeded he would dance about the room.'
Perhaps she was referring to other portraits he painted of her,
in which he succeeded better. A miniature deriving from one
of them (fig. 76) was supposedly worn by Augusta's lover,
General Sir Brent Spencer, round his neck until his death.
Another full-length shows her flushed with exercise, and out
on a walk on a coastline, as she really was – a healthy,

223

75. Henry Edridge, *Princess Elizabeth*, 1804. Watercolour.
RL 13867

energetic, and handsome woman, although no longer beautiful as in youth.

There are many stories illustrating the familiar footing on which artists lived with the royal family, when all the children were younger. But things changed once the King's eyesight deteriorated in the early 1800s. He commissioned no more portraits of his daughters, and was only grudgingly painted

76. British School, *Princess Augusta*, 1799. Watercolour on ivory.
RCIN 422246

himself. Furthermore, the King's health – ever since his first bout of apparent madness in the winter of 1788 – fluctuated, and as a result he and the Queen and the five daughters who were still at home lived in seclusion at Windsor a good part of the time from 1801 onwards, until the King's health gave way in 1810 and the Regency ensued. The King's years of patronage of the portrait painters of London were at an end.

But the Princesses' brothers, the Prince of Wales and the Duke of Sussex, obliged, and a whole new wave of royal portraiture ensued to enliven the days of the five Princesses at

77. Richard Cosway, *Princess Mary, Duchess of Gloucester, c.*1796. Watercolour on ivory. RCIN 420647

Windsor. The royal brothers commissioned, in addition to Beechey, the artists Henry Edridge, Richard Cosway (fig. 77), Andrew Robertson and Peter Stroehling to paint and draw the five Princesses at Windsor at intervals through the 1800s. And so these three artists had the privilege, like Beechey, of observing the royal sisters over a period of months – as it took so long to paint them all.

Joseph Farington noted in June 1802 that Edridge was 'at Windsor making drawings of the Princesses, but is obliged to wait their time and has them not to sit more than an hour in a day'. Hanging around Windsor, Edridge became a general favourite, 'from always, in his manners, keeping within the strict line of prudence and propriety'. He was at the Queen's House and at Windsor again in the sad year of 1804, when the King's mind was 'manifestly very unsteady'. For all his prudent manners with the King and the Princesses, Edridge kept Farington informed about what he observed in the royal households, and the latter committed it all to his diary. The King, ran one entry, acted like a 'humoured child', and was 'treated by everybody like one'. And again: 'The Princesses seem to have much affection for each other, but maintain strong distinction claiming superiority from age, etc. There does not appear to be the same feeling [among the Princesses] for the Queen as for the King. Her manner is more of a Governante which causes restraint.'

I was interested to find the artistic community in London so well informed in 1804 via Edridge about the King's illness and about the Queen's relations with her daughters. And here is Andrew Robertson, an artist to whom the Princesses sat repeatedly at Windsor at the request of the Duke of Sussex, writing in the spring of 1807:

> The easy, affable, and elegant manners of the Princesses are quite endearing. I already feel as if I had known them for years and almost forget who they are. They say it is very hard to be Royal Highnessed for ever. They wish people would let them feel they had a home. At St James's they may Royal Highness away as much as they please – there it is proper, but at Windsor they are at home.

He ends: 'The only difference I perceive between the Royal Family and other people is that on entering and leaving the room one makes a more profound bow – quite down, as much as to say, with all this familiarity, I do not forget whom I address.' But Robertson was mistaken in thinking the Princesses were like other people, or that their candid expression of their wish for privacy – or indeed the slap on the back that Princess Augusta gave him when praising her likeness – meant he was in their confidence. There were, to use an old-fashioned phrase, 'deep doings' at Windsor this spring. Caroline, Princess of Wales had been accused by the Prince, her husband, of adultery and of giving birth to an illegitimate son; a cabinet committee had met to consider the claims. The Princess of Wales was threatening, in turn, to 'bring forward' the misconduct of her sisters-in-law with their father's equerries, which she said the King condoned.

Fragments of this running sore penetrate Robertson's narrative, as when Augusta commissions a copy of her miniature to give to Caroline, once, the charges against her having been dropped, she appears again at court. But on the whole Robertson's narrative, while delightful and observant about the Princesses' mannerisms and appearances, is that of an outsider. He calls Princess Sophia (plate XVII) 'sensible, mild, reflective and good'. Now 'good' is a strange epithet to attach to someone who suffered all her adult life from the shame of its being known that she had given birth in 1800 to an illegitimate son. I am glad here to draw attention to Robertson's letters where he discusses the Princesses' sittings, but in the end neither Beechey nor Edridge nor Robertson can compare as witnesses to the Princesses' story to the 'insiders' of the Royal Household, whose letters reveal what was really going on. And so the sittings of the Princesses to these artists, and Farington's reflections on them, are absent from my text.

With Robertson's record, we end our look at the portraits of the Princesses, which tell one story while their letters tell another. After the King's power passed to his son as Prince Regent in 1811, and he lived under the care of attendants in the northern apartments of Windsor Castle until his death in January 1820, Queen Charlotte forbade her daughters to think of being painted or drawn again. It was unseemly, she said, given their father's affliction. Nevertheless Princess Elizabeth yearned to be drawn by Edridge again, while her sister Mary, who was more worldly and more beautiful, pined to be painted by Lawrence.

Mary had her wish eventually, on her marriage in 1816 to her cousin the Duke of Gloucester, when she was older and larger than she had been, and she may have regretted pursuing her dream on seeing the result. Lawrence's companion portrait of Princess Sophia, on the other hand, is the only one I know – of all the many images of the Princesses – to show a sexually attractive woman. To drive home this point, Sophia wears a red dress recalling Lawrence's earlier – and very sensual – portrait of Caroline, Princess of Wales, who was rumoured to have been the painter's lover. It makes you wonder about Sir Thomas and Princess Sophia . . .

To conclude, I admire the Princesses' childhood portraits without reservation and look happily in Sophia's round face as painted by Copley and Hoppner for the seeds of her later image – in spectacles – by Edridge, or without, by Robertson. Every edible image of Amelia as a baby, meanwhile, is tinged with sadness; the knowledge that she died young – and painfully, from tuberculosis – in 1810 obtrudes. Most of the glossy portraits of the Princesses made during their adult youth and beauty, however, seem at variance with what I know of them. I exclude the superb group of the three elder Princesses by Gainsborough, for I could stare at their young Royal Highnesses' enigmatic, blank expressions for ever. I am, in addition, always interested by those portraits and miniatures of the Princesses, of which multiple copies were made for the Princesses' brothers and sisters and friends, on the grounds that they must have been the most 'like'.

But it is when the Princesses – all but Amelia – grow old, it is when I look at their images from later years, commissioned from affection by nieces and nephews, that I seem to see the 'real' Princesses, the ones that I know from their letters. Admittedly they are in decline. Their hair is thinning, and their chins are double, or they themselves are bent double. But I find, when I look at these images of old age, some cheerful, some sad, that I recall best the Princesses' voices from their youth, before the family predicament that was their father's illness had arisen, and afterwards, during the years of endurance before emancipation.

So here's to Fischer and Voigt and Ross and Bone who also painted and drew the Princesses in the 1820s and '30s and '40s. (Princess Mary, astonishingly, survived until 1857, and was photographed twice in the preceding year, once alone, and once with her niece Queen Victoria and great-nephew and great-niece, the future Edward VII and his sister Princess Alice. I could not resist reproducing both images in my book.) In these humble, elderly portraits lurk the remains of great private passion, of terrible troubles borne stoically, and of faith in God. On a lighter note, having written *Princesses,* I now look askance at all family portraits and photographs of harmless great-aunts who stayed at home to be a support to their parents, and never married or – according to family legend – had a life of their own. God alone knows what they were really getting up to.

PRINCIPAL SOURCES

Farington Diary, III, V, VI and X
E. Robertson, ed., *Letters and Papers of Andrew Robertson,* (1895), pp. 136–51

I 2

Dining with
George III and Queen Charlotte

MATTHEW WINTERBOTTOM

Paul Pindar famously quipped that 'a leg of mutton and his wife'[1] were George III's chief pleasures in life, while Elizabeth, Duchess of Northumberland caustically described the royal table as 'neither sumptuous nor elegant & they always dined *Tête à Tête*'.[2] In James Gillray's caricature *Temperance enjoying a frugal meal* (fig. 78) the supposedly miserly King and his consort are depicted eating a miserable meal of boiled eggs and *sauerkraut* accompanied by liberal amounts of '*Aqua Regis*'. As this paper will show, the King was remarkably abstemious in his private dining habits. However, when occasion demanded, he and the Queen were capable of giving the most magnificent banquets – albeit not as regularly or perhaps quite so sumptuously as some of their courtiers.

The diaries of Elizabeth, Duchess of Northumberland, who was Lady of the Bedchamber to Queen Charlotte until 1770 and a personal friend, give a fascinating insight into the young royal couple's daily routine. She described the King and Queen's life as:

> very methodical & regular. Whenever it was in their power they went to Bed by 11 o'clock ... His Larum wked him before 5 o'clock when he rose & lighted the Fire himself & went to bed again till the Clock struck Five & by that Time the Fire being a little burnt up, he rose & dress'd himself & went into the Queen's Dressing Room where he wrote till 8 ... At eight he went down to his own Apartment to wash &c. The Queen rose about 6 or sometimes 7 and at 8 they

78. James Gillray, '*Temperance enjoying a frugal meal*', 1792. Engraving, published by H. Humphrey. RCIN 809343

breakfasted & that over the King went down stairs. . . . N.B. The King at Breakfast drank only one Cup of Tea, and never eat anything.[3]

A few years later she added that 'In Summer he even omits his Dish of Tea'.[4] This implies that the King ate nothing until his dinner in mid-afternoon as the concept of luncheon had

79. John Edwards III, *Egg boiler with ciphers of George III and his five youngest daughters*, 1803–4. Silver-gilt. RCIN 49122

yet to be introduced. An ingenious silver-gilt egg boiler (fig. 79) that forms part of a breakfast set given to the King by his five youngest daughters in 1804 suggests that the King developed a taste for more substantial breakfasts later in life.[5] After breakfast the fare for the remainder of the day depended on whether they were in London or the country. If in London the King might go to his study for an hour and then attend a levée or drawing room at midday in St James's Palace. Levées were held on Wednesdays and Fridays and were attended by men only. Drawing rooms took place on Thursdays and Sundays and were attended by both sexes. They were virtually compulsory for members of the royal family, ministers, MPs friendly to the government, and ambassadors.

The usual time for dinner, the main meal of the day, was four o'clock in the afternoon. However, if a levée was full, the King, who insisted on talking to everyone present, might not get back until five or six, in which case the Queen dined alone. Dinner was strictly a family occasion. In the early years of their marriage the young couple dined alone or with the Dowager Princess of Wales or the King's brothers as guests. Later they were joined by their daughters and any visiting sons. They rarely gave dinner parties and seldom dined out in London. Many years later Lord Melbourne recalled to Queen Victoria that:

> No one ever dined with George III except perhaps on very great occasions the Archbishop of Canterbury and the Lord Chamberlain ... George III introduced that very strict etiquette ... It suited him, he dined with great rapidity, was very temperate and hardly ate anything – it would not have suited him and he would not very probably have made it very agreeable to others.[6]

The Duchess of Northumberland described the King as living in the 'utmost Retirement, owing I believe to the Ascendancy Ld Bute had over him', and this was despite 'his cheerful even Socialble Disposition & a clear Understanding'.[7] On 4 April 1762 the Duchess recorded that 'Their Majestys constant Table at this Time' consisted of 'a soup removed with a large Joynt of Meat and two other Dish such as a Pye or a broyl'd fowl and the like. On the side table was a large Joynt, for example, a large Sirloin of Beef Cold and also a Boars Head and Sallad: 2nd Course always one Roast, one of pasty and Spinage and Sweetbreads, Macaron, Scollopt Oysters or the like.'[8] Of the King and Queen's drinking the Duchess remarked: 'Nor does he ever taste a drop of Wine except in hot weather when he sometimes has a Cup made 3 parts Water and one part Wine. The Queen always drinks one glass of Burgundy with her Dinner.'[9] Of the King's cup it was said that 'a monk of La Trappe might have drunk it without any infraction of his monastic vows'.[10]

After dinner the King went to his study and rejoined the Queen for tea at seven o'clock. Once again the Duchess of Northumberland provides a unique insight:

> went at seven to ye Queens House ... Tea was immediately call'd for (here I observ'd an Alteration). Formerly the Queen made Tea herself & the King carried it about to the Ladies, but now, The two Pages of the Back Stairs enter'd each with a single Cup of Tea with Cream pot &c. One was given to each of their Majestys & then the Pages made their appearance again with Tea upon a Waiter for Lady Holdernesse and myself.[11]

In the early years of their marriage the King and Queen visited the Princess Dowager at least two nights a week. They went to the theatre on Thursdays and opera on Saturdays and regularly attended the Concerts of Ancient Music. Most evenings, however, were spent at home playing and listening to music and playing cards with personal friends and courtiers such as Colonel Goldsworthy, the Courtowns, Lord Ailesbury and the Weymouths. They played 'whisk', pontoon, commerce and reverse except on Sundays, Good Friday, Christmas Day and on the anniversary of Charles I's death.

Supper was usually served around ten o'clock. This was a more modest meal than dinner and again rarely included guests. Once again the Duchess of Northumberland provides a helpful description: 'their supper consists of two made dishes usually composed of Poultry as Chickens, smore Turkey a la Bechomel, a joynt of Cold Mutton, Buttered Eggs, Custard and constantly Veal and Chicken broth.'[12] In February 1774 she noted that 'The King never sups, and indeed, in every Respect lives very abstemiously.'[13] By 1806 it was reported that 'Supper is set out but that is merely a matter of form, and of which none of the family partake'.[14]

In 1785 the King explained to Fanny Burney the reason for his strict eating habits. She recalled that 'the fault of his constitution was a tendency to excessive fat, which he kept, however, in order, by the most vigorous exercise, and the strictest attention to a simple diet; "I prefer eating plain and little to growing diseased and infirm"', he told her.[15]

The Lord Steward's ledgers in the National Archives include the Bills of Fare. These list the food served to the King and Queen, the royal children, their respective Gentlemen and Ladies, pages, Yeomen of the Guard and household officers such as chaplains and cooks. They run from 1660 through to the Regency. During the reign of George III they provide details of the dinners and suppers served at Buckingham House and St James's Palace, while a separate ledger lists meals served at Kew between 1780 and 1801. The King's dinner at St James's Palace on 7 September 1761 – the day before his marriage – consisted of two courses served in the usual *service à la française*. The first course comprised '*pottage Sante Noodles*', two pullets '*fillee* & broild' and roasted haunch of venison with one remove of a chine of lamb with mint sauce that would have replaced the soup. All would be then be cleared from the table and the second course brought in. This included a roasted partridge, four squabs, two of which were larded, four roasted 'peepers', stewed peas with sweetbreads, three buttered lobsters, two 'Chicks & Dry tongue', truffles and sweet dishes of plum tart, tartlets and eight jellies.[16] Obviously the King could not and was not expected to consume the entire substantial array of dishes set in front of him. What was left was referred to as returns and became the property of the servants, who would have divided them among themselves according to a strict order of hierarchy. Returns from the Danish King's table, for example, were sent to the chambermaids' table and from there to the parlour maids and other ladies' maids.[17]

According to the Duchess of Northumberland, on the day of his marriage the King dined with his bride, mother and eldest sister. She added somewhat disparagingly that 'They had only five and five for Dinner'.[18] She was referring to two courses of five dishes each. In an age when the number of dishes offered at each course was seen as an index of the splendour and expense of a dinner, this does seem modest for such an important occasion. However, the importance of the occasion is signified by the menu being entirely in French as opposed to the usual English with the occasional French dish listed. The first course included '*Pottage a la Cressy, Desperdeaux aux trouffle, pettit poulets aux pois, Un jambon glasse au vin*' and '*un pate mellee*' with two hot removes of '*Soles sauce blanc*' and '*Venison a la broche*'. The second course comprised '*Un poularde pique aux caille, faisandreux au cresse, Tourt Craquante, asperge sauce blanc*' and '*ris D'Agneau*' with 'lamb ribs cold' on the sideboard.[19]

The marriage ceremony was followed by a supper attended by the entire royal family which went on until three o'clock in the morning. For their first dinner together as man and wife, the young couple were offered '*Pottage Maigre*', boiled 'chicks' with mushrooms, '*Paté Fricando* & patties' with one remove of trout with shrimps and lobster followed by roast turkey cock, tart 'creamed' and tartlets, roast goose with prunes and apples, peas and lettuce, pigeons with tartare sauce, cold neck of mutton, salad and prawns.[20] The King and Queen's supper is listed for the first time below this dinner. Prior to his marriage the King never appears to have been served supper or, at least, it was not recorded. Their first supper included '3 chicks fricasy, Turks Cap Jelly, 6 quails roast, 30 Craviz cold', spinach with new laid eggs and glazed sweet bread and gruel. Gruel was later superseded by bread and milk. Bread and butter was a particular favourite of the King – during a visit to Whitbread's brewery in 1787 he is said to have declined their lavish hospitality and 'stood all the time and eat only bread and butter'.[21]

Included with the bills of fare are the Lord Steward's Wine Books. These list the types and quantities of wine sent to the royal table and to the tables of other members of the Household. Prior to his marriage, one or two bottles of

'Rhenish' wine were usually sent to the King's table for dinner. For his marriage day dinner, two bottles of claret, six bottles of Rhenish, one bottle of Burgundy, one bottle of champagne and one bottle of Madeira were sent.[22] In the early years of their marriage, around six bottles of wine, usually including claret and Hock, were listed as sent to the King and Queen's daily table. What is not recorded is how much of this was actually consumed by the King and Queen.

During the 1790s bad harvests and the war meant a shortage of grain. The King, as ever, was keen to set an example and according to Queen Charlotte's letters to her brother he insisted on potato or brown bread for the household. In 1801 she wrote: 'We eat only rice and a single piece of bread a day and the very word cake is unknown at present.'[23]

However, despite their personal preferences the King and Queen were capable of grand entertaining. The Garter celebrations of 1771 and 1805 and the state visit of the King of Denmark in 1768 were exceptional. On a more modest scale, balls were often held on royal birthdays. The Queen organised a surprise celebration for the King's twenty-fifth birthday at Buckingham House on 4 June 1763. This included 'supper of a hundred cold dishes followed by an illuminated dessert' lit by 4,000 lamps, with transparencies by Robert Adam.[24]

It was for such occasions that the King commissioned a magnificent new service of gilt dining plate (plate XVIII). The service formed part of an order for nearly 10,000 oz. gilt plate and 6,000 oz. white plate commissioned by the King shortly after announcing his betrothal in July 1761. Costing £8,783 6s 1d, this was the largest single order received by the Jewel House for several decades.[25] The service was supplied by Thomas Heming who, on the recommendation of Lord Bute, was appointed Principal Goldsmith to the King in 1760. He was the first working goldsmith to hold this appointment since the early seventeenth century. The style chosen for the service was a modified French rococo based on the designs of Pierre Germain, published in Paris in 1748 and republished in

England nine years later.[26] Most of the service survives in the Royal Collection, where it is known as the 'Coronation service'. So named since at least 1832, it was not actually delivered in time for the coronation banquet on 22 September 1761, when all the plate used on the royal table was hired.

The Queen's official birthday was celebrated on 18 January 'for the benefit of trade and public convenience' when all members of the court were to appear 'new dressed' twice.[27] The Queen's actual birthday on 19 May was thought to be too close to the King's. For the Queen's first official birthday in England in 1762 she served such German specialities as *metwurst* and *'schnusselles'*.[28] Twenty-seven different dishes, including *soup a la Reine*, plovers' eggs and ornamented Westphalia ham were served at the celebratory ball supper held at Buckingham House on 19 May 1794 – the Queen's actual birthday.[29] The birthday festivities ended at four in the morning and it is recorded that although the Queen stayed in bed the following day, the King was out riding by half past nine.

In contrast the King appears to have dined alone at Kew on his birthday on 4 June 1789. He was served haddock, roast haunch of venison, roast beef, 'a fowl cold', peas, spinach and jelly.[30]

The bill of fare for a typical family dinner at the Queen's House on 20 November 1793 lists *soup aux herbes*, boiled pheasants, beef 'collops' (escalopes), pigeon pie and loin of veal with removes of whiting, shrimps and oysters, mutton and chicken, followed by roasted pheasant and woodcocks, tarts, rice cakes, mushrooms, pancakes, stewed broccoli and buttered eggs. However, '1 fowl and Tart for the King' listed within the removes indicates what the King actually ate.[31] Throughout the 1790s the bills of fare frequently list the King's dinner as a simple roast and fruit tart.

This brief survey of the King and Queen's dining habits in public and in private concludes with a description of perhaps the most magnificent ball supper of George III's reign. Held by the Queen and Princesses in honour of the King's recovery at Windsor Castle on 1 May 1789, a full account of this magnificent supper, 'which exceeded any thing of the kind ever given in this kingdom', was published in the *Annual Register*. The supper was held in St George's Hall, with the royal family's table across one end 'raised above the rest'. The guests were seated at two long tables which ran down the entire length of the Hall:

> Her majesty's table was distinguished by gold plates, gold dishes, gold spoons, gold candle-branches, and gold knives and forks. On the ground-work of the royal table were the figures of Peace and Plenty, with the olive-branch and cornucopiae – the accompaniments various Genii weaving wreaths of flowers, – the pedestals presented vases of flowers. On one of the long tables, the platform was covered with dancing figures, – the other had emblematical figures, Hope, Charity, Peace, Plenty, Britannia ... which being done on sand, glistened with the reflected light of the candles. That part of the supper which was hot, consisted of twenty tureens of different soups, roast ducks, turkey pouts, cygness, green geese, land rails, chickens, asparagus, peas, and beans. The cold parts of the collation were the same kind of poultry boned, and swimming or standing in the centre of transparent jellies, which were supported by paste pillars ... This with the lights playing from the candles, and reflected on by the polish of the plates and dishes, made a most beautiful appearance. Crayfish pies of all kinds were distributed with great taste; and the ham and brawn in masquerade, swimming on the surface of pedestals of jelly, seemingly supported but by the strength of an apparent liquid, called for admiration. The ornamental parts of the confectionery were numerous and splendid. There were temples four feet high, in which the different stories were sweetmeats. The various orders of architecture were also done with inimitable taste ... The desert comprehended all the hothouse was competent to afford – and, indeed, more than it was thought art could produce at this time of year. There were a profusion of pines, strawberries of every denomination, peaches, nectarines, apricots, cherries of each kind, from the Kentish to the Morella, plums, and raspberries, with the best and richest preserved fruits, as well those that are dried as those that are in syrup. There were forty

silver branches, each holding two large wax tapers, on the long tables, and six gold branches on the queen's table and at the side-boards were two magnificent candelabra, which gave out a great light.[32]

NOTES

1. Exh. cat., *A King's Feast: the goldsmith's art and royal banqueting in the eighteenth century*, London, Kensington Palace, 1991, p. 107.
2. *Diaries of a Duchess*, p. 79.
3. *ibid.*, pp. 78–9.
4. *ibid.*, p. 100.
5. *George III & Queen Charlotte*, no. 377.
6. Viscount Esher, ed., *The Girlhood of Queen Victoria: a selection from Her Majesty's diaries between the years 1832 and 1840*, London, 1912, vol. II, p. 94.
7. *Diaries of a Duchess*, p. 79.
8. *ibid.*, p. 43.
9. *ibid.*, p. 199.
10. Quoted without reference in C. Hibbert, *George III: A Personal History*, London, 1998, p. 54.
11. *Diaries of a Duchess*, pp. 195–6.
12. *ibid.*, p. 43.
13. *ibid.*, p. 199.
14. Anon., *George the Third, His Court and Family*, vol. II, London, 1820, p. 385.
15. *Burney Diary*, II, p. 318.
16. TNA, PRO LS9/178.
17. *A King's Feast*, p. 107.
18. *Diaries of a Duchess*, p. 30.
19. TNA, PRO LS9/178.
20. *ibid.*
21. HMC, *Fifteenth Annual Report, Appendix, part VII: the manuscripts of the Duke of Somerset, the Marquis of Ailesbury and the Rev. Sir T.H.G. Puleston, Bart.*, London, 1898, p. 284.
22. TNA, PRO LS13/271.
23. O. Hedley, *Queen Charlotte*, London, 1975, p. 207.
24. *George III & Queen Charlotte*, no. 95.
25. *ibid.*, nos. 330–77.

26. See exh. cat., *Rococo: Art and Design in Hogarth's England*, London, Victoria and Albert Museum, 1984, nos. G46 and G47.
27. Hedley 1975, p. 67.
28. TNA, PRO LS9/178. I grateful to Melanie Doderer Winkler for her help in trying to uncover the meaning of the word *'schnusselles'*, although at present this remains a mystery.
29. *ibid.*
30. TNA, PRO LS9/226.
31. TNA, PRO LS9/214.
32. *Annual Register*, 1789, pp. 252–3.

Plate XVIII. Thomas Heming, *Centrepiece*, 1762. Silver-gilt. RCIN 51487

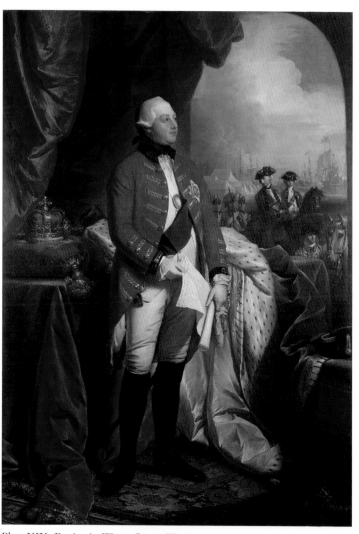

Plate XIX. Benjamin West, *George III*, 1779. RCIN 405407.

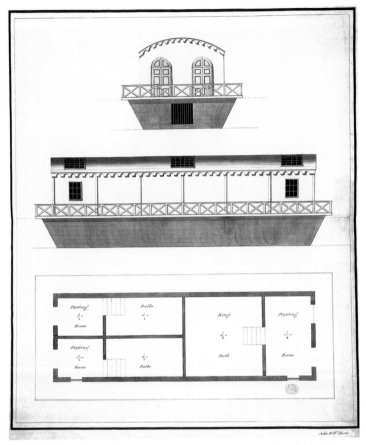

Plate XX. J.W. Hiort, *The King's floating bath at Weymouth*. British Library, London

Plate XXI. Dominic Serres, *Royal visit to the Fleet*, 1774. RCIN 404558

OBSERVATORY · RICHMOND GARDENS.

Plate XXII. G.E. Papendiek, *The Royal Observatory, Richmond Gardens, c.*1820. Yale Center for British Art

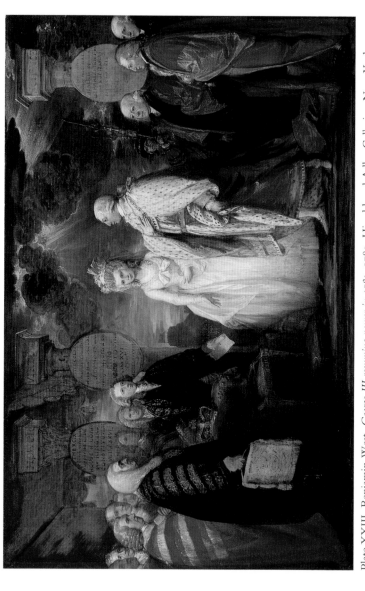

Plate XXIII. Benjamin West, *George III resuming power in 1789*, 1789. Hirschl and Adler Galleries, New York

Plate XXIV. James Stephanoff, *Buckingham House: East Library*, 1817. Watercolour.

Plate XXV. George Adams, *Silver microscope*, *c.*1763. Science Museum,
London

IV

GEORGE III AND
THE INSTITUTIONS

Detail of fig. 83

George III and the Royal Academy of Arts: the politics of culture

HOLGER HOOCK

If one had to single out George III's most important act of cultural patronage, it would perhaps be his role as founding patron of the Royal Academy of Arts. In my book *The King's Artists* I told the story of the forging of a national cultural institution: the Royal Academy's contribution to profession-alisation in the arts; its temporary dominance of the discourse and practices of a self-professedly patriotic English or British School of art; and its role as the national model and standard for art institutions across the British Isles and North America. I also considered the ways in which its national status was contested: its alleged failure to foster a native school of history painting and to represent all genres, media, and styles of 'national art'; and the gradual attenuation of academic aes-thetic authority, as national art was increasingly defined in terms of indigenous responses to British life and landscape rather than as art of universal quality.[1]

However, since the Academy's early history is usually written as the history of the ways in which British art was taught, practised, viewed and received, my main impetus in writing *The King's Artists* was to think, and to encourage thinking, about the politics of culture and the role of the arts in political life. I have sought to re-inscribe into Hanoverian history politics and political institutions as agents and sites of cultural change – thus relating the institutionalisation of academic authority to political culture, notions of national culture, and the process of state formation. Exploring some of the dimensions of the Academy's royal connection, this paper suggests, *en miniature*, an alternative version of Academy history which emphasises the politicisation of art and artists.

The story of the foundation of the Academy has often been rehearsed. It was the culmination of the quest by a generation of British artists for a prestigious, stable institutional platform for an indigenous school of art that would help overcome the long-standing sense of artistic backwardness vis-à-vis continental Europe. During 1767 and 1768, the Incorporated Society of Artists of Great Britain (the Royal Academy's immediate predecessor as an exhibition society) was torn apart by struggles over the direction which the Society, and with it British art, ought to take. While the ruling minority persisted with a high-minded educational mission, a majority aimed merely for an open trade association of artists and semi-artisanal practitioners. When this majority voted to alter the society's constitution and de-selected the President, Francis Hayman, and other directors, the remaining eight directors – all future Royal Academicians – resigned in protest. A keen supporter of plans for a national academy, George III had previously indicated to his new protégé Benjamin West that he 'would gladly patronise any association that might be found better calculated to improve the arts'.[2] Over the following months artists close to the King – West, George Moser (the King's former drawing master), Francis Cotes and, crucially, William Chambers drafted plans for an academy, recruited members – including some more who had had previous dealings with George III – and acclaimed Reynolds as their founding president. On 10 December 1768 George III signed the new Royal Academy's constitution.

In the eighteenth century the patronage of academies of art was widely seen to enhance the prestige of princes. In turn, academies benefited materially and symbolically from princely connections. Although far from uncontroversial, royal patronage was the most prestigious support which British artists could aspire to attract in the 1760s. By 1768 the King's art patronage and collecting had raised high expectations for an artistic renaissance. By seeking royal patronage, the founding Academicians employed a new method to achieve old ends – all foreshadowed in a series of abortive plans between 1748 and 1755 – namely the establishment of an art school, an artistic self-help organisation, and a prestigious, polite exhibition society and platform for an English or British School of Art.

Among Europe's national academies, the Royal Academy was a rare example of an institution that was largely independent of direct political interference: it bore no formal relationship to government or Parliament, and its royal recognition stopped short of a charter. Throughout his active life, however, George III closely involved himself in the Academy's administration. He drafted the academic diploma jointly with Chambers and established the office of Librarian and possibly the honorary professorships. He personally nominated Johan Zoffany and William Hoare; they can be seen on the extreme left and right of Zoffany's earliest group portrait of the Academicians (fig. 80). The King confirmed elections of members, the award of travel scholarships to students, and the appointment of regular and honorary officers as well as of household staff. Until spring 1810 he also sanctioned changes to the laws. Very occasionally, he intervened in the admission of students, the award of charity, and the selection of exhibits. From 1769 to 1780, after which the exhibition income made it self-financing, George III balanced the Royal Academy's books with a total of some £5,116 from the Privy Purse; he personally nominated William Chambers as Treasurer, considered himself responsible for any debts contracted by the Academy, and occasionally vetoed decisions involving supposedly undue diversions of funds. For the King, £5,000 over a decade was a negligible sum, if compared for instance with the £2,000 he spent each year on books, but the fledgling Academy was thus enabled to meet the running expenses of schools, salaries, and exhibitions, and to build up its study collections of casts.

It is important to note that the Academy never assumed any official role with respect to royal image-making and

80. Johan Zoffany, *The Academicians of the Royal Academy*, 1770–2.
RCIN 400747

ceremonial: it was keen not to be seen as a court department comparable to some of its continental counterparts. Any formal role for the Academy was also circumscribed by the prior existence of the King's Works, Lord Chamberlain's Office, Lord Steward's Department, and College of Arms. Thus, the royal family resorted to individual Academicians for their portraits and for building activities, simply because much of the country's artistic talent was concentrated in the Academy. But at no time did Academicians enjoy a monopoly of royal patronage, and the Academy never performed any official role with respect to royal ceremonial.

However, the King and his academy ostentatiously displayed their connection. After the Academy had initially resided in Pall Mall and the dilapidating Old Somerset House, George III and Chambers ensured that from 1780 it would be lavishly accommodated in the new Somerset House, the most prestigious public building raised in London in the second half

81. Thomas Malton Jr, *St Mary's Church and Somerset House in the Strand*. Aquatint, published 1801. Royal Academy, London

of the eighteenth century (fig. 81). The architecture of Somerset House celebrated Britain's arrival as a European cultural leader, both by echoing the themes of classical antiquity and Renaissance Italy, and by acknowledging contemporary French neo-classical examples. The RA was the first British art society to be housed in a publicly funded building, along with navy offices and revenue departments. The sculptural ornament of the Strand façade – executed mostly by the academic sculptors Wilton, Bacon, Carlini and Nollekens – celebrated the maritime, imperial and royal themes echoing throughout the decorative programme: the imperial arms are supported by the allegorical figures of Fame and the Genius of England, the latter being the symbol of the nation's intellectual and artistic creativity. Since 1789 the courtyard has been graced with John Bacon's bronze statue of the toga-clad George III against an antique prow, and holding a rudder (fig. 82). As in the iconography of Somerset House, in its annual calendar the RA associated itself with the King. Academicians dined publicly on the monarch's birthday, and presented loyal addresses on his recovery from illness in 1789, his survival of an assassination attempt in 1800, and his Golden Jubilee in 1809.

The Academy at Somerset House also became a stage for the performance of royal ceremonial, actual and imagined, especially on the occasion of private royal previews, as famously portrayed by Martini's engraving and etching after a drawing by the King's Hanoverian protégé Johann Heinrich Ramberg (1763–1840), to whom members of the royal family had sat (fig. 83). The centre of the Great Room at Somerset House is occupied by the King – highlighted by the rays of sunshine falling down from the skylight – the Queen, six royal Princesses arranged in a formal continuum to the royal couple's right, and the four oldest Princes led by the Prince of Wales to their left. Royalty is attended by an entourage in the background and a number of Academy officers, led by the President, Reynolds, and presumably the Treasurer, Chambers, standing at respectful distance towards the left of the royal family. Benjamin West and an unidentified second adult man are grouped with the three youngest Princes near the entrance. The engraving was published in spring 1789, when the King's recovery from the serious porphyria attack of the previous October ended the Regency crisis. It draws on the two main aspects of the self-presentation of the middle-aged George III: the splendour of majesty and the image of the *paterfamilias*. These combined to enhance the popularity of the King from the mid-1780s. His patronage of the RA allowed George III to be imagined like a continental-style monarch. One nineteenth-century French scholar tellingly misread the print as a visit by Louis XVI to the *Salon* (though the French king in fact never visited that exhibition). George III does not seem to have visited the Academy exhibition in 1789. Martini's print thus takes on added significance as a means of

82. Giovanni Battista Cipriani, *Design for the monument to George III in the courtyard of Somerset House, c.*1775. Pen and ink and wash. RL 13248

ensuring the monarch's virtual presence at his Academy in the season of his recovery.

While the link with the monarch as head of society enhanced the Royal Academy's standing, the King's political

83. Pietro Martini after J.H. Ramberg, *Their Majesties viewing the Exhibition at the Royal Academy*, 1788. Engraving. RCIN 750535a

role opened up the arts to political interpretations. Indeed, the Royal Academy was from the start not only an artistic but also a political body, and was understood as such by contemporaries. Artists, exhibits, and the Academicians' personal and collective activities were inextricably intertwined with the machinery and debates of British politics. In its early years a Hogarthian reading of 'the academy' as a continental concept and institution was related to a radical, Wilkesite critique of the Academicians as an exclusive, self-interested, corrupt, artistic oligarchy, which was destroying the more inclusive Society of Artists, and which colluded with a megalomaniac King, thus posing a threat to the profession at large and to English liberties. Throughout the Academy's first half-century the discussion of the arts reflected, and contributed to, wider political discourses: contests over the notions of royal authority, corruption, oligarchic monopoly, representation, and reform were all played out in the artistic sphere. In the remainder of this essay, the Academy's opening exhibition at Somerset House in 1780 will serve to exemplify the interplay between art and politics at and around the Academy.

One of the main attractions of the inaugural show was Benjamin West's full-length *Portrait of His Majesty, two general officers on horseback and the royal navy in the back ground* (plate XIX). It shows George III, standing in military uniform, with the star and sash of the Order of the Garter, and holding a scroll inscribed *Plans of the Camps of Cox Heath, Warley, St. Eden [Port]smouth and Plymouth with a General Return of Your Majesty's Forces in Great Britain Aug 18 1779*. A crown, orb, and sceptre are placed on a table behind the King. Through an arch on the right are visible two mounted officers, Lord Amherst and the Marquess of Lothian, as well as a groom in royal livery and three soldiers. In the far distance tents of a military camp stand by the sea-shore; among several ships the *Royal George* fires a salute.

Images of military camps were also exhibited at the 1779 and 1780 academy shows by de Loutherbourg in *A Landscape in which are represented the manoeuvres of an attack performed before their Majesties on Little Warley Common* (1779)[3] and *The Troops at Warley Camp reviewed by HM* (1780).[4] Such camps prepared the army and the population for the possibility of war, both militarily and psychologically. West's winning formula was to link royal portraiture with the commemoration of the preparations made during the French invasion crisis in 1778–9. West underlined the theme of the royal commander-in-chief with such exhibits as *Portraits of their royal highnesses, Prince William Henry, and Prince Edward*, painted to commemorate Prince William's entry into the navy as a midshipman, and *The Destruction of the French Fleet at La Hogue*, and *The Battle of the Boyne* (the defeat of James II and his French allies by William III), exhibited when another French invasion threat had only recently abated. Anti-war sentiment was growing. The Bourbon entry in the war seemed to show the inadequacy of British government policy. The Pennsylvania-born

West, who did not hide his sympathies for his rebellious compatriots, staked his claim as a loyal court painter. He tried to reassert the monarch's personal role in homeland defence and to imagine monarchical authority at its most splendid. West also sought to project the Academy as a site of royal authority and as a site for the display of Britain's cultural as well as military prowess.

Yet, as Horace Walpole commented wryly to a correspondent, West's painting of the King (plate XIX) served only to remind politically alert viewers that the King was 'at Coxheath when the French fleet was in Plymouth Sound'.[5] Far from representing an unambiguously successful projection of effective monarchical leadership, West's exhibit could just as easily be dismissed as an embarrassing record of poor royal timing at best, and, at worst, of downright incompetence.

In the same letter, Walpole then described a surprise encounter he had had in the Great Room: 'By what lethargy of loyalty it happened I do not know but *there* is also a picture of Mrs Wright modelling the head of Charles I, and their Majesties contemplating it.'[6] The painting in question was catalogue number 202, entitled *Mrs. Wright modelling a head in wax*, by Joseph Wright.

Wright, self-styled 'American Satan' (fig. 84), was a protégé of Benjamin West, the first ever American RA student, and a recent winner of an Academy silver medal. 'Mrs. Wright', his mother Patience, was an American Quaker who in the 1770s established a reputation as a modeller in wax and as a waxwork manager, at fashionable London addresses. Despite initial royal patronage, she soon alienated the King and government with her anti-monarchical pronouncements, radical contacts, and military espionage on behalf of the American rebels.[7]

According to press reviews, *Mrs. Wright modelling a head in wax* showed Patience modelling a head of Charles I, *either* observed by (the heads of) George III and Queen Charlotte *or* looking towards the portraits of that royal couple. The picture, which was hung high up, in a corner, polarised

YANKEE - DOODLE. or the American SATAN.

Ask me what provocation I have had
That strong antipathy Good bears to Bad.
Ask by Clarence's Scalp'em on the Banks of the Ohio.

84. Joseph Wright, *Yankee-Doodle, or the American Satan, c.*1780. Engraving. The John Carter Brown Library, Brown University, Providence

commentators on political rather than aesthetic grounds. Within two days of the opening, the *London Courant* described the exhibit as a 'very striking likeness' with 'exactly the features of that incorrigible tyrant, Charles the First', and 'caricatura's, of *the two first personages in the kingdom*' looking on. The review went on to praise Patience Wright and her political stance in terms which chimed with those strands in late eighteenth-century political discourse that warned of the potential consequences of bad government and the subversion of English liberties, in England and America, but stopped short of threatening the trial or killing of a Hanoverian king.[8]

Some reviews described Mrs Wright as looking towards George III and his queen, apparently expressing a desire to see the historical fate of one king repeated by another. For instance, the *Gazette* on 16 May printed an epigram which read the painting in unambiguously regicidal terms as far as the wax modeller was concerned, though without committing the paper itself to any political stance: 'Mrs Wright on her lap sustains a trunkless head,/ And looks a wish – the King's was in its stead!'[9] This interpretation of the picture resonated with the rhetoric of regicide not uncommon in radical political discourse since the late 1760s. Many writers accused George III of directing a neo-Stuart attempt to impose tyranny on Britain and warned the King that the early Stuarts' fate might be repeated. During the American Revolutionary War, there was an unusually violent tone about the attacks of the parliamentary opposition against the corrupt, 'secret influence' of the crown.

The three royal heads in Wright's painting were at the centre of one of the most elaborate of the printed responses to the exhibit. The reviewer for the *London Courant* first criticised moral and political corruption and upheld the didactic function of art in reforming the individual and the polity. He then praised the Academy for exhibiting

the picture of Mrs. Wright, modelling . . . the *bleeding* head of the tyrant Charles the Ist, with two striking figures in the back ground, meanwhile contemplating the execution of this celebrated Artist. The male portrait is exhibited [in] seeming likeness of somebody, in a gloomy sullen surprize at the public exhibition of such an unusual representation, whilst the female form ... looks on ... rather disgusted at the strange conceit of employing so much time and art in modelling a horrid subject, which Mr. .... Voltaire some time said jocosely, was apt to give every King in Christendom an annual crick of the neck on every thirtieth of January. I asked many of the spectators ... what all this meant; but I could find none who challenged any intimate acquaintance with either of the portraits, though all confessed there was the most striking likeness of Mrs Wright, and her wonderful art in such terrific exhibitions.[10]

This reviewer thus played with the language of 'execution' – the double meaning of the word itself, the bleeding head, the 'annual crick' in royal necks, and Mrs Wright's 'terrific exhibitions'. By involving the imaginary audience in the futile identification of the royal personages – who were of course all too easily identifiable – the reviewer suggested that the picture was likely to attract attention, but also that it might seem impolitic to discuss it in public, or with strangers, or someone appearing to write for the press.

By describing Charles I's modelled head as 'bleeding' – and hence rendered in colour – the *London Courant* supported Joseph Wright's clever subversion of academic hierarchies through the exhibition of the image of the wax modeller practising her art. Patience Wright was generally considered the leading practitioner in her field. Academy laws, however, banned models in coloured wax because of the association with the supposedly debased sculptural form of life-sized, clothed wax figures (fig. 85). The Wrights' *Charles I* subverted both the Academy's aesthetic hierarchies and the royalist-loyalist site of culture it supposedly provided.

Joseph Wright and his exhibited mother Patience thus displayed a robust, anti-British, American patriotism, one that was violently critical of the King's and government's colonial and religious policies and of their subversion and suppression of English and Protestant liberties. 'America in defiance' (fig. 86), the second sculpture from the left on the courtyard façade

85. Catherine Andras, *Lord Nelson*, 1805. Wax.
Westminster Abbey, London

of Somerset House (next to those of Europe, Asia, and Africa
with cornucopiae) (fig. 86), must have appeared a very
ambiguous ornament during the 1780 opening season of the
RA.

But Wright's picture also attracted very different reactions
from the ones quoted so far. One of the strongest loyalist

86. Joseph Wilton, *The Four Continents: America*, 1778–80. Portland stone. Somerset House, London

patriotic critiques of Wright's exhibit appeared at the climax of the Gordon Riots. On 2 June, at least 20,000 followers of Lord George Gordon's Protestant Association marched towards the Houses of Parliament to demand the immediate repeal of the Roman Catholics Relief Act of 1778. The

Academy show closed the following day, when the capital was relatively quiet. The day after, 4 June, the King's birthday, violence broke out. For four days London was at the mercy of a fanatically destructive mob, which attacked prominent Catholics, their properties, and chapels. On 7 June, 'Black Wednesday', the mob was running amok in large parts of London, assaulted the Bank of England, and set the King's Bench and Fleet prisons alight. That same day a 'Lover of Decency', writing in the *Public Advertiser*, condemned Joseph Wright's work and the Academy for displaying it. An 'Insult to Decency' in any public exhibition, the fact that the painting was displayed in the *royal* show added 'Ingratitude to Insult and Indecency'. When the *Public Advertiser* gave column inches to a review of a painting in a show already closed, and at a time of an emergency in the capital, the political drama outside Somerset House was clearly influencing editorial policy and the author's stance and language.[11]

In sum, Wright's picture had attracted immediate, sustained and disproportionate attention, quite independent of its artistic merit, but due to several factors: the spatial and institutional contexts in which it was exhibited at Somerset House; the political background of the artist; and the wider political context, namely George III's deficit of legitimacy during the American Revolution, and anti-monarchical tendencies in British politics. Art was an immensely useful resource to represent political positions, partly because there was such a high degree of uncertainty about the reading of exhibits such as West's and Wright's royal imagery. Throughout George III's reign, a period when the idiom of patriotism was frequently contested between radicals and loyalists, critics of the Academy and the King found opportunities to exhibit and discuss works that lent themselves to partisan interpretations. During the 1790s acute divisions within the Academy itself, between radical and loyalist-royalist factions, almost led George III to close down the Academy. Whilst it survived that temporary crisis of royal confidence, the fact that George III seems to have come quite close to doubting his wisdom in founding the Academy tells us much about the politics of culture during his reign.

NOTES

1. *The King's Artists. The Royal Academy of Arts and the Politics of British Culture 1760–1840*, Oxford, 2003. The material for the present paper is taken from chapter 5. I am grateful to the publisher, Clarendon Press, for allowing me to draw on this material here.
2. Royal Academy of Arts Archives, General Assembly Minutes, I, 2f.
3. *George III & Queen Charlotte,* no. 163, and Millar 1969, no. 932.
4. Millar 1969, no. 933.
5. *Walpole Correspondence*, XXIX, p. 33, Horace Walpole to William Mason, 19 May 1780.
6. *ibid.*
7. See M.H. Fabian, *Joseph Wright, American Artist 1756–1793*, Washington DC, 1985, and C.C. Sellers, *Patience Wright, American Artist and Spy in George III's London*, Middletown, CT, 1976.
8. *London Courant*, 3 May 1780.
9. *Gazette*, 16 May 1780.
10. 'A Lover of the Arts', *London Courant*, 12 May 1780.
11. *Public Advertiser*, 7 June 1780. The Wright family was in disgrace at court. Patience went into exile in Paris. Her daughter Phoebe married the painter John Hoppner, who shortly afterwards lost his crown pension. Joseph Wright, without much prospect of a career in the Academy, departed via France to America. His infamous RA exhibit was lost in a shipwreck off the coast of Maine. See Fabian 1985, pp. 41–2.

87. George Knapton, *The Family of Frederick, Prince of Wales* (detail), 1751.
RCIN 405741

14

George III and his geographical collection

PETER BARBER

King George III's geographical collection is less well known than his other collections of paintings, drawings, scientific instruments and the 'King's Library'. Yet his relationship with it was in many ways more personal and intimate. The geographical collection is now divided between the British Library and the Royal Library in Windsor Castle, with small fragments to be found, often unidentified, in the British Museum's Department of Prints and Drawings and in the Admiralty Library in Portsmouth. Though frequently thought of as part of the King's Library, it has always been distinct and was certainly a distinct entity in the King's own mind. Largely assembled during his lifetime, but with many printed maps and views dating back to the mid-sixteenth century, items continued to be added until March 1824, more than a year after George IV had offered the collection, with his father's library, to the British Museum. The collection consists largely of loose items. These were formerly gathered into folders which were placed in large boxes disguised to look like volumes of an atlas, but since about 1950 they have been mounted into approximately 260 large guard-volumes. In addition there are about another 200 individually bound manuscript and printed atlases and volumes of printed views.

Before 1811 the collection seems to have formed a single unit, combining maps and views, a few estate maps, military plans, maritime charts, and topographical ephemera arranged in a geographical sequence and loosely referred to by area (e.g. 'the Scotch topography'). Only what ultimately became eight boxes of large- and medium-scale official mapped surveys of the King's Hanoverian dominions were kept separate before their incorporation into the Topographical Collection, probably in 1826. The overall geographical collection was divided into the present constituent parts – the Topographical Collection, the Military (sometimes known as the Cumberland) Collection and the Maritime Collection – after 1811. The Topographical Collection numbers about 50,000 images; the Military Collection, now in Windsor Castle and consisting predominantly of maps of battles, sieges and encampments with accompanying texts, 4,000; and the Maritime Collection, consisting mainly of eighteenth- and early nineteenth-century printed charts and sea atlases, but with some notable seventeenth-century manuscript and printed exceptions, approximately another 3,000.

The King and His Geographical Collection

George III's relationship with his geographical collection was an amalgam of the official and the intensely personal. In this it differed from his other collections – of books, scientific instruments, paintings and drawings – which were both less official and more obviously intellectual in nature and where he generally left the detailed collecting to librarians and experts in the various fields.[1]

Geography was enmeshed with George's perception of his role as monarch. It was a commonplace in the eighteenth century that geography was particularly the science of kings since it conveyed important information on the frontiers, peoples and towns of the world, and the strengths and weaknesses of fortresses and harbours. At the end of the previous century, a Savoyard writer had asked rhetorically 'Peut-on sans la Géographie parler des affaires du temps?' while in 1691 the Abbé de Vallemont in his *Elemens de l'histoire* had written that 'la Géographie est sans doute une de ces connaissances qui entrent par tout ... pourroit-on sans renoncer au bon sens, négliger la Géographie, dont les affaires du Prince et de la Patrie même, reçoivent des lumieres si avantageuses?'[2] Over the following decades atlases with maps showing the classical and modern worlds had been dedicated to the heirs to the English and French thrones supposedly as part of their education.[3] Later, as Jill Shefrin has recently shown, George III and Queen Charlotte themselves, through Lady Charlotte Finch, pioneered the educational use of dissected maps, the earliest known jigsaw puzzles, primarily in order to teach their children about political frontiers and world politics.[4]

This was the educational milieu in which George III had grown up. Family portraits by Wilson and Knapton of the late 1740s and early 1750s, now owned by the National Portrait Gallery, the Royal Collection and the Yale Center for British Art, New Haven, show him and his brothers in the vicinity of a globe or, in Prince George's case, actually holding a plan of the town and fortifications of Portsmouth (fig. 87 and plate II).[5] His early correspondence with Bute demonstrates that from the start of his reign he was using maps as an important source of information on foreign affairs.[6] In the 1820s, when arguing against the transfer of 'the great & valuable collections of Geography & Military Plans' to the British Museum together with the main library, the King's Librarian, Frederick Augusta Barnard, hinted at their political importance by describing them as one of the 'conveniencies to which the Crown has the strongest right of Preference & most undeniable Claim'.[7] There can be little doubt that Barnard was reflecting his late master's views. Until at least 1800 George III seems to have regarded his geographical collections as an indispensable neutral source of political information that would enable him to achieve the objective, as John Brooke has emphasised, of keeping himself independent of faction and exercising his prerogative, not least as supreme commander of British forces with ultimate responsibility for the country's security.[8]

The King probably also believed that geographical collections ought to form part of a proper royal library – as presumably did Emperor Charles VI and his daughter, Maria Theresia, when they acquired for the Imperial library in Vienna the magnificent multi-volume Blaeu-Van der Hem atlas from the heiress of Prince Eugene of Savoy in the late 1730s and Philip von Stosch's 324-volume atlas of maps, prints, drawings and architectural plans in 1769.[9] His confidence was probably further increased by Samuel Johnson's enthusiastic endorsement of such collecting. Indeed the Doctor set some guidelines for the collection when in 1768 he assured Barnard that he would bestow particular distinction on it if he concentrated on acquiring large-scale mapping and particularly locally produced depictions of towns, buildings and gardens in the course of a forthcoming buying expedition to the Continent.[10]

The geographical collections would not have expanded as they did, however, if George III's attitude had simply stemmed from regal conscientiousness. The special characteristics of his collections can be attributed to his personality and interests. Geography appealed to the King's love of facts for their own sake. A contemporary observed in about 1770 that 'topography is one of the King's favourite studies: he copies every capital chart, takes models of all celebrated fortifications, knows the soundings of the chief harbours in Europe and the strong and weak sides of most of the fortified towns.'[11]

Not surprisingly, given the King's well-known enthusiasm for architecture, the collection contains an abundance of architectural plans and elevations. His love of science is reflected in the presence of maps of hitherto unparalleled accuracy that had been surveyed using extremely sophisticated instruments of the kind represented elsewhere among his collections. These include the latest large-scale English county maps that had won Royal Society of Arts prizes for their accuracy. The manuscript drafts and neat copies, drawn and colour washed by the young Paul Sandby, of William Roy's groundbreaking survey of Scotland of 1747–55,[12] probably secured following Roy's death in 1791, and examples of Ordnance Survey one inch to the mile maps which were acquired as they were published from 1801, bear witness to the King's interest in the work of and his sustained support for General Roy and Jesse Ramsden, the pioneers of the Ordnance Survey.[13] The surveys of the Hanoverian lands commissioned by George III from teams led by Georg and Joshua du Plat after 1764 – at scales that were to be undertaken by the Ordnance Survey only after 1840 – resulted in extensive large-scale manuscript mapping still to be found in the Hanoverian sections of the King's Topographical Collection.[14] At the other end of the geographic spectrum, the King was a keen supporter of the voyages of exploration. Although there is virtually no original material relating to Cook's or Vancouver's voyages of discovery – a point to which we shall be returning later – the collection seems to include all the published mapping and charting.

The geographical collections betray other aspects of the King's character. His patriotism and love of the past[15] are intrinsic to them, though any mid- and late eighteenth-century topographical collection with a world-wide coverage, regardless of country of origin or inclinations of the collector, would have been flattering to Britain, which then stood at the apex of power and international fashion. Nevertheless, the topographical views do particularly reflect popular conceptions of British Roman and Gothic antiquity and of modern British civilisation, 'liberty' and power in its widest sense. One can see the fertile countryside, romantic hills and dales, landscaped parks and Palladian country houses, the booming towns and nascent industry, flourishing colonial towns and the powerful fleet, all underpinned by a military power expressed through the innumerable plans of British forts scattered throughout the world, and of British victories increasing in number as the eighteenth century progresses, that are also to be found in the collections.[16] Even outside his dominions, British influence was present through the depiction of English landscape gardens throughout Europe and through the silent testimony of the number of maps and aquatints of places beyond the King's dominions that were printed in England: a reflection of

Britain's rise to a position of world dominance in the map and print trade during the course of George III's reign.

The collections also shed light on the King's insatiable curiosity, which was repeatedly alluded to by his contemporaries. George was notoriously not a traveller. He never left southern and central England. This was almost certainly because, as a creature of habit, he disliked the disruption that inevitably accompanies extensive travel. The collections nevertheless suggest an enormous desire to find out all he could about his own dominions and about faraway places. It made him into an enthusiastic armchair traveller. In this context, almost anything with a topographical connection seems to have been grist to the mill. As well as atlases, travel accounts, topographical plate books, individual maps and views, the King was happy to acquire any sort of ephemera so long as it contained a view, be it an annual report of the Hereford Infirmary, advertisements for schools or wire-fence manufacturers in Chelsea, depictions of disasters like the collapse of the west front of Hereford Cathedral, or admission tickets to assembly rooms at Epping (fig. 88).[17]

The thousands of loose items in folders must have resembled nothing so much as a vast scrap album, presenting the King with few obvious and potentially intimidating aesthetic or intellectual challenges, unlike his other more rigidly categorised collections. As a result they came to reflect, in a way that the other collections could not, the private and personal inclinations of a person at his ease.

Acquisition

Inheritance

On his accession George III inherited a considerable collection of maps, atlases, and official reports illustrated with maps that had been owned and used by his predecessors. They may have come to his notice in the early 1760s when the contents of the older royal palaces, such as Hampton Court and Kensington,

88. Admission ticket for the Epping Assembly, 1725.
British Library, London

were being moved into newer residences, most notably
Buckingham House. Certainly by 1774 the King was so
impressed by one such document, Edmund Dummer's manuscript survey of the royal dockyards undertaken for William III
in 1698, that he commissioned a modern supplement, which
Celina Fox discusses in her contribution (pp. 290–312). The
maps and atlases had formed part of the monarchs' working
libraries, as opposed to the moribund [Old] Royal Library that
had been presented to the newly founded British Museum by
George II in 1757. The maps and atlases extended back to the
Restoration and up to 1714. They included the enormous
Klencke Atlas of seventeenth-century Dutch wall maps presented to Charles II on his restoration by a consortium of
Dutch sugar merchants headed by Joannes Klencke.[18] It had

been kept separate from the old Royal Library only because Charles II placed it in his cabinet of curiosities. It is still said to be the largest book owned by the British Library.

Most of the collection, however, consisted of maps and atlases presented to the monarchs in the course of official business. Among many relatively humdrum maps there are several that are ornately decorated, like the 'Duke's' plan of New Amsterdam, probably executed in London by draughts-men working near the Thames on the basis of maps made in America and presented to James, Duke of York, the future James II, in 1665, at the time of its change of name.[19] There was nothing from the private libraries of George's grandfather and great-grandfather, though at some point after 1760 George acquired miscellaneous maps, atlases and loose items, such as plans of the palace of Ansbach and an address from Queen's College, Oxford, from the library of his grandmother, Caroline of Ansbach, that had passed to Queen Charlotte from George II.[20]

In 1765 the King inherited the extensive map collection of his uncle, the Duke of Cumberland (fig. 89). As Yolande Hodson has shown,[21] this consisted predominantly of plans of forts and encampments, marching routes, and siege and battle plans acquired in the course of his career (including maps purchased from a spy in the French ministry of foreign affairs in Versailles).[22] It almost certainly also embraced a considerable number of Board of Ordnance plans dating back to 1715. But there were other elements demonstrating that Cumberland was not the militaristic dunderhead or monster of legend, such as plans and elevations of Holkham Hall in Norfolk by Matthew Brettingham[23] and plans for the lay-out of Virginia Water and his gardens at Windsor.[24] Of equal importance with the items themselves, however, was the structure of the collection that Cumberland bequeathed to his nephew. It was modelled on the arrangement that the bookseller John Innys imposed on the universal geographical collection that he had assembled in the 1730s and 1740s, which is now in Holkham Hall.[25] Although this was

89. John Elphinstone, Frontispiece to a selection of plans and views of Glamis Castle, *c.*1746 dedicated to the Duke of Cumberland. Ink and wash. British Library, London

modified in the early 1790s and again after 1811 to accommodate the enormous increase in items, the King's Topographical Collection in the British Library, the largest element of his geographical collections, is still arranged along the same lines.

Purchase

As Francis Russell's study of Lord Bute shows, George III had been buying maps and atlases, through agents such as his librarian Richard Dalton, since before his accession. Indeed in 1759–60 Bute seems seriously to have contemplated the purchase on his behalf of the Stosch Atlas, which was then being hawked around Italy at a price equivalent to £3,000.[26] This would at a swoop have brought a collection of over 30,000 printed and manuscript maps, views and architectural

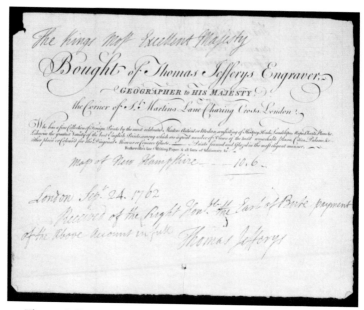

90. Thomas Jefferys, Receipt for a map, 1762. British Library, London

plans (including the largest single set of drawings by Borromini). The sole surviving paper relating to the acquisition of the geographical collections dates from September 1762 (fig. 90). It is a receipt from Thomas Jefferys, Geographer to His Majesty, for 10s 6d, paid to him by Bute on the King's behalf for a map of New Hampshire by Joseph Blanchard and Samuel Langdon which had been published by Jefferys in the previous year. George's correspondence with Bute in this period[27] strongly suggests that it was acquired so that the young King could inform himself about the North American colonies. They had become of particular interest because of the peace negotiations with France that were to lead to the Treaty of Paris (1763) and the outbreak of the first rumbles of discontent at the Grenville ministry's attempt to tax the colonists.

In the same months the purchase of the Consul Smith and Albani collections enormously enriched the geographical

91. Bernardo Bellotto, *View of Lucca*, 1741–2. Pen and ink. British Library, London

collections (see pp. 106–8). The former brought not only manuscript and printed atlases, volumes of Venetian architectural plans,[28] and books of etchings by Visentini after Canaletto (now mainly in the British Museum's Department of Prints and Drawings), but possibly also a group of five drawings of Lucca by Bellotto (fig. 91),[29] though these may have been bought by Dalton in the course of his travels through Italy. The Albani collection included the enormous holdings of material relating to modern Rome and numerous sixteenth-century Italian maps, and early engravings and etchings of all kinds, that stemmed from the Cassiano del Pozzo 'Paper Museum'.[30]

The King's agents and librarians continued to purchase maps, views and atlases, both manuscript and printed, throughout the rest of his reign. Detailed records of individual purchases are lost after the Privy Purse accounts finish in 1773, but annotations and endorsements on the items themselves

92. Jacques Callot, *The gardens at Nancy*, 1625. Engraving.
British Library, London

show that material from Francis Grose's working collection
was purchased shortly after his death,[31] and further purchases
were made at one of the sales of General William Dowd-
eswell's antiquarian collections[32] and in the sale that followed
Alexander Dalrymple's death in 1805.[33] Many of the grand
Dutch, French and German atlases that form an important part
of the collections, as well as other sets of the same atlases that
were dismembered, with the maps being scattered in the
appropriate place in the geographical sequence, were also
presumably purchased. At some point, too, the King's agents
seem to have bought the complete contents of a print shop,
which are recognisable from the inventory numbers, descriptive titles and prices on their versos. In addition to this, locally
produced material was picked up as the occasion offered,
accounting for much of the ephemeral material in the
collections.

What is particularly striking about the later purchases,
however, is their modesty. This is a characteristic reflected in

the King's instructions to his librarians, not to challenge serious collectors at auction.[34] While he made sure that he or his agents acquired the latest atlases and volumes of topographical prints as they were published, there were no spectacular coups on the auction room floor. As a result, with the exception of the items from the Smith and Albani collections, the most precious manuscript and antiquarian printed atlases, maps, views and ephemera came by inheritance, by presentation, and through incorporations made by the King in his official capacity and from his private papers. It is to these last three categories that we shall now turn.

Presentation

In the course of his reign, George III was presented with a wide variety of material which he thought appropriate for his geographical collections. He felt no qualms about using his special position as monarch in this respect, even if he seems to have been reluctant at a private and personal level to make a direct request for a gift. This may explain the absence from the collections of any original maps or views created during the great Pacific voyages of Captain Cook, even though the King had provided considerable, if indirect, support for them through a substantial donation that he made to Cook's sponsors, the Royal Society. A royal request to Cook, at his audience with the King in August 1771, would have been very difficult to refuse.[35] It seems never to have been made.

By contrast the King utilised his official position at the apex of the constitutional pyramid to the full. At one end of the spectrum he was presented with maps of obvious military and political importance. Perhaps the most notable is the copy of the revised, 1775 edition of John Mitchell's wall map of North America, first issued in 1755, that had been used by the British negotiators in Paris in 1782–3 when settling the borders of the United States of America. Generally known as the 'Red-Lined Map', because of the red lines drawn across it to mark out the differing boundary interpretations, it was almost certainly presented to the King by Richard Oswald, who had been secretary to the British legation, in the course of the 1780s.[36] Almost as politically sensitive were the maps of the coastlines of southern and south-western Ireland and forty miles inland surveyed between 1776 and 1782 by General Charles Vallancey, an Irish equivalent, as far as it went, of Roy's map of Scotland. These were presented to the King by Vallancey between 1782 to 1790 in a successful attempt to win the King's support for the remapping of the whole of Ireland.[37]

In a similar vein, but well illustrating the way in which George used his royal position to obtain a geo-political reference library of his own, is the little volume of 'Plans of all the Fortified Places in the Kingdom of the Two Sicilies exactly drawn from originals in the possession of His Sicilian Majesty (upon a smaller scale for the ease of conveyance)'[38] that Sir William Hamilton, the British minister to the Neapolitan court, sent him in September 1766. Hamilton had been transmitting full-size versions, copied from originals commissioned in 1743 by the King of the Two Sicilies and obtained clandestinely through the services of the Sardinian minister in Naples, to Lord Shelburne, the Secretary of State for the Southern Department, over the previous year.[39] Evidently, however, the King was not prepared to rely on the administration for continued access and he let Hamilton know that he wanted copies of his own. There is probably a similar story behind the two volumes of exquisitely executed plans of military encampments in Britain for the years 1756–62 and 1778–82 that were presented in about 1784 by the Quartermaster-General George Morrison, containing work by himself and by Daniel Paterson.[40] These were doubtless duplicates of originals prepared for the Board of Ordnance – examples of some of the plans are also to be found among the map collections of the Royal United Services Institution now owned by the British Library.

The presentation material, however, also catered for George's more general curiosity about the world. In May 1786 the somewhat eccentric antiquary, David Erskine, 11th Earl of Buchan (1742–1829), sent a series of 62 etchings and drawings of Scottish scenes to the King's Librarian, Barnard, for presentation to the King. Executed by John Clerk of Eldin (1728–1812), a dilettante naval theorist as well as a former pupil of Paul Sandby, several of them are tinted by Clerk's brother-in-law, the architect Robert Adam.[41] The wider world was also well represented. On the return to England in 1794 of George Macartney's politically unsuccessful mission to the Chinese court at Peking, the Secretary to the Legation, Sir George Staunton, presented the King with an album of ravishing watercolours of Chinese life and people by William Alexander, one of the official artists, and rather less skilled but no less fascinating views and diagrams by Lieutenant Henry Woodbine Parish, commander of the artillery company accompanying the mission.[42] In the same year Elizabeth Postuma Simcoe, the wife of the Lieutenant-Governor of Upper Canada, presented the King with picturesque ink and wash drawings in the style of William Gilpin of the country-side and settlements around Lake Ontario, including the earliest views of what was to become Toronto. As if to emphasise the Rousseau-like simplicity implicit in the images, they are executed – quite unnecessarily from a practical standpoint – on birchbark.[43]

Incorporation from official papers

If George III was unable to obtain what he felt he needed or wanted through presentation, he was quite prepared to take advantage of his constitutional position to retain official reports, surveys, maps and illustrative material, even if addressed to his minsters, that crossed his desk.[44] Thus the collections are replete with manuscript plans of fortifications in Britain and abroad prepared for the Board of Ordnance. Typical among them is Thomas Hyde Page's manuscript report to the Board of Ordnance on the forts along the

Medway, dated 6 June 1778, with plans of Sheerness, Gravesend, Tilbury and Landguard forts,[45] and the Montresor plan of Philadelphia of 1777 showing the additional defences created during the American War of Independence.[46] Nor were the plans confined to fortifications. No doubt because they appealed to the King's architectural inclinations, there are also numerous plans and elevations of barracks.

George III's interests extended far beyond the purely military. In 1767 the Lords of the Admiralty ordered that the fair draft of Captain Cook's survey of St Pierre and Miquelon of 1763–7, executed in an attempt to chart the extent of French fishing rights off the coasts of Newfoundland re-established under the terms of the Treaty of Paris, 'be laid before the King'. It was not returned and is now K. Top. 119.111. A further two charts by Cook of 1764 showing the whole and the northern coasts of Newfoundland, apparently presented on the same occasion, remain in the Royal Collection, never having apparently been incorporated in the geographical collection.[47] In 1790 the King detached four manuscript charts showing Botany Bay, Broken Bay and Port Jackson, copied by Henry Brewer (1743–96) after originals by John Hunter, from a dispatch of 13 February 1790 sent by Governor Phillip to the Home Secretary, Lord Sydney. They are now in the King's Topographical Collection,[48] while the original dispatch is in the National Archives. In 1794 the King similarly extracted a coastal chart and profiles of King George's Sound off South Australia,[49] originally sent by George Vancouver to Governor Phillip, and three drawings of Port Jackson by Fernando Brambila (fig. 93),[50] that the Spanish navigator Alessandro Malaspina had presented to Francis Grose the younger, the Lieutenant-Governor of New South Wales, from the dispatch dated 30 May 1793 of Grose to the then Home Secretary, Henry Dundas. Again, the charts and views are now in the King's Topographical Collection while the original dispatch, with the astronomical observations made by Malaspina and his colleagues, which

93. Fernando Brambila, *A view of Sydney*, 1793. Pen and ink.
British Library, London

George evidently found less appealing, are in the National
Archives.

Private papers

George III seems to have been particularly busy with his
geographical collections during the late 1780s and throughout
the 1790s. Perhaps, in the wake of his first bout of illness, they
were a form of relaxation from the pressures of official life.
The then-elegant embossed boxes, the backs of some of which
still survive in the King's Library in the British Museum, the
rolls, many of the atlases, and the terrestrial and celestial globes
by the scientific instrument-maker George Adams, were
accommodated in or around enormous wooden map cabinets,
surrounded by shelves of books, in the centre of the Great or
West Library immediately next door to his bedchamber in the
Queen's House (fig. 94).[51] The King felt few qualms about
incorporating some of his private papers if they contained
maps or views. There are several plans and views of royal
properties. These range from Thomas Richardson's elegant
plan, in its original gold-embossed wooden case, of Richmond

94. *The West Library, Buckingham House*. Woodcut.
Frontispiece to F.A. Barnard, *Bibliothecae Regiae Catalogus*, 1820.

and Kew Gardens drawn in 1771,[52] to a little pencil drawing of Frogmore House dating from between 1795 and 1804 (fig. 95), perhaps by one of the princesses.[53] There are plans and elevations by James Adam for the observatory at Kew that was finally commissioned from William Chambers[54] and a plan and elevation of 1791 for a 'Strawberry-Hill gothick' pew to be occupied by the King, Queen and Duchess of York, presumably for a celebration of one of the Duke of York's military successes, at St Margaret's Church, Westminster.[55] The collection also includes an elevation and plan of the new palace in Queen Charlotte's home town of Neustrelitz[56] as well as numerous plans of palaces and royal parks in Hanover.

Relics of the King's role as a country squire are also to be found. There is a plan by his agricultural adviser, landscape guru and land agent Nathaniel Kent, datable to December 1797, relating to the King's proposals for the enclosure of land around Cranbourne Lodge in Windsor Great Park.[57] A letter dated 15 May 1799 accompanying a drawing for a proposed iron bridge over the Thames between Windsor and Datchet also sheds light on George III's activity as a local landowner. The design was a response to the King's expressed 'determination of having a bridge over the Thames at Datchet in the course of the ensuing summer. If so,' wrote its designer, John Stickney, 'I think that he would be pleased with this plan, as

95. *Frogmore House*, possibly by a daughter of George III, *c*.1795–*c*.1804. Pencil. British Library, London

it would make an elegant appearance & has combined simplicity, durability and strength.'[58] One might add that, though the bridge was never built, it probably particularly appealed to the King because it would have utilised the latest industrial technology. What is now the Topographical Collection also includes numerous canal plans; one of 1770, showing a canal that would have passed near Windsor,[59] was sent as a form of lobbying to George III in the hope of securing his support for a parliamentary bill.

There are souvenirs of George III's official activities. Two large watercolours by Samuel Hieronymus Grimm show the distribution of the royal Maundy in the Banqueting House, Whitehall, in 1773.[60] The King made several attempts to get hold of the watercolours after seeing them on display at the Royal Academy in 1774, but their owner, Sir Richard Kaye, the King's Sub-Almoner, kept him waiting and they reached the Royal Collection only in 1810 under the terms of his will.[61] The collection also includes a large print showing the thanksgiving service held at the King's insistence in St Paul's Cathedral on 23 April 1789 to celebrate his first recovery.[62]

Less formal occasions, such as the regular late summer trips to Weymouth between 1789 and 1805,[63] are commemorated in a handsome little volume of the early 1790s bound in red morocco showing the route from the Queen's House, London, and from Windsor, in the style of Cary's road books,[64] and in an elevation and plan of the King's floating bath (plate XX).[65] There is even a letter of 1778 from the former Commander-in-Chief, Lord Amherst, to the King with instructions on how to reach his country seat, Montreal, near Westerham in Kent, with an accompanying plan of the surrounding country and the suggestion that the King and Queen should give the ladies and gentlemen of the neighbourhood the equivalent of what would today be called a photo-opportunity by driving slowly as they passed through the gates of the mansion.[66]

Finally, there are occasional hints of George III's own personal tastes and affections. A watercolour of the Staubbach Fall in Switzerland by William Pars dating from the early 1770s is a duplicate of one forming part of the first sequence of alpine watercolours to be publicly exhibited in London. They caused something of a sensation at the time and mark a milestone in the acceptance and popularity of the 'sublime' in England. The King's possession of a copy suggests that he too had been impressed.[67] Even more personal is a set of drawings of fictitious defence installations by students of fortification in Hanover in the 1790s. Almost certainly they owed their place in the collection to the presence of one dated 1792 by the King's son, Adolphus Frederick (later 1st Duke of Cambridge), who was then serving with the Hanoverian forces against Revolutionary France.[68]

Evidence that George III did actually consult the maps and volumes of his geographical collection for private as well as official purposes has come to light in the form of what must be the most poignant item in the whole collection. Some folded sheets found in a volume of manuscript plans of

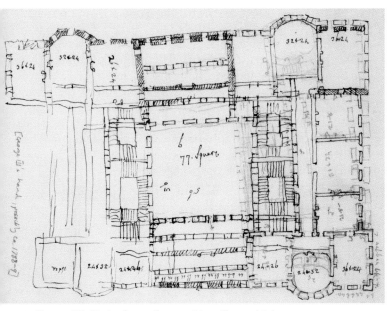

96. George III, *Design for a palace*, c.1788–9. Pen and ink.
British Library, London

Hanoverian palaces contain the order of a service at St
George's Chapel, Windsor, for 10 July 1785 and a series of
architectural plans in pencil in the King's hand. One, its
outline reinforced in ink, is a rather disturbing plan for a
grand palace, probably dating from the period of his illness
in 1788–9 (fig. 96): it shows no less than four grand staircases
leading from a central courtyard and a series of corridors
instead of an enfilade of rooms occupying the wings.[69] It was
probably accidentally left in the volume in about 1789 when,
following his recovery, the King was contemplating a trip to
Hanover.[70]

After 1800 the sense of the King's active involvement in his
geographical collections ceases. There are no more manuscript
maps and plans with an official provenance, with the exception of a survey of Hesse Homburg of 1818 that was
presumably added by the Prince Regent at the time of his

sister Elizabeth's marriage to the Landgrave.[71] There are no more intensely personal items. The collections themselves continued to grow; indeed, after 1811, at an increased pace as additional resources were devoted to them and to the King's Library as a whole. But this was all the work of the King's librarians. As his sight dimmed and his political influence waned, his physical condition worsened and his living quarters contracted, it seems that the King also lost his hitherto insatiable curiosity about the wider world.

NOTES

1. Brooke, p. 307.
2. Quoted in M. Milanesi, 'Note sull' "Epitome Cosmografica" di Vincenzo Coronelli (1692–1693)', in *La Cartografia tra primo Rinascimento e fine dell'Illuminismo*, ed. D. Ramada Curto, A. Cattaneo and A. Ferrand Almeida, Florence, 2003, pp. 69–70, n. 21.
3. e.g. E. Wells, *A new sett of maps both of antient and present geography*, Oxford, 1700, dedicated to Queen Anne's son, William, Duke of Gloucester; 'N. De Fer', *Atlas Royale*, 'Paris' [actually Mortier, Amsterdam], 1695, with maps by Jaillot dedicated to Louis XIV's eldest grandson, the Duke of Burgundy (see M. Pastoureau, *Les Atlas français XVIᵉ–XVIIᵉ siècles: répertoire bibliographique et étude*, Paris, 1984, pp.189–93).
4. J. Shefrin, *Such Constant Affectionate Care: Lady Charlotte Finch, Royal Governess, & the Children of George III*, Los Angeles, 2003. There is no evidence, however, that the King used his geographical collection for his children's education.
5. J. Kerslake, *National Portrait Gallery – Early Georgian Portraits*, 2 vols., London, 1977, no. 1165; Millar 1963, no. 573; exh. cat., *Richard Wilson: The Landscape of Reaction*, London, Tate Gallery, 1982, pp. 151–2; *George III & Queen Charlotte*, fig. 4. The plan held by George in Knapton's family group of 1751 probably derives from the Desmaretz plans of the previous year, a set of which forms part of the King's Topographical Collection (BL, Maps K. Top. 14.29, 30, 41).

6. R. Sedgwick, ed., *Letters from George III to Lord Bute, 1756–1766,* London, 1939, pp. 133–4 (letter dated 6 September 1762).

7. F.A. Barnard to the Duke of Clarence, 27 February 1828 (BL, Add. MS 46358, ff. 53–4).

8. Brooke, pp. 309–10.

9. P. van den Krogt and E. de Groot, *The Atlas Blaeu-Van der Hem of the Austrian National Library,* 5 vols., t'Goy-Houten, 1996–; F. Wawrik *et al.,* eds., *Kartographische Zimilien: Die 50 schönsten Karten und Globen der Österreichischen Nationalbibliothek,* Vienna, 1995, pp. 5, 6, 122; R. Kinauer, *Der Atlas des Freiherrn Philipp von Stosch der Österreichischen Nationalbibliothek,* unpublished PhD thesis, University of Vienna, 1950; L. Lewis, *Connoisseurs and Secret Agents in Eighteenth-Century Rome,* London, 1961, particularly pp. 60–1, 64, 192–3.

10. Samuel Johnson to F.A. Barnard, 28 May 1768, quoted in *Bibiliothecae Regiae Catalogus,* I, pp. v–vi.

11. I. Cobbin, *Georgiana: or Anecdotes of George the Third,* London, 1820, p. 16. I am most grateful to Tony Campbell for bringing this quotation to my attention.

12. BL, Maps C. 96.

13. e.g. Survey of the Isle of Thanet at two inches to the mile, 1808 (Maps K. Top. 16.29).

14. These surveys, in boxes, volumes and as single sheets, are scattered throughout Maps K. Top. 99 and 100. The principal large-scale survey of Hanover, once K. Top. 99.29–2, is now in the Staatsbibliothek zu Berlin, but the reduction from it remains: Maps 6 Tab. 33 (K. Top. 99.29.3).

15. Brooke, p. 285.

16. P. Barber, 'George III's topographical collection: a Georgian view of Britain and the world', in *Enlightenment,* pp. 158–65.

17. BL, K. Top. 15.96-t; 28.4-ee; 15.96-4; 28.4-ff-4; 13.36-1.

18. Now BL, Maps K.A.R.

19. BL, Maps K. Top. 121.35.

20. BL, Maps K. Top. 96.79 a-c; 35.10-q. For the Ansbach plans and drawings by Leopoldo Retty see K. Raschzok, *Lutherischer Kirchenbau und Kirchenraum im Zeitalter des Absolutismus, dargestellt am Beispiel des Markgraftums Brandenburg Ansbach 1672–1791,* [European University Studies, Series XXIII, Theology vol. 328], Frankfurt-am-Main, Bern, New York and Paris, 1988, I, pp.

238–40; II, plan no. 28. I am grateful to Dr Josef Maier for this reference.

21. Y. Hodson, 'Prince William, royal map collector', *The Map Collector*, XLIV (autumn 1988), pp. 2–12. Dr Hodson is preparing a detailed catalogue of the King's Military Collection.

22. BL, Maps K. Top. 67.80-2-a, c, d-g; for the agent see R. Whitworth, *William Augustus, Duke of Cumberland: A Life*, London, 1992, p. 173.

23. BL, Maps K. Top. 31.42-b-h. The published version, *Plans and Elevations of the late Earl of Leicester's House at Holkham* (1761), was dedicated to Cumberland. Brettingham's introduction emphasises the active interest that Cumberland took in the completion of the building.

24. BL, Maps K. Top. 7.38-2-a; 7.38-2-b-1-3; J. Roberts, *Royal Landscape: The Gardens and Parks of Windsor*, New Haven and London, 1997, pp. 31–52 and esp. p. 38.

25. This can be deduced from a comparison between the numbering on fragments of Cumberland's stamps and in orange crayon on some items and Innys's explanation of the structure of his collection in BL, Lansdowne MS 685, ff. 48–56, as well as Cumberland's acquaintance with the Cokes of Holkham Hall.

26. *Bute*, pp. 33, 36, 220–24 and particularly p. 36 and p. 223 (Richard Dalton to Bute, 3 March 1759).

27. *Letters from George III to Lord Bute, 1756–1766*.

28. BL, 71.i.1-3 or K. Top. 78.65-a, still retaining Smith's arms on their title pages.

29. BL, Maps K. Top. 80.21-a-e.

30. For a general introduction, see exh. cat., *The Paper Museum of Cassiano del Pozzo*, London, British Museum, 1993.

31. Endorsement, BL, Maps K. Top. 42.22-lv.

32. Annotation, BL, Maps K. Top 41.6-c.

33. Annotation, BL, Maps 7 Tab. 127 and K. Mar. VII.3*.

34. J. Brooke, 'The Library of King George III', *Yale University Library Gazette*, LII, 1978, p. 38.

35. For Cook's probable gift to the King on that occasion see *George III & Queen Charlotte*, no. 485.

36. BL, Maps K. Top. 118.49-b.

37. BL, Maps 6 Tab 38 and Maps K. Top. 51.31-2. For Vallancey's survey and its connection with his maps of the whole of Ireland, the spur to which was defensive, see J.H. Andrews, *Shapes of*

Ireland: Maps and their Makers 1564–1839, Dublin, 1997, pp. 224–5 and 250–60.

38. BL 118.d.1; also Maps K. Top. 83.76.

39. See G. Pagano de Divitis and V. Giura, eds., *L'Italia del secondo settecento nelle relazioni segrete di William Hamilton, Horace Mann e John Murray*, Naples, 1997, particularly pp. 41 (n. 44), 47, 173, publishing the text of Hamilton's letter to Secretary of State Conway, Naples, 6 August 1765. Espionage worked both ways, however. For an example of Neapolitan spying activities in the British royal dockyards during the delivery of a diplomatic gift to George III in the late 1780s, see *George III & Queen Charlotte*, no. 329.

40. The volumes are now in the Military Collection at Windsor (*George III & Queen Charlotte*, no. 211). The British Library has an identical set of the plans, though in a different and less luxurious binding (Add. MSS 15533–15534).

41. BL, 191.g.6 and Maps K. Top. 48. 23-1-1. For Clerk of Eldin, see most recently K. Sloan, *'A Noble Art': amateur artists and drawing masters c.1600–1800*, exh. cat., London, British Museum, 2000, pp. 107, 133–4.

42. Now BL, Maps Tab 8.c.8.

43. BL, Maps K. Top. 119.15.

44. See Brooke, p. 313, for the King's treatment of official correspondence.

45. These have now been separated from the report and inserted in their appropriate geographical places. See BL, Maps K. Top. 17.16-b (report); K. Top 17.16 (Sheerness); 16.56-b (Gravesend); 13.55 & 56 (Tilbury); 39.62 (Landguard).

46. Although of a type which is normally found in the King's Military Maps, this map is included in the King's Topographical Collection (BL, Maps K. Top. 122-6-2).

47. RCIN 710058a and b. I am grateful to Lieutenant-Commander Andrew David for his kindness in allowing me to read the manuscript of his unpublished article 'Further light on James Cook's survey of Newfoundland' which discusses these and other charts.

48. BL, Maps K. Top. 116.59, 60, 61, 62.

49. BL, Maps K. Top. 116. 64, 65.

50. BL, Maps K. Top. 124, Supp. 43, 44, 45. See also P. Barber, 'Malaspina and George III, Brambila and Watling: Three Dis-

covered Drawings of Sydney and Parramatta by Fernando Brambila', *Australian Journal of Art*, XI, 1993, pp. 31–56 and particularly pp. 33–6.

51. The room also appears in the frontispiece woodcut to *Bibliotheca Regiae Catalogus*.

52. BL, Maps K. Top. 41.16-k-2. For the context and a related plan still in the Royal Collection, see *George III & Queen Charlotte*, no. 119.

53. BL, Maps K. Top. 7.39-c.

54. BL, Maps K. Top. 41.16-r.

55. BL, Maps K. Top. 23.24-e.

56. BL, Maps K. Top. 101.22-d.

57. BL, Maps K. Top. 7.31-3, and see Roberts 1997, plate 285.

58. BL, Maps K. Top. 8.28-c, letter from John Stickney to William Vaughan, 15 May 1799; and see Roberts 1997, p. 143.

59. BL, Maps K. Top. 6.42-2.

60. BL, Maps K. Top. 26.5-r, t.

61. R.M. Clay, *Samuel Hieronymus Grimm of Burgdorf in Switzerland*, London, 1941, pp. 56–8.

62. BL, Maps K. Top. 23.36-g, and see Brooke, p. 343.

63. Brooke 1972, pp. 343–4.

64. BL 18.c.18 and Maps K. Top. 5.98-1.

65. BL, Maps K. Top. 12.12-h.

66. BL, Maps K. Top. 17.43.

67. BL, Maps K. Top. 85.65-2a. The first version, prepared for the first Viscount Palmerston during a Swiss tour in 1770, is now in the British Museum (1870-5-4-1218). See also A. Wilton, *William Pars' Journey through the Alps*, Bubendorf, 1979, particularly pp. 20, 22 and 65, n. 19, where the British Library example is dated to shortly after Pars's return from Switzerland, and exh. cat., *Switzerland 700*, London, British Library, 1991, pp. 54–5.

68. The drawings, with the golden British Museum stamp containing the GIII monogram denoting their origin, were transferred back to the Map Library from the British Museum's Department of Prints and Drawings in 2002 and incorporated into Maps K. Top. 124 (supp.). See also R. Fulford, *Royal Dukes*, 2nd edn, London, 1973, pp. 283–5.

69. For architectural plans drawn by George during his illness of 1788–9 see *George III & Queen Charlotte*, p. 129, referring to R. Fulke Greville's *Diaries*, ed. F. Bladon, London, 1930, pp. 119,

152. The sheets are to be found on guards in the third plan in 'Plans der königlichen Schlösser in und bey Hannover' (BL, Maps 7 Tab. 17 (Maps K. Top. 100.57-a)). I am grateful to the Hon. Lady Roberts for supporting my hunch that the plans were in the hand of George III and to Dr Eileen Scarff, the archivist at St George's Chapel, for identifying the date of the service.

70. Brooke, p. 314.
71. BL, Maps K. Top. 94.51-3.

97. Thomas Gainsborough, *John Montagu, 4th Earl of Sandwich, First Lord of the Admiralty*, 1783. National Maritime Museum, London

15

George III and the Royal Navy

CELINA FOX

George III's continuing interest in the practical application of mechanics, arising from his scientific education, is evident from his acquisition in the 1760s of sophisticated astronomical clocks which showed not only international time but also high and low water at seaports round the coasts of Britain and Western Europe (fig. 98).[1] But the King's mechanical bent extended beyond the clockwork toys displayed within the confines of his palaces, or even his Richmond observatory completed in 1769. He went out into the real world to the heart of the country's greatest operation in applied mechanics, the Royal Navy. I propose to demonstrate the extent and importance of this commitment by focusing on the visit the King made to Portsmouth from 22 to 26 June 1773.

Before describing the visit itself and the material evidence arising, I shall place the occasion in a national context and show it was not a gadfly amusement to divert and entertain a bored court. It had a more serious function: to provide support for the country's chief bulwark against foreign attack and thereby also to identify the Crown with the interests of the nation.

The Royal Navy had the advantage over its rivals in France and Spain in the consistency of state support it received, being financed through taxation and, at times of war, through government borrowing.[2] In return, the country expected it to maintain national security, wealth and strength. This was the root of its popularity, as manifest in such songs as 'Rule Britannia', first performed in 1740. The Navy, personified in

98. Christopher Pinchbeck, Sir William Chambers and others, *Astronomical clock*, 1768. Tortoiseshell, oak, gilt bronze, silver, brass, steel and enamel. RCIN 2821

its famous admirals and jack tars, enjoyed a privileged position among the symbols that represented this island race. People were fascinated not only by acts of heroism and sacrifice but also by prize money. Commerce, profit and plunder were inextricably mixed with imperial and maritime power. Given such a high popular profile, it was at least as much in the interest of the Hanoverian dynasty to identify itself with the Navy as it was for the Navy to be identified with its titular head.

It is not clear who first proposed the visit to Portsmouth, but it was probably John Montagu, 4th Earl of Sandwich (fig. 97), who was appointed First Lord of the Admiralty for the third time in 1771 and for whom the Navy was his first love and in many ways his life's work.[3] He resumed the practice of annual inspections of the six royal dockyards by the Admiralty Commissioners as a body; this had not taken place for twenty years, and no detail was too small to escape his attention. He pushed through intensive programmes of shipbuilding using seasoned timber, insisting it was properly stored in sheds, not left to rot in the open around the yards.

No sooner was Sandwich back in office than he arranged for the King to see the launch of the *Grafton* at Deptford. Under his guidance, George III developed an informed enthusiasm for his Fleet and conscientiously sought to learn as much as possible. The royal visit to Portsmouth marked the climax of this induction process, a *tour de force* of organisation and marketing which advertised to the world the King's interest in and support for the Royal Navy and by extension for Sandwich himself. Nothing like it had been devised for nearly a century.

Nevertheless, in 1773 neither the Crown nor the Navy was on top, buoyant form. The Crown was emerging from a prolonged period of assault by John Wilkes and his supporters while the Navy's claims on the country's tax revenues were somewhat battered. On 2 December 1772 Edmund Burke had launched a devastating attack in parliament on the Navy Estimates for 1773.[4] Given that the country had been at peace for the preceding two years, why, Burke enquired, did the ministers not revert to the old peacetime establishment? The Estimates (which stood at nearly £2 million, compared with less than £900,000 prior to the war) were passed, but Sandwich might well have calculated the time was ripe for some positive public relations.

News received on 28 May 1773 of an impending royal visit to Portsmouth provoked the Navy Board into frenzied activity, which underlines the novelty of the occasion. Colours in store were to be sent from all the yards to dress the ships. An entire new suit of silk colours at a cost of £211 10s 9d was ordered for the *Barfleur*, the 90-gun second rate ship on board which the King was to dine each day, and she was to be 'painted, trophied and freezed'. Mr Kuhf, cook and confectioner, was contracted to supply 31 covers a day on board; linen and plate were delivered from St James's Palace. The Commissioner's House was prepared for the King's residence; bedding and a bedstead were sent down from the Wardrobe. Stables were cleared for the Horse Guards, the mould loft and hemp house for the men. Spare beds in officers' houses were commandeered for the Commissioners as well as the 'noblemen and persons of distinction' attending upon His Majesty. The officers of the yard were ordered to prepare capital pieces of work in each branch of shipbuilding, the work to be in hand when the King viewed the yard, so that shipwrights, caulkers, ropemakers, sailmakers, smiths, boatbuilders and mastmakers were all seen to be busy.[5]

Meanwhile, Sandwich was no less assiduous in his briefing of the King though 'fearful of offending your Majesty by troubling you about trifles; but my desire [is] that everything . . . should give satisfaction when you honour us with your appearance.'[6] Both King and First Lord of the Admiralty were united in their desire to exclude the French Ambassador, the duc de Guisnes, from the yard. The King wished only a small suite to accompany him, the better to 'enable me so thoroughly to see things that I may form some idea of the wonderful mechanism that is concerned in forming the amazing machines that float on the sea.'[7] Sandwich hinted heavily as much to the Ambassador, reporting back: 'I am persuaded he thoroughly understood my meaning.'[8]

Sandwich assured the King that the Commissioner's House was 'extremely quiet, and though low and by no means spacious, is well aired and warm.' He also reported that a new red cloak had been made for the King ('cloaks being always used in boats belonging to men of war') and asked him to order a larger than normal Garter Star for the outside be sent down before his arrival.[9] Ever accommodating, the King was obliged for the scarlet cloak but added, 'if it is warm shall hope to be excused wearing it.' He further insisted on retaining the custom of sitting alone at the head of a long dinner table rather than at the more commodious horseshoe table Sandwich had proposed: 'You know very well I am not very rigid as to form but some cannot be broken through.'[10]

As the momentous occasion drew closer, Sandwich expressed his fears that one morning would not be sufficient time to see the dockyard.[11] The King agreed to stay another day so that he could see everything without confusion 'for I do not mean a visit of empty parade but to come back *au fait* of the mode of conducting so complicated an affair as the fitting out a ship.' He also found 'very agreeable' the proposed order of the visit, going round the dockyard first, 'as it will give me an insight before my arrival [at Spithead], and enable me the better to comprehend the many curious and entertaining objects I shall then view.'[12] The King's language combined a genuine desire for knowledge with an appreciation of polite forms of amusement.

Fashionable society flocked to Portsmouth. As early as 12 June, Edward Gibbon was predicting, all too accurately, 'The world is going down to Portsmouth, where they will enjoy the pleasure of smoke, noise, heat, bad lodgings and expensive reckonings.'[13] On 22 June the King set out from Kew at four o'clock in the morning and by eleven reached Portsmouth, where he was received by the Mayor and Corporation with a 21-gun salute.[14] He immediately held a levée at the

Governor's house, then travelled by barge past the coastal forts to dine on board the *Barfleur* at Spithead, accompanied by more 21-gun salutes. At six o'clock he descended once more into the barge to review the Fleet, each ship saluting as he passed. He then boarded the yacht *Augusta* and sailed back to Portsmouth harbour, arriving at a quarter to nine.

The King rose at the crack of dawn on succeeding days to inspect the dockyard: the ships lying in ordinary; the gun wharf, magazines, artillery and provisions; the victualling department; and the town's new works and fortifications. Sailings on the *Augusta* were followed by a great number of yachts and other vessels, 'many of them full of the nobility and gentry'. During the King's visit to the yard on 24 June, a group of 30 shipwrights 'who formed a society of vocal and instrumental church music' sang 'God save the King', 'which was a signal for all the other workmen to leave off and face about, which they did do accordingly, and stood with respectful silence with their adzes on their shoulders, and made a pretty appearance.' The King was much pleased and stayed to hear a second song with the refrain, 'Great George is King'.[15] On 26 June His Majesty returned to Kew 'in perfect health', having disbursed £2,120 in bounties to the workers in the yard and seamen and boys on the ships in ordinary (covering 2,355 men in total, including 849 shipwrights).

The King's enthusiastic reception was not confined to naval personnel. Patriotic feeling was skilfully orchestrated among the people at large. Throughout the visit the houses in Portsmouth and Gosport were illuminated every evening. When the King was rowed into Portsmouth harbour from a becalmed *Augusta* on 23 June, he was greeted by 'the acclamations of multitudes, the firing of cannon, the ringing of the bells, and all the tokens of joy which could be shewn.' At the civic reception held on 24 June, the Mayor and Corporation delivered a gratifyingly fulsome address. When the King left Portsmouth bright and early on 26 June, 'Many thousands of people attended the chaise' and all the way back to Kew, 'there were numerous assemblies of people ... expressing, in the warmest manner, their duty and affection, and their joy at seeing their Sovereign amongst them.' According to the correspondent from the *Gentleman's Magazine*, 'Thus ended the Royal visit to Portsmouth; a measure that has endeared the King to his faithful subjects more than I can possibly express, and does honour to those who presided over the different departments.'

Horace Walpole's reaction to these 'games on the oceans' or 'Georgics at Portsmouth', struck a sourer note:

> The mob were unbounded in those exultations which the first sight of a king always excites in a distant province. Mistaking giddy joy for affection, he [the King] said: "I do not mind abuse, I am grown accustomed to it; but I own these sentiments of applause touch me". It was a pity he did not reflect that the silent suffrages of approbation founded on merit were the only testimonies of affection that are lasting and worth coveting.[16]

Certainly, buried in the Navy Board's accounts for the visit, (including the cook's bill of £2,994 3s and £1,293 8s 6d for wine), in a total cost of £7,103 19s, is the sum of £250 for the poor of Portsmouth, Portsea and Gosport who doubtless contributed to the throng.[17] But the King's pleasure in being identified with his Fleet, and no doubt his relief at not having to endure more booing and cries of 'No Lord Mayor! No King!' from Wilkite mobs, was to take a more permanent form.

Dominic Serres (1722–93), Marine Painter to the King, executed four paintings of the visit.[18] The first, depicting His Majesty saluted by the Fleet at his arrival on board the *Barfleur*, was exhibited at the Royal Academy the following year (plate XXI). When the Academicians held their annual dinner at Somerset House on 4 June that year, to mark the King's birthday, Serres himself commanded a 21-gun salute from a yacht moored in the Thames alongside, to coincide with Reynolds's proposal of the toast to the King's health.[19] In 1775 two more paintings of the occasion were shown,

99. Dominic Serres, *The Royal visit to the Fleet, 22 June 1773*, 1775. Watercolour. RL 27980

depicting the King on board the *Augusta*, sailing from Spithead towards St Helens on 25 June with the Plymouth Squadron, and then back to Spithead. In one of the associated watercolours in the Royal Collection (fig. 99) you can clearly make out the King in the stern of the *Augusta*, with the nobility and gentry packed into other yachts all around.

The occasion also provoked more mechanical forms of record. On 5 July 1773 Sandwich wrote to the King to thank him for the loan of 'a very curious and valuable work' which would 'be particularly useful in pointing out the original design of the several structures in the different yards; and give us better grounds for ascertaining the utility of the improvements that have been made from time to time since the Revolution.'[20] The King's response makes it clear that the book in question was a grand Survey of the Royal Dockyards made in 1698 by the then Surveyor of the Navy, Edmund Dummer, and deposited in the King's Library: 'I am glad the description of the yards in 1698 has proved some amusement, and it may have given birth to some new ideas from seeing the improvements that have been made, and suggesting what further may be done.'[21] In August the King intimated he would be 'much pleased at having added to it the subsequent improvements that have been made.'[22] By the following March a sample account and drafts relating to Sheerness had been prepared for comment.[23]

Thus Dummer's Survey of 1698 inspired the production of a Supplement of 1774 and they are now shelved next to each other in the King's Library, as King's MS 43 and 44 at the British Library. This is not the place to go into the lengthy and fascinating history of Edmund Dummer; suffice it to say that he was one of the first to try to introduce an element of rationality to the royal dockyards. His greatest claim to fame lies in his design and construction of a new model dockyard at Plymouth, and his introduction of the first stepped stone dry docks at both Portsmouth and Plymouth. Although his abilities as a shipbuilder and project manager were criticised, nobody could fault his outstanding skills as a draughtsman. The 1698 Survey of the Royal Dockyards represents his visual apologia. It combined allegory in the frontispiece with prospects of the ports and surrounding countryside in the manner of Hollar, plans showing changes to the dockyard which had taken place between the Glorious Revolution and 1698, engineering drawings showing his construction of the dry docks in Portsmouth and Plymouth, and meticulously detailed elevations and plans of every single aspect of every single one of the buildings that were jumbled into the royal dockyards, some in wood dating back to Tudor times, the more substantial and more recent in brick and stone.

Superficially the 1774 Survey was a continuation of its predecessor, although the frontispiece was more overtly patriotic, with Neptune bowing to the royal standard of Great Britain (fig. 100). The explanation on the facing page is placed in a cartouche replete with patriotic motifs, signed by Thomas Mitchell (1735–90), whose career as both shipwright and artist suggests he might have been responsible for much of the succeeding matter.[24]

However, the 1774 Supplement differs in a number of respects from its predecessor. Rather than detailing every new

100. Thomas Mitchell, *Frontispiece of the Supplement to a Survey . . .*, 1774.
British Library, London

building constructed in the intervening decades, it concentrated more on an overview of the advantages and disadvantages of each dockyard and port from the sailing navy's

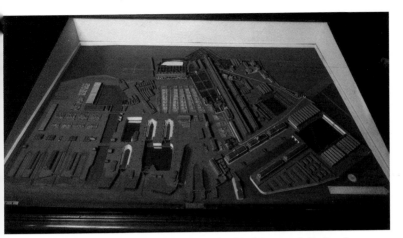

101. Nicholas Vass Jr and John Doughty, *Model of Portsmouth Dockyard*, c.1774. National Maritime Museum, London

viewpoint. This was because the dockyards' expansion was being recorded in other ways.

On his visit to Plymouth in June 1771, Sandwich had checked progress on the ground against the great plan of improvement commissioned in 1761 and 'by a very ingenious model of the whole carved in wood by the foreman of the yard.' Notes in the margin of his report indicate that, as a result, models of the same type were ordered for the Admiralty from the other royal dockyards, which are now in the collection of the National Maritime Museum (fig. 101).[25] They may be seen as the naval equivalent of the great relief maps of military fortifications commissioned from 1668 onwards by Louvois, Louis XIV's Minister of War, and used to plan changes and simulate sieges.[26] By the time the models were complete, in 1774, so was the Supplement.[27] In fact, the Supplement states that its plans of 1774 (on a 1 inch to 220 foot scale) 'agree with the models of the yards prepared and herewith sent for His Majesty's use showing all the buildings, docks, slips &c in their due proportions and each distinguished whether of brick, stone or timber.' In

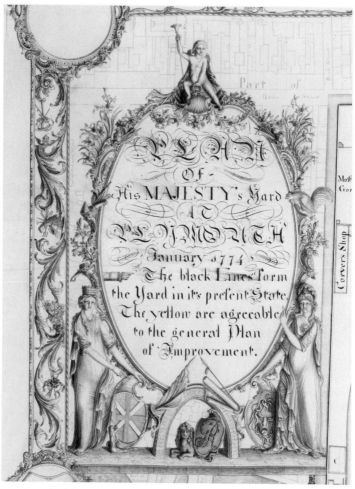

PLAN
OF
His MAJESTY's Yard
AT
PLIMOUTH
January 1774
The black Lines form
the Yard in it's present State.
The yellow are agreeable
to the general Plan
of Improvement.

102. Detail of the large-scale plan of Plymouth, from the 1774 survey. British Library, London

other words, the models were intended to serve as a substitute for the plans and elevations of all the buildings detailing the materials included in the 1698 Survey. Furthermore, the King's Topographical Collection, now in the British Library, contains large-scale plans drawn to the same

1 inch to 40 foot scale as the models themselves, and also dated 1774 (fig. 102).

Somewhere between 1771 and 1774 the decision was made not to keep the models and plans in the Admiralty but to present them, along with the Supplement, to the King to form part of what he would describe as his 'Naval Collection'. Sandwich had commanded their manufacture on the grounds that it was 'proper' to have them made, which scarcely suggests a driving practical purpose. Their value to the Navy must have been less, he calculated, than as objects of prestige for the King, works of art which demonstrated the country's naval power to foreign visitors. He had agreed to have the Supplement to Dummer's Survey made to show subsequent alterations and additions, a process achieved to a larger scale and in greater detail through the models and plans. It therefore made sense for them all to be kept together. Perhaps Sandwich realised the impracticality of housing six huge horizontal relief plans – three of which were over two metres in length – within the confines of the Admiralty or the Navy Office. Presumably he saw these products more as a means of maintaining royal support for his proposals and their financial implications than as useful management tools. We can consider them together, as they are so closely related, informed by the accounts made of Sandwich's annual visitations between 1771 and 1774.[28]

Significantly, instead of starting with the Thames and Medway yards, the Supplement commenced with Portsmouth followed by Plymouth, where the greatest rebuilding programmes had been initiated in the 1760s. The sums involved were colossal: the original 1764 estimate for Portsmouth was £352,240 4s 3d, of which £299,917 had been spent by the end of 1773.[29] The Portsmouth model was made by two house carpenters in the yard, and precisely accorded with the large-scale plan of the yard in the King's Topographical Collection.[30] It was the last to be completed, although a version (unfinished?) was on display in the Commissioner's House during the 1773 visitation. Perhaps because it was also the biggest, it is the most schematic, detailing construction works that had yet to be undertaken.

Plymouth followed in the Supplement, its advantages being attributed to the more modern style of buildings and the more efficient layout of works, a belated tribute to Dummer's planning. But by 1761 there were proposals to sweep away virtually all trace of his dockyard, at an estimated cost of £379,170 1s 2d, of which £153,585 had been spent by the end of 1773. The Supplement frankly stated Plymouth had serious disadvantages – the crooked, narrow and dangerous passage into the harbour and lack of a spacious, safe roadstead – which meant it could never be the principal rendezvous for great fleets at times of war.[31] Perhaps it was because of these handicaps that the yard had sought to promote its chances of government investment through the production of the first wooden model.[32] This was certainly very detailed, with named model ships in the docks and slips, and two removable sections which could be lifted out with brass handles and substituted for projected developments: one of a new dry dock and the other of new warehouses. The 1:40 scale plan was the most elaborate of all the dockyard plans, with a cartouche depicting Britannia triumphant (fig. 102) and, of course, proposals for growth indicated in yellow – further propaganda for the dockyard's redevelopment.[33] But Sandwich's visit to Plymouth in 1774 indicated that he was not entirely won over by the extent of the proposals, querying whether the sums allowed would not be better spent at Chatham than employed in 'useless magnificence' and needless demolition of strong stone buildings.[34]

The model of Chatham was made by a Sheerness shipwright and joiner, and the dockyard Commissioner was so pleased with it that, according to a contemporary report in the *Kentish Gazette*, it was placed on display before being sent to the Admiralty.[35] It showed the Commissioner's House and officers' houses with their gardens, several ships under construction or repair, and a first rate ready to launch, as well as the timber rope sheds and storehouses that were in need of replacement, as Sandwich constantly stressed on his visits.[36]

The Sheerness model was the first to be finished, in March 1774, and is arguably the best, made by a professional ship model maker, with a wealth of detail including piles of rope and shot and two teams of bullock, and even tiny men wearing cocked hats.[37] Here the ships in slip and dry dock and even the ancient hulks serving as breakwaters were named on the large-scale plan.[38] Sir Thomas Slade, late Surveyor of the Navy, had produced a scheme (unexecuted) to enlarge the yard, which was included in the 1774 Supplement. Deptford was the largest naval victualling store, and the great storehouse is the most prominent element in the beautiful model built by a yard shipwright and joiner.[39] The model of Woolwich – called the 'Mother Dock' as the first royal dockyard – was signed on the underside by its makers; but as at Deptford, there were no proposals for new works indicated either on it or on its large-scale plan.[40]

On 19 August 1773 the King wrote to Sandwich requesting him to direct the Surveyor of the Navy 'to have a Book containing the plans of the most capital Ship of each Rate to be made. This I think would thoroughly compleat the Naval Collection.'[41] In his response Sandwich intimated that he and the Surveyor were not sure what the King had in mind: standard ship's profiles and plans or painted perspectives of models of the ships along the lines of examples submitted.[42] The King replied he would like both: 'I give you infinite trouble but it is from a desire of being a little *au fait* of ship building.'[43]

Thus encouraged, Sandwich bombarded the King with ship models and plans. In September he received a model of a third rate: 'the timbers are all marked with their proper appellations, and Lord Sandwich flatters himself that nothing can be more likely to give your Majesty a thorough idea of a ship's construction than this model.' It was delivered by its maker, Joseph Williams, a Navy Board draughtsman on the books at Deptford, who explained it thoroughly to the King. 'The

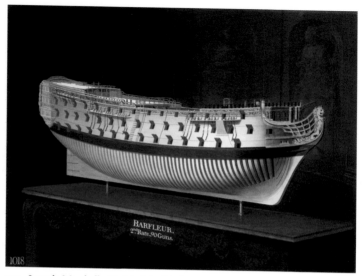

103. Joseph Marshall, *Model of the* Barfleur, 1773–5. Oil on panel. The Science Museum, London

more I reflect on,' wrote the King, 'the more it shews the perfection to which mechanicks has arrived.'[44] The framed model Williams made is possibly that of the *Intrepid*, now in the National Maritime Museum.[45]

At the same time Sandwich sent a model of ships' masts (including the mainmast which could be taken to pieces), made by the Master Mastbuilder in consequence of orders given to him on the King's visit to Portsmouth.[46] In January 1774 the King received the 'geometrical draughts' of the ships with an account of the number of guns and weight of metal on each deck, as well as an account of their recent alterations and improvements, prepared by the Surveyor of the Navy, Sir John Williams.[47] In July another Williams model arrived with its maker, this time of the frigate *Winchelsea*, as a present for the Prince of Wales.[48] By August 1775 the painted panel perspectives of twelve different ship models were complete.[49] Executed by Joseph Marshall with the assistance of Joseph Williams and John Binmer, they ranged from the 100-gun first rate

Royal George and second rate *Barfleur* (fig. 103) down through the rates to a bomb vessel and fire ship. The ships selected had nearly all been launched in the late 1760s or 1770s to the design of Sir John Williams. All were depicted in two views, taken from the stern and the prow, as unrigged models, sitting mounted on tables in room settings, some elegantly appointed.

The King's interest in his dockyards was capitalised upon in February 1775, when the marine painter Richard Paton waited on him with some pictures including two – views of Deptford and Chatham – which were finely engraved by Woollett and Canot. 'His Majesty was pleased to honour the artist with his approbation, and to express satisfaction in his performances', even to the point of purchasing the works and three others, representing Portsmouth, Woolwich and Sheerness.[50] The figures were painted by John Hamilton Mortimer. Thomas Jones reported Paton and Mortimer going off to Portsmouth in July 1770. So the series was probably inspired by the magnificent paintings of the Ports of France executed by Joseph Vernet between 1753 and 1765, more widely known through the engravings by Cochin and Le Bas published between 1760 and 1778.

George III's models of the royal dockyards, ships and fortifications were displayed at Buckingham House, where Sophie von la Roche saw them in 1786, in a Marine Gallery specially built above the East Library in 1774. 'The great care bestowed on the preservation of these works', she observed, 'proves that the owners can appreciate art.'[51] Sadly it was not recorded in a view, but the wind-dial over the mantelpiece is visible in James Stephanoff's depiction of the East Library in 1817 (plate XXIV).[52] Its workings were described to Sophie by François-Justin Vulliamy, father of the maker, Benjamin Vulliamy: 'a large semi-sphere set in the wall [on which] he can follow which parts of the world are affected if a heavy gale is sweeping England; while the weather-vane on the house, with its eminent situation, calculates and records so accurately on this sphere that the King can conjecture how his fleet is faring.'[53]

104. Francesco Bartolozzi and Paul Sandby, after Benjamin West, *Prince William as a midshipman on board* HMS Prince George, 1782. Stipple engraving. RCIN 605494

If Sandwich's assiduous sourcing of the Naval Collection was intended to retain the King's interest in his Navy, it certainly worked. He continued to visit the royal dockyards and review the Fleet until at least 1797. These visits further demonstrated that, in the King's words, no one was 'more hearty in the cause' than himself.[54] It was an enthusiasm he failed to pass on to his eldest son, as was demonstrated all too conspicuously in 1781 during a review of the Fleet at the Nore, off Sheerness, when the Prince of Wales and his chums behaved appallingly.[55] Fortunately for royal honour, sailing with the Fleet was the King's third son William (fig. 104), who saw active service for the first time in 1779, shortly before his fourteenth birthday.[56] William was with Rodney's fleet in January 1780 when it captured a Spanish flagship, immediately renamed the *Prince William* in his honour; a full-scale battle followed and William, who behaved courageously throughout, became a national hero.[57]

Nevertheless, while the King entrusted his son to the seamanship of the British Navy, he was less impressed by its scientific training.[58] By 1783 William had been long enough at sea to pick up some bad habits and the King determined that as soon as he returned he would be sent to the Continent 'that your manners and behaviour be formed fit for shore, and that you may be in time an officer. Lord Howe who certainly is a scientific officer assures me that he thinks in our service the attention is carried so long alone to seamanship that few officers are formed, and that a knowledge of the military is necessary to open the ideas to the directing large fleets.'[59] Consequently, William was packed off to Hanover to learn the German language as well as 'the law of nations, the grounds of civil law, engineering, artillery and military tactics, which last three branches will open his ideas and enable him to pursue his profession as an officer, not a mere sailor.'[60] As I hope I have demonstrated, George III accomplished a successful transit in the opposite direction, from scientific theory to maritime practice, thereby identifying the Crown with the Royal Navy for the benefit of the Nation at large.

NOTES

1. For the clocks by Norton and Pinchbeck, see *George III & Queen Charlotte*, nos. 300 and 302.

2. D.A. Baugh, 'The Eighteenth Century Navy as a National Institution 1690–1815', in *The Oxford Illustrated History of the Royal Navy*, ed. J.R. Hill, Oxford, 1995, pp. 120–60.

3. N.A.M. Rodger, *The Insatiable Earl: A Life of John Montagu, Fourth Earl of Sandwich, 1718–1792*, London, 1993.

4. P. Langford *et al.*, eds., *The Writings and Speeches of Edmund Burke*, Oxford, 1981–91, vol. I, pp. 374–7.

5. The best account of the visit from the viewpoint of the Navy Board is given in '"An Account of the Preparation made for and the Entertainment of the King at Portsmouth in June 1773 . . . minuted and collected by George Marsh, one of his Majesty's principal Officers and Commissioners of the Navy", communicated by one of his Descendants [Commander Duke Crofton]', *Colburn's United Service Magazine*, 1887, part 1, pp. 433–49, 517–30 (hereafter Marsh).

6. Both sides of the correspondence survive: Sandwich's letters in the Royal Archives, published in *The Correspondence of King George III*, ed. J. Fortescue, London, 1927–8 (hereafter Fortescue), and the King's responses in the Sandwich Papers deposited at the National Maritime Museum (hereafter NMM). Fortescue, vol. 2, pp. 501–3, letter 1272, 12 June 1773.

7. NMM, San 45/c/5–6, 6 June 1773.

8. Fortescue, vol. 2, pp. 494–5, letter 1263, 7 June 1773.

9. *ibid.*, pp. 501–3, letter 1272, 12 June 1773.

10. NMM, San 45/c/7, 13 June 1773.

11. Fortescue, vol. 2, pp. 506–7, letter 1279, 14 June 1773.

12. NMM, San 45/c/13, 19 June 1773.

13. J. E. Norton, ed., *The Letters of Edward Gibbon*, London, 1956, vol. 1 (1750–73), p. 367.

14. The fullest account of the proceedings, besides that of Marsh, is given in an appendix to the *Annual Register* for 1773, pp. 202–7.

15. A broadside with the words of 'Two Loyal Songs proposed to be sung before His Majesty, on his Arrival at Portsmouth Dock; By the Workmen of that Yard', printed by R. Lee, Tea-Kettle Alley, Portsmouth Common, marked in manuscript 'was sung', is in the Royal Archives, GEO/1594.

16. A.F. Steuart, ed., *The Last Journals of Horace Walpole during the Reign of George III from 1771 to 1783*, London, 1910, vol. 1, p. 238; *Walpole Correspondence*, XXXII, pp. 129, 132.

17. Marsh, p. 523.

18. Millar 1969, nos. 1072–5.
19. Royal Academy Archives, Critiques, vol. 1, 1774.
20. Fortescue, vol. 3, pp. 1–2, letter 1290.
21. NMM, San 45 c/13.
22. NMM, San 45 c/18, 14 August 1773.
23. Fortescue, vol. 3, p. 82, letter 1420.
24. K. Sloan, 'A Noble Art': Amateur Artists and Drawing Masters c.1600–1800, London, 2000, pp. 118–19, no. 78. The drawing by Mitchell, catalogued as Deptford, is of Chatham.
25. NMM, San V/5, 5 June 1771. B. Lavery and S. Simon, Ship Models: Their Purpose and Development from 1650 to the Present, London, 1995, pp. 36–7.
26. I. Warmoes, Musée des Plans-Relief, Paris, 1999.
27. Fortescue, vol. 3, p. 81–2, nos. 1418, 1420.
28. NMM, San V/5–11.
29. J.G. Coad, The Royal Dockyards 1690–1850: Architecture and Engineering Works of the Sailing Navy, Aldershot, 1989, pp. 132–6, quoting TNA, PRO, ADM/B/183, 21 May 1770. NMM, San V/6, 12–21 June 1773.
30. NMM, SLR 2156. BL, K. Top. XIV: 45–2.
31. NMM, San V/5, 5 June 1771.
32. NMM, SLR 2149. It is thought to be a copy of the 1771 original which was perhaps retained by the yard.
33. BL, K. Top. XI: 88.
34. NMM, San V/8, 25 June 1774.
35. NMM, SLR 2151; Lavery and Simons, pp. 155–8.
36. NMM, San V/5, 13 May 1771.
37. NMM, SLR 2148.
38. BL, K. Top. XVII: 15–2.
39. NMM, SLR 2906.
40. NMM, SLR 2905; BL, K. Top. XVII: 24–1 (Woolwich) and XVIII: 17–10 (Deptford).
41. NMM, San c/19.
42. Fortescue, vol. 3, pp. 8–9, letter 1303.
43. NMM, San c/20.
44. Fortescue, vol. 3, p. 10, letter 1305. NMM, San c/21.
45. NMM, SLR 0525; Lavery and Stephens, pp. 119–20.
46. Fortescue, vol. 3, p. 10, letter 1305.
47. ibid., pp. 55–9, letter 1378. Unfortunately I have not been able to trace them: they do not appear to be in the National Maritime

Museum, Science Museum, British Library, Admiralty Library or the Royal Collection.

48. *ibid.*, p. 118, letter 1490.
49. *ibid.*, p. 250, letter 1700. In 1864 they were presented by Queen Victoria to the South Kensington Museum and are now in the Science Museum.
50. Millar 1969, p. 90, nos. 980–84.
51. *Sophie in London*, pp. 145–6.
52. *George III & Queen Charlotte*, nos. 118 and 307.
53. *Sophie in London*, p. 146.
54. Fortescue, vol. 4, p. 130, no. 2325, on the occasion of the controversial royal visit to Portsmouth in May 1778, when the French fleet had left for America and the British fleet was about to leave in hot pursuit.
55. F. McKno Bladon, ed., *The Diaries of Colonel The Hon. Robert Fulke Greville*, London, 1930, pp. 32–47. The Prince's lack of enthusiasm for the Navy may help to explain the transfer in 1822 of his father's model collection – including the ship and dockyard models – to the Museum of Artillery at Woolwich.
56. For the King's instructions to Rear-Admiral Sir Robert Digby regarding the naval education of his son see A. Aspinall, ed., *The Later Correspondence of George III*, Cambridge, 1962–70, V, pp. 654–5, no. 4265.
57. P. Ziegler, *King William IV*, London, 1971, p. 34.
58. Before he left Portsmouth in 1773 the King declared his intention of establishing addition scholarships at the Royal Naval Academy for the sons of naval officers, but in 1778 he noted there were only 14 scholars attending (Fortescue, vol. 4, p. 129).
59. Aspinall, V, pp. 697–8, no. 4296.
60. *ibid.*, pp. 699–700, no. 4298.

16

George III, scientific societies, and the changing nature of scientific collecting

JANE WESS

On display at the Science Museum, London, is a considerable part of the King George III Collection of Scientific Instruments (fig. 105). A number of items also feature in the Enlightenment gallery in the British Museum. Within this collection of collections are two very important sets of eighteenth-century apparatus: that made for George III when he came to the throne, and that formerly belonging to an itinerant lecturer, Stephen Demainbray (1710–82), who taught the Prince of Wales before he became king.[1]

This paper looks at the type of collecting exemplified by George III's scientific instruments, which was relatively new when he came to the throne in 1760.[2] The word 'relatively' denotes a comparison with the longer established natural-historical or antiquarian form of collecting exemplified by collections of natural specimens, pieces of antiquity, anthropological material and curiosities. The paper will also explore the position of two 'scientific' societies – the Royal Society and the Society for the Encouragement of Arts, Manufacture and Commerce – with respect to this new form of collecting and the experimental attitude towards nature that it entailed. It will look at the place of the royal collection of scientific instruments and the royal family in this context.

As James McClellan has explained, the eighteenth-century scientific societies were straddling two revolutions[3]: the 'scientific' revolution of the seventeenth which broke from

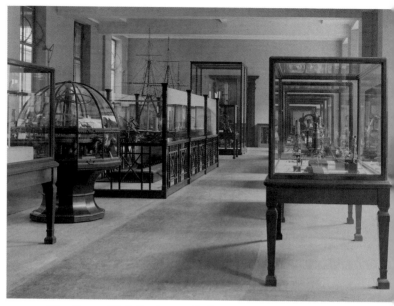

105. The George III Collection on display at the Science Museum, soon after its arrival in 1927

the earlier scholastic learning, and the nineteenth-century revolution in organised science which saw the modern discipline-based professional activity centring around the universities or research laboratories. In breaking from the older tradition, the new emphasis on experiment was progressive and productive. However, the type of collecting exemplified by George III's collection of scientific instruments had a finite role in society, mirrored to an extent by the general scientific institutions, such as the Royal Society, which dominated the organisation of science during this period.

I will argue that the two attitudes towards scientific collecting present at the time – the antiquarian and the experimental – co-existed both at the Royal Society and within the Royal Collection. This was more problematic at the Royal Society than at court, and eventually gave rise to the formation of the Society for the Encouragement of Arts,

Manufacture and Commerce, which took over part of the Royal Society's underlying remit.[4] George III, meanwhile, took an active part in experimental collecting, and was able to influence the new science of his day, but by the 1780s his collection of scientific instruments had become an example of antiquarian collecting under the care of a curator rather than a practising 'scientist'.[5]

I will start where Marie Boas Hall does, with the statutes of the Royal Society from 1663.[6] According to these:

> The business of the Society in their Ordinary Meetings shall be to order, take account, consider and discourse of philosophical experiments and observations ... and also to view, and discourse upon, rarities of nature and art; and thereupon to consider, what may be deduced from them, or any of them, and how far they, or any of them, may be improved for use or discovery.

This statement embodies the dichotomy between the active experimentation and the passive viewing of objets d'art, both sitting together in one overarching aim of the sole society devoted to 'scientific' learning that existed in this country at the time.

The balance of this rather uncomfortable dualism was difficult to maintain. Even under Sir Isaac Newton's presidency in the early years of the century, when experiments were encouraged at the meetings,[7] there was scope for satire from those impatient with antiquarianism. Joseph Addison in 1711 wrote, 'I would certainly not have a scholar unacquainted with these secrets and curiosities of nature (as the generation of a mite), but certainly the mind of man, that is capable of so much higher contemplations, should not be altogether fixed on such mean and disproportionate objects.'[8] Perhaps the most explicit statement of the tension from within the society comes from James Jurin who, in the power struggle following Newton's death in 1727, wrote in the *Philosophical Transactions*: 'the Great Man was sensible, that something more than knowing the Names, the Shape and obvious Qualities of an Insect, a Plant, or a Shell, was requisite to form a Philosopher . . . Natural History was not Natural Philosophy.'[9] John Hill in similar vein in 1751 poured scorn on the increasingly antiquarian *Philosophical Transactions* under Martin Folkes's direction. He asked why the *Transactions* contained articles such as 'The Incontestible Proof of a Strange and Suprising Fact, namely that Fish will Live in Water'.[10]

Very little has been written on the Royal Society in the eighteenth century, compared with the attention that its early years, and more recently its nineteenth-century history, have received.[11] By the mid-eighteenth century the energy and experimentation of the Royal Society's beginnings appeared to have been lost,[12] even though it continued to play an important role as a state service, providing a technical base of expertise to help solve problems that were related to the longer-term historical interests of the nation.[13] It had a role too in legitimising and communicating science, but the momentum of progressing knowledge, especially experimental knowledge, was faltering.[14]

Fortunately the future King was influenced both by his father, Frederick, Prince of Wales, and by the Earl of Bute, and as a result received a good grounding in experimental philosophy. Frederick's influence in scientific matters was largely exercised through his patronage of John Theophilus Desaguliers (1683–1744; fig. 106), who had a room on the top floor of the Prince's house at Kew. It was here that he kept some of his apparatus and performed demonstrations for the royal family.[15] He was a prolific experimenter and lecturer, and the last effective curator of experiments at the Royal Society, ceasing in 1743, only shortly before his death.[16] Desaguliers had met Willem Jacob Van 'sGravesande in 1716,[17] while 'sGravesande was taking part in a celebratory visit which began in 1715, arranged to celebrate George I's accession to the throne.[18] He is reported to have been much influenced by Desaguliers, but the reverse was also true.

With Newton's backing, 'sGravesande became professor of mathematics and astronomy at Leiden in 1717, and in 1724

I. T. Desaguliers Legum Doctor, Regiæ Societatis Londinensis
Socius, Honoratissimo Duci de Chandos à Sacris, Philosophiæ Naturalæ
Experimentorum ope Illustrator.

106. P. Pelham after H. Hysing, *John Theophilus Desaguliers*, 1725.
Engraving. The Science Museum, London

professor of physics.[19] He promoted the use of experiment in
teaching, and was an ardent supporter of the Newtonian
philosophy.[20] He had a substantial private collection of

scientific instruments,[21] and his published course of 1720 became the blueprint for this particular body of knowledge, digesting Boyle and Newton for a wider audience.[22] Desaguliers took aspects of 'sGravesande's work further, particularly adapting it to the English situation; for example there was less emphasis on barges and canals and more on raising water and on wheeled transport.[23] A number of the items in the George III Collection appear to have come directly from Desaguliers and feature in his magnum opus, *A Course of Experimental Philosophy* (1744–5),[24] for example a model Newcomen engine and a machine for finding the maximum of a man's power.[25]

The other strong influence was of course John, 3rd Earl of Bute, who had wide-ranging interests, among them scientific instruments. The catalogue of his collection, unfortunately dispersed at his death in 1793, revealed a grand orrery, air pumps, electrical machines, the latest barometers and thermometers, sets of artificial magnets, a new equatorial telescope by Ramsden and a lucernal microscope by Adams.[26] Bute appears to have maintained his active interest throughout his life. In 1755 he arranged a course of experimental philosophy for the two elder Princes, George and Edward, from an itinerant lecturer, Stephen Demainbray.[27] This commission was to change Demainbray's fortunes in both the short and long term.

When George III came to the throne in 1760 he appointed his instrument maker, George Adams (plate XXV), to construct a collection based on Bute's.[28] It is known from a dated sketch of the philosophical table in the accompanying manuscript that Adams was actively employed designing the instruments in January 1761.[29] The pneumatics instruments (fig. 107), and the complementary set of mechanics instruments, form the core set of apparatus that has come into the extant collection directly from George III. The growing number of instruments was remarked upon by Demainbray, who wrote to Bute suggesting that he should act as 'Keeper of the same', but was unsuccessful on this occasion.[30]

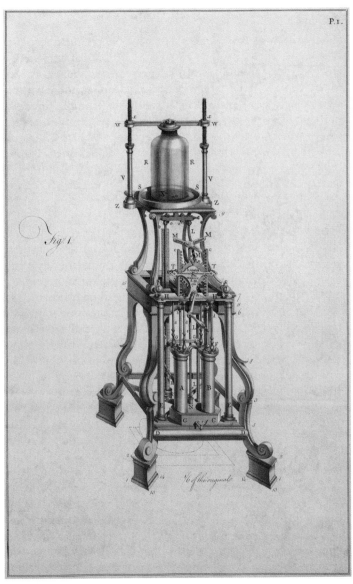

107. George Adams, *Sketch of an air pump*, c.1761. The Science Museum, London

George III and Queen Charlotte were not the first members of the royal family to take an interest in the fledgling science. In the George III Collection there is a pocket dial with a William and Mary monogram, the magnificent grand orrery which was enlarged by George II, and an armillary sphere made for Frederick, Prince of Wales.[31] We also appear to have the theodolite which was used by the Duke of Cumberland in his survey of the Highlands in 1747.[32] However, it was not until George III's reign that a royal collection of scientific instruments became a major acquisition project.

The King George III Collection of Scientific Instruments embodies not just a change in scale, but a change in approach which departs from the earlier natural-historical attitude towards objects of interest in a number of ways. While philosophical instruments were still considered objets d'art, they had an additional role. These newly designed artefacts did not in themselves represent knowledge, but were used as active tools, even apparatus, to tease out the underlying principles of nature. The natural world was interrogated through a series of experiments, not simply reflected by passive specimens.[33] A knowledge of these underlying principles could then be used to explain a whole range of other phenomena and be applied in a whole range of applications. The Enlightenment confidence in man's ability to control and order nature was inherent in these experiments, as was the desire to provide useful knowledge for the benefit of mankind.

Adams prepared two courses to accompany the instruments. They were copied out by George III's Writing Master, a Mr Champion,[34] and drew heavily on the works of the 1740s and 1750s: in particular those of 'sGravesande, Desaguliers and the French experimental philosopher, Abbé Nollet.[35] The subject matter of the first is pneumatics, which includes hydrostatics and some chemical experiments. The second covers mechanics, which also includes the attraction of bodies, so including magnetism and capillarity. It appears that a third course on electrostatics was planned but not completed, although an elegant cylinder electrical machine was constructed.[36] The royal collection addresses debates of the time less frequently than does the collection contributed by Demainbray, but items such as the model hay cart (fig. 108), with its interchangeable wheels and cobbled roadway, and the model Archimedean screw (fig. 109), do relate to contemporary issues.[37]

The pneumatics experiments centred around the magnificent double-barrelled air pump, which could evacuate or condense.[38] All the standard experiments of the day were incorporated: the bell *in vacuo*, the Magdeburg hemispheres, the crushing of glass phials, and also some more adventurous ones: the mixing of chemicals to produce cold effervescences, measured *in vacuo* with thermometers also made by Adams, and the comparison of airs.[39] It is not clear whether animals were used; although animal experiments are described in the course. The mechanical alternative, bladders, were also included and have survived.

The mechanics course centred around the Philosophical table, to which could be attached the collision apparatus, the isochronous pendulum, and the straight pendulum. Other pieces of apparatus and instruments were placed on the table for demonstration: for example the path of projectile apparatus, the central forces machine or the tidal motion machine. The framework of the course followed 'sGravesande's *Mathematical Elements of Natural Philosophy*, translated by Desaguliers and published in 1747.[40]

Anecdotal evidence of George III using his instruments supports a view that he was interested for over ten years. In 1761 he awarded James Ferguson, a lecturer specialising in astronomy, a pension of £50 a year. Ferguson relates that he had never even applied for it.[41] In 1762 the King was apparently 'extremely busy in a course of experimental philosophy, but not under the direction of any real philosopher.'[42] The following year the French astronomer Jerome Lalande, who was on a visit to England, reported that the

108. George Adams, *Model of a hay-cart*, 1762. The Science Museum, London

King had asked for Lalande's large air pump to be demonstrated to his guests.[43] On another occasion Adam's assistant, John Miller, is reported to have shown the King the experiment where a guinea and a feather are dropped simultaneously in a near-vacuum.[44] In 1765 there were still new additions being made to the collection, such as a magnetic toy which aligns itself to show 1 7 6 5, presumably the date.[45] The King's continued interest in scientific pursuits is shown by his decision to build the Royal Observatory at Richmond (plate XXII) in order to view the transit of Venus in 1769, a considerable outlay. Demainbray was installed there as its superintendent, a post which supported him in his declining years and which he held until his death in 1782.[46]

There is less evidence for Queen Charlotte's involvement in experimental philosophy, but that does not necessarily indicate less interest. Gibbes Rigaud asserts that 'Queen

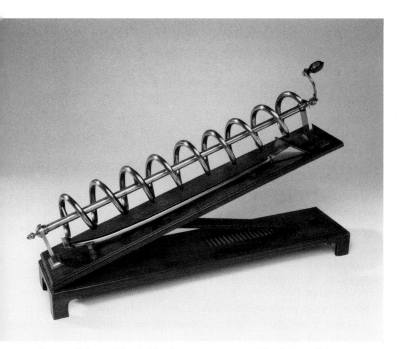

109. George Adams, *The Archimedean screw*, 1761–2. The Science Museum, London

Charlotte, after her marriage with the King, also became [Demainbray's] pupil and listened to his lectures in philosophy, and to her he gave his manuscripts, which were afterwards sold with her Library.'[47] In an undated manuscript known as the Queen's Catalogue, it is stated that the Queen deposited 'apparatus and philosophical instruments' in the royal observatory.[48] Here are listed the items which appear to have come from Demainbray into the extant George III collection, together with various other pieces that had been presented to her.

This manuscript shows clearly the co-existence of the antiquarian with the experimental in the royal collection, without the tensions that this caused in the Royal Society. There is listed 'a petrified turtle placed by Her Majesty', 'A

Rattle Snake's Skin. Her Majesty', 'a piece of Marble from Ceasar's Tomb. Her Majesty', and about 60 other similar antiquarian and natural-historical items.[49] Sadly, much of this antiquarian material has not survived.

The expeditions to view the transit of Venus in 1769 represented a triumph for the Royal Society, but also a considerable cost.[50] George III granted a sum of £4,000 to send Captain James Cook to the South Seas, Jeremiah Dixon and William Bayley to different sites in north Norway, and Charles Mason to Donegal in Ireland, all with matching sets of instruments.[51] The transit was a crucial event because it provided a method of determining the size of the solar system, but it was also an opportunity to explore 'Terra Australis'. Political and scientific ambitions happily coincided. After analysis of hundreds of reports from around the globe,[52] a respectable figure was found for the size of the solar system, to within 1 per cent of today's value,[53] but more importantly, a new continent was explored, plants and animals were discovered, and new avenues for trade opened up. At home the King viewed the transit with a discreet group which included the instrument-makers John Cuff and Jeremiah Sisson, and the clockmaker Benjamin Vulliamy.[54]

George III also took an interest in other pressing scientific issues of his day. His support of the ageing John Harrison in 1773 is well known.[55] He reputedly was heard to say, 'By God! Harrison, I'll see you righted!'[56] and certainly ensured that £8,750 was paid to him. The chronometer known as H5 had been tested at the Royal Observatory the previous year.[57] Another pressing concern was the design of lightning conductors. George III championed the rounded conductors promoted by Benjamin Wilson, much to the disgust of Benjamin Franklin. It is likely that bad feeling between England and America played as much a role as dispassionate experiment on that occasion.[58]

However, as was suggested earlier, the eighteenth-century collections of experimental apparatus, the lecturers such as Demainbray who made them accessible, and the general scientific societies that were dominant simultaneously, had their problems. An early recognition of one of the problems came from Desaguliers in the mid-1720s, when his initial burst of enthusiasm as curator of experiments at the Royal Society was on the wane.[59] When criticised for letting the number of experiments performed at meetings slip, he rejoined that he expected to perform only when he had something new to show.[60] He was struggling to reconcile novelty and entertainment with frequency and utility.

Outside the Royal Society, the itinerant lecturers who toured this country and the Continent giving courses similar to that prepared by Adams for George III were doomed to face similar difficulties. Alan Morton has studied the circumstances around Demainbray's complaint in 1756 that his countrymen were 'inattentive' to scientific pursuits.[61] In some respect the lecturers were victims of their own success – polite society had already attended the lecture courses and were satiated. Morton also points to the founding of a new society, the Society for the Encouragement of Arts, Manufacturing and Commerce, which attracted over 2,000 members within ten years of its founding in 1754.[62] The Society of Arts appears to have taken the audiences from the lecturers and contributed to the decline of experimental philosophy as exemplified by collections such as the King's.

What did the new society offer? It was set up to reward 'Ingenuity in the Polite and Liberal Arts, useful Discoveries and Improvements in Agriculture, Manufactures, Mechanicks and Chemistry'.[63] Like the Royal Society it hoped to put aside all Party distinctions. Its relevance for its time was advocated by H.B. Wheatley, who wrote:

> As the condition of England in the middle of the seventeenth Century brought about the foundation of the Royal Society and the popular and widely-spread interest in the investigation of science, so the condition of the country in the middle of the eighteenth century brought about the formation of the Society of Arts for the encouragement of the application of science for the general good.[64]

The annual premiums encouraged experimentation with, for example, optimising manure, combating smoke from chimneys, transporting timber, and providing ventilation for jails.[65] The society was directed, centralised, rewarding, and addressed immediate issues. For a time at least it filled a role in the eighteenth century 'between revolutions' scenario, appearing more vibrant and relevant than the more academic experimental philosophy.

To return to the royal collection: Demainbray had been installed at Richmond Observatory in 1769 to look after George III's instruments, and George III had promised the position to Demainbray's son after his father's death. When that moment came in 1782, Joseph Banks, then president of the Royal Society, lobbied the King to give the position to William Herschel, who had discovered the planet Uranus the previous year.[66] Indeed, the King had welcomed Herschel at court and had ordered telescopes from him.[67] He granted Herschel £200 pounds a year to pursue astronomy 'independent of music', in order that Herschel could devote his time to studying the heavens rather than have to earn a living playing the organ. This was an offer which prompted Banks to write: 'Was every kingdom blessed with a sovereign as capable of distinguishing and as ready to reward merit as ours is, Philosophy would indeed be a Fashionable study ....'.[68] However, George III kept his promise with regard to the post at Richmond, an honourable action but one which contributed to the loss of this magnificent observatory for progressive science, and saw his collection of scientific instruments, once the height of fashion, become, by the end of the century, equivalent to Queen Charlotte's antiquarian miscellany.

George III took an interest beyond the call of duty in the science of his day. He enjoyed his collection and the pursuit of science,[69] patronised developments where he thought fit, and acted generously towards both individuals and the Royal Society. As a man of his time, his collection and his attitudes are imbued with the progressive, experimental side of the new philosophy, but also with the limitations of this type of collecting, and the general societies, such as the Royal Society in this country, that existed simultaneously. More immediate economic concerns were the focus of the new Society for the Encouragement of Arts, Manufacture and Commerce, and the growing specialisation required to absorb the increasing body of knowledge in the latter part of the century also mitigated against general courses and general societies.

Fortunately for us, unlike Bute's collection, George III's was not lost. In 1841 it was passed to King's College London by Queen Victoria, who decreed that it must not be broken up, and there it formed the George III museum. In 1927 King's College kindly lent it to the Science Museum, where it is now enjoyed by many in a purely antiquarian manner, the only way it could have survived.

NOTES

1. For a comprehensive discussion and catalogue of George III's collection of scientific instruments see A.Q. Morton and J.A. Wess, *Public and Private Science: The King George III Collection*, Oxford, 1993.

2. S. Ackermann and J.A. Wess, 'Between Antiquarianism and Experiment: Hans Sloane, George III and collecting science', in *Enlightenment*, pp. 150–57.

3. J.E. McClellan III, *Science Reorganised: Scientific Societies in the Eighteenth Century*, New York, 1985, p. xix.

4. For a discussion of the impact of the Society for the Encouragement of Arts, Manufacture and Commerce on science lecturing see A.Q. Morton, 'Lectures on natural philosophy in London, 1750–1765: S.C.T. Demainbray (1710–1782) and the "Inattention" of his countrymen', *British Journal for the History of Science*, XXIII, part 4, 1990, pp. 432–3.

5. The term 'scientist' was coined by William Whewell in 1834 and so is anachronistic for this period. What is meant by this term is someone who is expanding the boundaries of knowledge of the natural world.

6. M. Boas Hall, *Promoting Experimental Learning: Experiment and the Royal Society, 1660–1727*, Cambridge, 1991, p. 1.

7. See J.L. Heilbron, *Physics at the Royal Society during Newton's Presidency*, Los Angeles, 1983.

8. See D. Stimson, *Scientists and Amateurs: A History of the Royal Society*, London, 1949, p. 128.

9. See D. Atkinson, *Scientific Discourse in Sociohistoric Context: The Philosophical Transactions of the Royal Society of London, 1675–1975*, Mahrah, NJ, 1999, p. 25.

10. See Stimson 1949, p. 141.

11. M. Hunter, *Establishing the New Science: The Experience of the Early Royal Society*, Woodbridge, 1989, pp. 356–68, and M. Boas Hall, *All Scientists Now: The Royal Society in the Nineteenth Century*, Cambridge, 1984, p. x.

12. C. Russell, *Science and Social Change, 1700–1900*, London, 1983, p. 76, and Boas Hall 1991, p. 131.

13. McClellan 1985, p. 25.

14. This was especially true under Folkes's presidency from 1741 until 1752. See C.R. Weld, *A History of the Royal Society*, London, 1848, p. 483.

15. R. King, *Royal Kew*, London, 1985, p. 55.

16. Boas Hall 1991, p. 124.

17. J.T. Desaguliers, *A Course of Experimental Philosophy*, 2 vols., London, 1744–5, vol. 2, p. 484.

18. E.G. Ruestow, *Physics at Seventeenth and Eighteenth Century Leiden*, The Hague, 1973, p. 116.

19. *ibid.*, p. 118.

20. [W.J. 'sGravesande] *G.J. 'sGravesande's Philosophiae Newtoniae institutiones: in usus academicos*, Leiden, 1723.

21. P. De Clercq, *The Leiden Cabinet of Physics: A Descriptive Catalogue*, Leiden, 1997.

22. W.J. 'sGravesande, *Mathematical Elements of physicks, proved by experiments: being an introduction to Sir Isaac Newton's Philosophy*, trans. J. Keill, London, 1720.

23. J.A. Wess, 'Lecturing and the Real World: the case of cartwheels', *British Journal for the History of Science*, XXVIII, 1995, part 1, pp. 79–90.

24. Desaguliers 1744, pp. 143, 464, 503–4; Morton and Wess, 1993, pp. 155 and 182.

25. Desaguliers 1744, pp. 143, 464, 503-4.

26. G.L.'E. Turner, ' "A Catalogue of the Capital Collection of optical, mathematical and philosophical instruments and

machines: late the property of the Right Hon the Earl of Bute, Deceased. 1793": The auction sales of the Earl of Bute's instruments, 1793', *Annals of Science*, XXIII, pp. 213–42.

27. Morton and Wess 1993, p. 17.

28. TNA, PRO, LC/3/67, p. 30; Morton and Wess 1993, p. 18.

29. Science Museum, MS 203, p. 17.

30. Bute MSS: Demainbray to Bute, November 1760.

31. Morton and Wess 1993, E34, E35 and E46.

32. Morton and Wess 1993, E25.

33. Ackermann and Wess 2003, p. 154.

34. Morton and Wess 1993, p. 22; J. Millburn, *Adams of Fleet Street, Instrument Maker to King George III*, Aldershot, 2000, p. 100.

35. *A Description of an Apparatus for explaining the principles of mechanicks made for His Majesty King George III by George Adams in Fleet Street, London, 1762*, Science Museum Library, MS 203/1, and plates, MS 203/2; *A Description of the pneumatics apparatus made for His Majesty George III by George Adams in Fleet Street, 1761*, Science Museum Library, MS 204.

36. Morton and Wess 1993, E189.

37. Wess 1995, and see pp. 342–3.

38. Morton and Wess 1993, P1.

39. Morton and Wess 1993, P1–P63.

40. Morton and Wess 1993, M1–M114.

41. J. Millburn, *Wheelwright of the Heavens: The Life and Work of James Ferguson, FRS*, London, 1988, p. 140.

42. G. Harris, *The Life of Lord Chancellor Hardwicke*, London, 1847, vol. 3, p. 291. This quote is attributed to Dr Birch.

43. J. le F. Lalande, *Journal d'un Voyage en Angleterre*, ed. H. Monod-Cassidy, Oxford, 1980, p. 72.

44. T.N. Clarke, A.D. Morrison-Low and A.D.C. Simpson, *Brass and Glass: scientific instrument making workshops in Scotland as illustrated by instruments from the Arthur Frank collection at the Royal Museum of Scotland*, Edinburgh, 1989, p. 54, n. 29, from a document in the Scottish Record Office, SRO GD 76/464/3-4.

45. Morton and Wess 1993, E71.

46. G. Rigaud, 'Dr. Demainbray and the King's Observatory at Kew', *The Observatory*, V, p. 282.

47. *ibid.*, p. 281.

48. *A Catalogue of the Apparatus of Philosophical Instruments, Her Majesty has deposited in the Royal Observatory at Richmond, with an*

account of the Presents, by Sundry Persons made to her Majesty's Collection (hereafter The Queen's Catalogue), Science Museum Library, MS 348.

49. The Queen's Catalogue, pp. 20–3.

50. H. Woolf, *The Transits of Venus: a study of Eighteenth-century science*, Princeton, 1959, p. 166.

51. D. Howse, *Nevil Maskelyne: The Seaman's Astronomer*, Cambridge, 1989, p. 110.

52. Woolf 1959, p. 190.

53. *ibid.*, p. 196.

54. King's College Archives, K/MUS/1. See Morton and Wess 1993, pp. 28–9.

55. D. Howse, *Greenwich Time and the Longitude*, Oxford, 1997, p. 75; R.T. Gould, *The Marine Chronometer, its History and Development*, London, 1923, p. 65.

56. Originally from a publication under the name of Johann Horrins (an anagram) by Harrison's grandson in 1835.

57. Howse 1997, p. 124.

58. Morton and Wess 1993, p. 29, and J.L. Heilbron, *Electricity in the Seventeenth and Eighteenth Centuries: A Study of Early Modern Physics*, Berkeley, 1979.

59. See Boas Hall 1991, pp. 128–31.

60. Heilbron 1979, p. 24.

61. Morton 1990.

62. D.G.C. Allen and J.L. Abbott, eds., *The Virtuoso Tribe of Arts and Sciences*, Athens, Georgia and London, 1992, p. 365.

63. *ibid.*, cover.

64. D. Hudson, *The Royal Society of Arts, 1754–1954*, London, 1954, p. 28.

65. *Premiums offered by the Society Instituted at London for the Encouragement of Arts, Manufactures and Commerce*, London, 1778.

66. Morton and Wess 1993, p. 35.

67. C.A. Lubbock, ed., *The Herschel Chronicle: The Life-Story of William Herschel and his Sister Caroline Herschel*, Cambridge, 1933, p. 114.

68. *ibid.*, p. 122: letter from Banks to Herschel, 28 August 1782.

69. *ibid.*, p. 118.

17

George III: Enlightened monarch?

DAVID WATKIN

George III was characteristic of the Enlightenment in his intense intellectual curiosity which led, for example, to his concern with topics such as the measuring of time and the universe, and to his promotion of the global explorations of Captain Cook, the revolutionary discoveries of the astronomer William Herschel, the manufacture and design of Josiah Wedgwood and Matthew Boulton, the researches of the botanist Joseph Banks, and the agricultural reforms of Arthur Young.[1] Of course, there were many ways in which he was not a typical figure of the Enlightenment: in his deep religious faith, his conservative and traditional character, and the interest in chivalry which encouraged him to employ Wyatt to remodel Windsor Castle in the Gothic style once he had decided to return to reside there, the first monarch to do so since Queen Anne. His very role as an *ancien régime* monarch seems uncharacteristic of the Enlightenment, yet that movement was itself a product of the *ancien régime*.

As Prince of Wales, he was introduced to the new world of exploration by William Chambers (1723–96), his tutor in architecture and the new archaeology, who put into his hands that great Enlightenment text, *Les ruines des plus beaux monuments de la Grèce* (1758), by Chambers's friend, Julien-David Le Roy (1724–1803). Containing the first accurate record of the Parthenon and other monuments on the Acropolis, this book illustrates constructional details which are close to plates of machinery in Diderot's *Encyclopédie*. Indeed, Chambers had been trained in Paris by Jacques-François

Blondel (1705–74), the principal contributor of essays on architecture to the *Encyclopédie*. Chambers, at home in Rome, Paris, Gothenburg, and Canton, was the kind of pan-European figure admired by the Enlightenment. 'Always see with Your own Eyes,' he instructed his pupils, and do not rely on the judgements of others; also, do not mingle merely with the English when abroad but 'Converse much with artists of all Countrys, particularly foreigners, that you may get rid of national prejudices.'[2] There is a contrast with George III who never got much further than Weymouth, to which he had an improbably strong attraction, though the court of Queen Charlotte, as we are now learning, had a remarkably cosmopolitan nature. Moreover, the fabulous collection which George III assembled of maps, plans and topographical views enabled him, through virtual reality, to be a world traveller.[3]

In his student days he was set by Chambers to study the most up-to-date archaeology, as we know from drawings by him such as that based on Le Roy's engraving of the Tower of the Winds in Athens, probably made in the year the book was published, 1758.[4] Chambers also set the Prince to study Robert Wood's pioneering books of the 1750s on the Roman cities of Palmyra and Baalbek. Thus, in one drawing,[5] the Prince transferred the temple of Baal Shamin at Palmyra to an English watery landscape: nature and architecture combined through the medium of new Picturesque practice and of modern archaeological research.

In this context we can place the King's early interest in neo-classical painting. In 1761 he admired Nathaniel Dance's *Death of Virginia* (untraced), a stoical portrayal of the daughter of a Roman centurion, preferring death to dishonour. The painting contained numerous temples and public buildings all in the Doric order, a favourite of the king, who had been taught by Chambers that, according to Vitruvius, it was the most appropriate for heroes. The King acquired from Dance in 1765 his *Timon of Athens*,[6] showing Timon throwing gold coins at two female companions of Alcibiades and wishing that the gold may damn them. This moral essay on the rejection of society and wealth blended with George III's religious and moral feelings, as well as his enthusiasm for the classical virtues of heroism and self-sacrifice, a common topos of the Enlightenment cult of civic virtue, as in the paintings of Jacques-Louis David.

In the Warm Room in his suite at Buckingham House the King hung seven paintings which he had commissioned from Benjamin West (see p. 87), the artist whom he used to make public statements, as opposed to Zoffany and Gainsborough whom he employed for private commissions. The seven paintings by West included *The Departure of Regulus from the Senate and his Return to Carthage* of 1769 (fig. 31).[7] A Roman Consul, Regulus is shown in the Senate House, again sternly Doric, rejecting the pleas of his family and the Senate to accept the Carthaginian peace terms. His heroic refusal to do so led inevitably to his death. Admired by writers such as Cicero and Horace as a frugally living martyr, Regulus, a figure of the third century BC, was a prominent part of Roman Republican history, and so he was an unexpected hero for George III. But this reminds us that West, a Quaker with a strong moral sense, was curiously close in outlook to the King. His mixture of sophistication and simplicity also seemed to reflect the eighteenth-century concept of the noble savage. Indeed, West often pointed out that, 'though he socialised with courtiers and kings, he had been raised in the Pennsylvania wilderness.'[8]

West celebrated the King's recovery in 1789 with a remarkable allegorical painting dominated by three large columns which bear shields carrying inscriptions (plate XXIII).[9] Three groups of figures stand in front of the symbolical columns which recall Masonic iconography, as in the frontispiece to Batty Langley's *The Builder's Jewel* (1741) where three columns are hung with symbolic labels, the plinth below the Doric column marked W for Wisdom, the Tuscan S for Strength, and the Corinthian B for Beauty. In West's painting, the tablet over the left column, in the richest order, the Corinthian, is inscribed Honour and represents the

110. J. H. Ramberg, '*Sketch to a curtain for His Majesty's Theatre at Hannover*', 1789. Watercolour, pen and ink. British Library, London

members of the House of Lords who had supported the King's cause during his illness. Next to it is a stern Doric column, inscribed Virtue, representing his supporters in the House of Commons. The right column, also Doric, is inscribed Science and refers to the doctors who cured him. The association of the classical orders with public virtue, as in Dance's *Death of Virginia*, can be seen as an Enlightenment concept.

The King's concern for the arts is demonstrated in the curtain for His Majesty's Theatre in the Leineschloss at Hanover of 1789, showing the Muses with the King as Apollo who, as the caption explains, 'enlightens the world' (fig. 110).[10] This was painted by Johann Heinrich Ramberg (1763–1840), who had studied under Benjamin West at the Royal Academy in the 1780s, under George III's special protection.

Around the mid-eighteenth century, the early stirrings of the Industrial Revolution began to make London the leading centre in Europe for the design and manufacture of scientific instruments. These were tools used in experiments to discover the underlying principles of nature, all part of the Enlightenment's confidence in man's ability to control and order his environment. The King played his part in this process by forming a remarkable collection of scientific instruments, models of engines and steam pumps, barometers and hygrometers, microscopes and orreries. He gave employment to the manufacturer, Matthew Boulton, and discussed manufacturing industries at Buckingham House with Josiah Wedgwood, the ceramics manufacturer and industrialist who became Potter to Her Majesty. Wedgwood's watchword, 'All things yield to experiment', was a classic Enlightenment statement, and led him to develop an export trade with Europe, America, and the Indies.

John Adams, the first American Minister to Great Britain, visited the royal gardens at Kew with Thomas Jefferson and also inspected Wedgwood's manufactory in 1783. Wedgwood's partner from 1768, the Liverpool merchant, Thomas Bentley, was invited to an audience with the King in 1771, after which he noted that:

> The King is well acquainted with business, and with the characters of the principal manufacturers, merchants and artists and seems to have the success of all our manufacturers much at heart, and to understand the importance of them.[11]

Wedgwood was to be a radical in politics who supported the American War of Independence and even the French Revolution.

George III has been described as 'undoubtedly the most scientifically and cartographically interested monarch that Britain has ever had.'[12] With his insatiable curiosity about the world, he gave key support to John Harrison who devised a marine chronometer capable of determining longitude at sea. By the later eighteenth century England had fallen behind some other European countries in map-making, and it was thus important that George III gave financial and moral assistance from 1784 to the Trigonometrical Society, the fledgling Ordnance Survey, which had long carried out enquiries into determining longitude. The King's interest in machinery and the measuring of time found expression in his handsome collection of clocks, some of which provided him with international time.[13]

Related to this was the King's fascination with astronomy, in which context we should note that his father and also the courtier Lord Weymouth had both created planetaria. In 1768 the King commissioned Chambers to build an up-to-date observatory at Richmond in time to observe the transit of Venus on 3 June 1769 (plate XXII). This was important because when Venus, the earth and the sun were, unusually, in a straight line, it was possible to measure the scale of the solar system. In this year English and French astronomers undertook this task in rivalry with each other, discovering the universe to be ten times bigger than supposed (see p. 324). This observatory was one of the most striking demonstrations of the King's enquiring mind: indeed we should recall that the ostensible reason for Captain Cook's journey to Tahiti, subsidised by the King, was to take astronomers there to observe the transit of Venus.

The King's most striking contribution to the scientific revolution of the eighteenth century was his patronage of the German astronomer William Herschel, whose discovery of a new planet, Uranus, on 13 May 1781 overthrew the entire conception of the solar system, which had been believed since the earliest times to consist of the sun and six planets, each capable of being seen by the naked eye. In 1782 the King invited Herschel to come with his telescope to an audience at Windsor, where he subsequently became a regular visitor. In view of the observations made by the astronomer which led to the theory of the galaxies and the modern concept of the universe, it has been suggested that, 'Perhaps the biggest thing King George ever did was to patronise Herschel.'[14] He paid £4,000 for an immense telescope of 40 feet focal length and 49 inches aperture, the

111. *William Herschel's telescope at Slough*, artist unknown, 1786–7.
Watercolour. Herschel family archive

largest of its day (fig. 111). Housed in a field near Herschel's
house at Slough, it was supported within a towering pyramid
of scaffolding which had some claim to be one of the most
imposing constructions for which George III was responsible.
It became an object of amazement, being compared in
popular journals to the Seven Wonders of the World such as
the Colossus at Rhodes, or to the Porcelain Tower of
Nanking. Herschel described George III to Sir Joseph Banks,
as 'the best of Kings, who is the liberal protector of every
art and science', in a letter in which he proposed naming the
planet he had discovered 'Georgium Sidus', in honour of
George III.[15]

Another area of experiment in which the King was interested was new techniques in agriculture, in which England was now leading Europe. Known as the farmer king, he used to be presented merely as someone tickling the back of a pig, but as a young man he wrote an essay in which he claimed agriculture as 'that greatest of all manufactures'. He even contributed letters on crop rotation to Arthur Young's seminal journal *Annals of Agriculture and Other Useful Arts*, published from 1784. Such new developments brought many foreigners to England, notably that great Enlightenment patron Prince Franz of Anhalt-Dessau, who was a frequent visitor to England between 1763 and 1785. He attended the baptism at St James's Palace of Prince Frederick, later Duke of York, and described England as his 'second homeland'. He ran his state of Anhalt-Dessau almost along the lines of one large country estate in England which was for him the model for the programme of domestic reform, including the introduction of the latest developments in architecture, agriculture, gardening, manufacture and industry, with which he wished to transform his state of Anhalt-Dessau where the local economy had been destroyed by the Seven Years' War. On all his travels he was accompanied by his friend the architect Friedrich Wilhelm von Erdmannsdorff, in an association like that between George III and Chambers, though closer to that between Burlington and Kent. Erdmannsdorff built Schloss Wörlitz for him at Dessau in 1769–73 (fig. 112). It was similar to Chambers's Duddingston House, and to Claremont House by the royal gardener, 'Capability' Brown, for which Chambers also made designs. The library contains portraits of key thinkers and writers including Locke and Rousseau. Prince Franz had met Chambers in England and owned his books on Chinese design and gardening.[16]

A Calvinist, promoting self-improvement and practical good among his subjects, Prince Franz was a defender of the Holy Roman Empire, founding the *Fürstenbund* or League of Princes within it in 1783 with the active support of George III as a founder member. He saw the Empire as an umbrella

338

112. Karl Kuntz, *Schloss Wörlitz*, 1769–73. Aquatint. Schloss Wörlitz, Dessau

which protected small states such as his own. Seeing English agricultural improvement as a new expression of enlightenment, Prince Franz created a model farm at Wörlitz, run along English lines, bringing back clover seeds from England in 1763–4, as introduced by George III in clover-based crop rotation.

Visiting France on his return from England in 1775, the Prince met Rousseau at Ermenonville and later built a monument to him in the park at Wörlitz based on Rousseau's tomb on the Ile des Peupliers at Ermenonville. The extensive stylistic and cultural range of his garden buildings at Wörlitz was intended to educate his subjects in the history of architecture and world history. Such buildings as the Gothic House were a parallel to buildings at Kew like the Alhambra and their relation to the architectural instruction of the Prince of Wales. The garden at Wörlitz has recently been related to the federal concept which Prince Franz found in the *Fürstenbund*.[17] The purpose of the last of his visits to England in 1785 was principally to persuade George III to reveal to him the secret clauses of the *Fürstenbund*.

Queen Charlotte was close to her brothers, especially Prince Carl, later ruling Duke of Mecklenburg-Strelitz, with whom she maintained an intimate correspondence. She was painted with her brothers and children by Zoffany in 1771–2 on a rustic seat at Kew or Richmond (plate XIV).[18] Mention of Prince Carl introduces the question of the relation of the continental passion for the *jardin anglais* to the ideals of Rousseau on nature, morality, and sensibility. Having studied at Geneva in 1758, where he read Rousseau, Prince Carl 'instigated a Rousseauesque festival for the local population in 1796 at a consecrated forest altar' in the Picturesque English garden he had created at Hohenzieritz.[19]

Several of Queen Charlotte's associates and her relatives in Germany were friends or followers of Rousseau. Among the close friends of the King and Queen were Lord and Lady Harcourt, whose flower garden at Nuneham Courtenay was inspired by Julie's flower garden in Rousseau's *Julie, ou la Nouvelle Héloïse*. It was designed by William Mason, royal chaplain from 1757 to 1772, and was much admired by George III. When Rousseau was in England in 1766, Lord Harcourt, then still Lord Nuneham, offered him lodgings on the estate at Nuneham; he added a bust of Rousseau in the flower garden in 1777, the year in which he employed 'Capability' Brown to remodel the landscape. Rousseau's initial sponsor in Britain was the historian, diplomat, and agnostic philosopher of the Enlightenment, David Hume. Hume wrote in 1762: 'We are happy at present in a king who has a taste for literature, and I hope M. Rousseau will find the advantage of it, and that he will not disdain to receive benefits from a great monarch, who is sensible of his merit.'[20] This was because Rousseau had been offered pensions by Louis XV and Frederick the Great, George III's second cousin, but had declined both on grounds of his republican principles.

While Rousseau was in England, Hume commissioned a striking portrait of him in Armenian dress by Allan Ramsay

113. Allan Ramsay, *Jean Jacques Rousseau*, 1766. The National Gallery of Scotland, Edinburgh

(fig. 113),[21] who had painted the finest portrait of George III, his coronation portrait. Indeed, such was the fame of Rousseau that the King asked to see this portrait and Lord Harcourt commissioned a copy. George III now granted Rousseau a pension of £100 a year, which was even paid after Rousseau's death in 1778 to his mistress, Thérèse Levasseur.[22] It was decided, significantly, that it should not be a Treasury

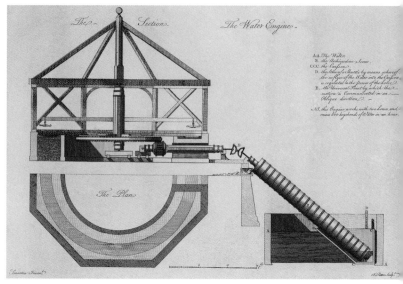

114. F. Patton after J. Smeaton, *The Water Engine, Kew Gardens*, 1763.
Engraving, from Sir William Chambers, *Plans, Elevations, Sections and Perspective Views of the Gardens and Buildings at Kew in Surry*.
RCIN 1150769

pension but should come from the Privy Purse. The King's interest in agriculture and farming, and his easy familiarity with his humbler subjects, were somewhat Rousseauesque: indeed, he made plans for a cottage for a labourer at Windsor in 1793, 1793–4 being *An II* of the Terror in France. This could be seen as revealing George III's real concern for the poor, in contrast to Revolutionary rhetoric.

A further link with the Enlightenment is suggested by comparing the King to his near contemporary, Thomas Jefferson (1743–1826), President of the United States of America from 1801 to 1809. Jefferson spent six weeks in London in 1786, including a week in April touring the country to inspect Picturesque parks.[23] Visiting the King's gardens at Kew, Jefferson admired an Archimedes screw for raising water, to which he devoted two diagrams and

115. *Omiah the Indian from Otaheite presented to their Majesties at Kew by Mr Banks and Dr Solander*, 1774. Engraving. National Library of Australia, Canberra

numerous detailed notes.[24] With his own interest in machinery, George III would have been in complete sympathy with this response to Kew. This ambitious water engine, designed by the famous civil engineer John Smeaton (1724–92), was illustrated in the book which Chambers dedicated to the King's mother, *Plans, Elevations, Sections, and Perspective Views of the Gardens and Buildings at Kew in Surry* (1763) (fig. 114). Jefferson thought that such a device might be used for the springs at Monticello, the experimental house he designed for himself near Charlottesville, full of mechanical devices which George III would have loved. He noted in 1786 that, 'The mechanical arts in London are carried to a wonderful perfection.'[25]

During this visit Jefferson was presented to the King and Queen at St James's Palace but he was not well received in view of the insults hurled at the King in the Declaration of Independence. Nonetheless, even in the first year of the American War of Independence, Jefferson had declared that, 'there is not in the British Empire a man who more cordially loves a Union with Gr. Britain than I do',[26] while rejecting totally the current proposals of the British parliament for maintaining that union. The marked similarities between George III and Thomas Jefferson included their interests in architecture, gardening, music, science, and machinery; their devotion to their family; and their dislike of ostentation and preference for the simple life of the country gentleman. Like George III, Jefferson was an amateur architect although, in contrast to the monarch, he had to teach himself architectural draughtsmanship. He is supposed to have declared that, 'architecture is my delight, and putting up and pulling down one of my favourite amusements.'

George III had even been pleased to welcome Omai, the South Sea Islander, when he was brought in 1774 to England. He was seen as one of Rousseau's real 'noble savages', as in the portrait of him by Reynolds of 1776 (formerly Castle Howard, Yorkshire). He remained for two years in England before returning to Tahiti with Captain Cook, and was introduced to the expert on the Pacific, Sir Joseph Banks, who presented him to the King at Kew in July 1774, three days after his arrival (fig. 115). A contemporary noted that 'The King very familiarly took him by the hand, and made several very kind enquiries concerning him', giving him an allowance, and recommending that he be inoculated.[27] His treatment of Omai surely shows 'the wisdom of George III': curiosity combined with courtesy.

NOTES

1. For a fuller account of this topic, see D. Watkin, *The Architect King: George III and the Culture of the Enlightenment*, London, 2004.

2. William Chambers to Edward Stevens, 4 August 1774, Sir John Soane's Museum, Private Correspondence i.c.7.1.

3. See Peter Barber's contribution to this volume.

4. Royal Library, RL K 214.

5. Royal Library, RL K 206; *George III & Queen Charlotte*, no. 56.

6. Millar 1969, no. 725.

7. *George III & Queen Charlotte*, no. 158.

8. J. Galt, *The Life and Work of Benjamin West, Esq.*, Part II, London 1820, pp. 189–90.

9. *Architect King*, pp. 134–5; H. Von Erffa and A. Staley, *The Paintings of Benjamin West*, New Haven and London, 1986, no. 107.

10. *Architect King*, fig. 3.

11. Brooke, p. 304.

12. Peter Barber, 'Maps and Monarchs in Europe, 1500-1800', in *Royal and Republican Sovereignty in Early Modern Europe: Essays in Memory of Ragnhild Hatton*, ed. R. Oresko *et al.*, Cambridge, 1997, p. 106.

13. For example, *George III & Queen Charlotte*, nos. 293–306.

14. Brooke, p. 303.

15. *Philosophical Transactions*, LXII, 1783. See C.A. Lubbock, ed., *The Herschel Chronicle: The Life-Story of William Herschel and his Sister Caroline Herschel*, Cambridge, 1933, p. 124.

16. See *For the Friends of Nature and Art: The Garden Kingdom of Prince Franz von Anhalt-Dessau in the Age of Enlightenment*, exh. cat., Dessau Wörlitz, 1997, pp. 37–71.

17. M. Umbach, *Federalism and Enlightenment in Germany, 1760–1810*, London and Rio Grande, 2000, p. 191.

18. *George III & Queen Charlotte*, no. 10.

19. Information from Professor Marcus Köhler, cited in C. Campbell Orr, 'Queen Charlotte, Scientific Queen', in *Queenship in Britain, 1660–1837*, ed. C. Campbell Orr, Manchester and New York, 2002, p. 257.

20. Letter to Madame de Boufflers, 1 July 1762, cited in R.A. Leigh, 'Rousseau's English Pension', in *Studies in Eighteenth-Century French Literature: presented to Robert Niklaus*, ed. J.H. Fox, Exeter, 1975.

21. A. Smart, *Allan Ramsay: A Complete Catalogue of his Paintings*, ed. J. Ingamells, New Haven and London, 1999, no. 451.

22. R.A. Leigh, 'Rousseau's English Pension'. David Hume was another recipient of such a pension.

23. J. Boyd *et al.*, eds., *The Papers of Thomas Jefferson*, 27 vols, Princeton, 1950–97, IX, 1954, 'Notes of a Tour of English Gardens', pp. 369–75.
24. *ibid.*, Jefferson to John Page, Paris, 4 May 1786, p. 373.
25. *ibid.*, p. 445.
26. *ibid.*, I, p. 269, Thomas Jefferson to John Randolph, Philadelphia, 29 November 1775.
27. *Gentleman's Magazine*, XLIV, 1774, p. 330.

Contributors

PETER BARBER joined the British Library in 1975, and worked in the Department of Manuscripts until 1987, when he transferred to the Map Library. He has been Head of Map Collections since 2001. A diplomatic historian by training, Peter Barber has curated several exhibitions and has published extensively on medieval and early modern mapping in their historical context and on the British Library's map and topographical collections.

CLARISSA CAMPBELL ORR is a graduate of Girton College, Cambridge with a combined degree in English and the History and Philosophy of Science. After doing post-graduate work on the history of science, she joined Anglia Polytechnic University in 1980, and is currently a Senior Lecturer in History, specialising in gender, Enlightenment and court studies. Among other essays and articles, she has published four collections of essays which she has edited and to which she has contributed: *Women in the Victorian Art World* (Manchester University Press, 1995); *Wollstonecraft's Daughters: Womanhood in England and France 1780–1920* (Manchester University Press, 1996); *Queenship in Britain 1660–1837: Royal Patronage, Court Culture and Dynastic Politics* (Manchester University Press, 2002); and *Queenship in Europe 1660–1815: The Role of the Consort* (Cambridge University Press, 2004).

CELINA FOX trained as an historian at Cambridge, Harvard and Oxford, specialising in the nineteenth century. Subsequently, she worked as Keeper of Art Collections at the Museum of London, from which she was seconded in 1990–2 to organise the *Metropole London/London World City 1800–1840* exhibition at the Kulturstiftung Ruhr, Essen. Her research interests have extended backwards into the eighteenth century and she is currently writing a book on the art of industry in the age of Enlightenment, while acting as a museums consultant for the Heritage Lottery Fund and other institutions both in this country and abroad.

FLORA FRASER has been a professional writer ever since leaving university. Her books include a romantic thriller, *Double Portrait*, in a series called *Nightshades: The Darker Side of Love* (1983); an illustrated *History of the English Gentlewoman* (1987); and two historical biographies, *Beloved Emma: The Life of Emma, Lady Hamilton* (1986) and *The Unruly Queen: The Life of Queen Caroline* (1996). Her latest book, *Princesses: The Six Daughters of George III*, was published by John Murray in September 2004, and in the USA by Knopf in spring 2005. Fraser recently co-founded the Elizabeth Longford Prize and Grants for Historical Biography in affectionate memory of her grandmother, the noted biographer. A Trustee of the National Portrait Gallery since 1999, and a member of the Friends of the National Libraries Executive Committee, Fraser lives in London with her husband and three children.

JOHN HARRIS is Curator Emeritus of the Drawings Collection of the Royal Institute of British Architects, where he served from 1956 to 1986. He is a historian of architecture, gardens and architectural drawings, and is the author of many books and catalogues. He has organised exhibitions – notably more than 30 at the Heinz Gallery – and, with Marcus Binney, was responsible for the celebrated *Destruction of the English Country House* exhibition staged by Sir Roy Strong at the Victoria and Albert Museum in 1974. He was a member of Paul Mellon's London Acquisitions Committee and one of the founder members of the International Confederation of Architectural Museums, of which he is Honorary Life President. The first volume of his memoirs, *No Voice from the Hall*, was published in 1998, and the second volume, *Echoing Voices*, in 2002. He lives with his historian wife Eileen in London and Badminton.

HOLGER HOOCK is a historian of eighteenth- and early nineteenth-century Britain with a doctorate from Oxford University. A fellow of the Royal Historical Society, he has held Fellowships at the Huntington Library in California, Yale University, and the Paul Mellon Centre for Studies in British Art, London. He is currently a British Academy Postdoctoral Fellow at Selwyn College, Cambridge and a Research Curator for the Nelson and Napoleon exhibition at the National Maritime Museum, Greenwich (2005). He has published articles on the history of collecting, artists' dinner culture, and the history of naval and military commemoration. His cultural and political history of the early Royal Academy, *The King's Artists: The Royal Academy of Arts and the Politics of British*

Culture, 1760–1840 (Oxford, 2003), won *proxime accessit* in the RHS Whitfield Prize, 2003.

MARCUS KÖHLER studied art history at the Free University, Berlin (1987–1992) and at the Courtauld Institute of Art; his Masters thesis covered early German landscape gardens. His dissertation was on Johann Busch, gardener to Catherine II of Russia (1997). In 1995 he was made Fellow at Harvard University (Dumbarton Oaks). This was followed by an Assistancy at the University of Hanover, and since 1998 he has been a professor at the Fachhochschule Neubrandenburg. He has published on architectural and garden history, and interior decoration. His interests include the mid-eighteenth-century Anglo-German-Russian exchange, about which he has written three articles in English.

CHRISTOPHER LLOYD worked in the Department of Western Art of the Ashmolean Museum at Oxford University (1968–88). During that time he was appointed by Harvard University to a Fellowship at Villa I Tatti (Centre for Renaissance Studies) in Florence and was Visiting Research Curator of Early Italian Painting at the Art Institute of Chicago. He was made Surveyor of The Queen's Pictures in 1988. His publications include monographs on painters, official catalogues of museum collections and general surveys of the Royal Collection, including *The Paintings in the Royal Collection: A Thematic Exploration.*

JONATHAN MARSDEN worked on the preparation of the *Treasure Houses of Britain* exhibition for the National Gallery of Art, Washington DC from 1984 until 1986, and subsequently worked for ten years for the National Trust as a Historic Buildings Representative. He was appointed Deputy Surveyor of The Queen's Works of Art in 1996. He has contributed to several exhibition catalogues for the Royal Collection, including *George III & Queen Charlotte, Patronage, Collecting and Court Taste.* His catalogue of the sculpture in the Royal Collection is in preparation.

HUGH ROBERTS is Director of the Royal Collection and Surveyor of The Queen's Works of Art, posts he has held since 1996. He joined the Royal Collection in 1987 and was previously a director of Christie's. He has written extensively on the Collection, and in 2001 he published *For the King's Pleasure. The Furnishing and Decoration of George IV's Apartments at Windsor Castle.*

JANE ROBERTS joined the Royal Collection as Curator of the Print Room in 1975. She has written extensively on the Old Master drawings and watercolours in the Collection. Her publications include *Royal Landscape. The Gardens and Parks of Windsor* (1997). She has edited the catalogues for several exhibitions at The Queen's Gallery and elsewhere, most recently *Royal Treasures* (2002) and *George III & Queen Charlotte* (2004).

STEPHEN ROE is Director of the European Book Division at Sotheby's and responsible for Music worldwide. He has written widely on the music of the Bach family, particularly Johann Christian and Carl Philipp Emanuel. He is Honorary Research Associate at Royal Holloway College, London and a member of the Kuratorium of the Bach-Archiv, Leipzig.

JUDY RUDOE has worked in the Department of Medieval and Modern Europe at the British Museum since 1974, specialising in jewellery and engraved gems, and nineteenth- and twentieth-century decorative arts. She is co-author of the two-volume *Catalogue of the Hull Grundy Gift of Jewellery to the British Museum* (1984), and author of the catalogue of the exhibition *Cartier 1900–1939*, which she organised at the British Museum in 1997. She has written widely on nineteenth-century jewellery and contributed to the *Catalogue of the Gilbert Collection: Micromosaics* (2000).

FRANCIS RUSSELL has been a Director of Christie's since 1977, and is now a Deputy Chairman, Christie's International UK Ltd. He is a member of the Arts Panel of the National Trust and the author of numerous articles in the *Burlington Magazine*, *Country Life*, *Apollo*, *Master Drawings*, and other scholarly publications and exhibition catalogues. He published *Portraits of Sir Walter Scott* in 1987 and *John, 3rd Earl of Bute, Patron and Collector*, in 2004.

DAVID WATKIN is Professor of the History of Architecture at the University of Cambridge and a Fellow of Peterhouse. He is Vice-Chairman of the Georgian Group, an Honorary Fellow of the Royal Institute of British Architects, and a Fellow of the Society of

Antiquaries. His many books include *Sir John Soane. Enlightenment Thought and the Royal Academy Lectures* (1996), and (with Richard John) *John Simpson. The Queen's Gallery, Buckingham Palace, and Other Works* (2002). His book, *The Architect King: George III and the Culture of the Enlightenment*, was published by the Royal Collection in September 2004.

JANE WESS has a first degree in theoretical physics from York University and a Masters degree in the history and philosophy of science from King's College, London. She joined the staff of the Science Museum in 1979 and has worked with the science collections in various capacities since then. She was involved in producing the 'Optics' gallery in 1986, the 'Science in the 18th Century' gallery in 1993, and the 'Making of the Modern World' gallery in 2000. She was co-author, with Dr A.Q. Morton, of *Public and Private Science* (1993), a detailed catalogue and interpretation of George III's collection of scientific instruments, and has since published a number of papers on aspects of the collections under her care. She is currently Senior Curator of Science.

MATTHEW WINTERBOTTOM is Assistant Curator, Works of Art, in the Royal Collection, where he has worked for six years. He was formerly a curatorial assistant in the Metalwork and Furniture Departments at the Victoria and Albert Museum. His particular interest is silver but he has carried out extensive research in different areas within the Royal Collection, and contributed an essay on Queen Charlotte's will to the *George III & Queen Charlotte* catalogue.

Photographic Acknowledgements

All works reproduced are in the Royal Collection unless indicated otherwise below. The Royal Collection is grateful for permission to reproduce the following:

fig. 3 BFI Stills, Posters and Designs, London; fig. 6 RIBA Library Photographs Collection; fig. 9 The National Trust for Scotland Photolibrary; figs. 10, 11, 13, 14, 15 Private Collection; fig. 12 © Tate London 2005; fig. 16 The Huntington Library, Art Collections, and Botanical Gardens, Bequest of Florence M. Quinn; fig. 20 MS Typ 576 (31), Department of Printing and Graphic Arts, Houghton Library, Harvard College Library; fig. 18 V&A Images/Victoria and Albert Museum; figs. 19 and 22 © Queen's Printer and Controller of HMSO, 2005. UK Government Art Collection; figs. 23, 24, 49, 88, 89, 90, 91, 92, 93, 94, 95, 96, 100, 102, 110, plates VI and XX By permission of the British Library; figs. 25 and 26 Photographs: Photographic Survey, Courtauld Institute of Art; fig. 30 Akademie der Wissenschaften zu Göttingen; fig. 32 The City of Westminster Archives Centre; fig. 35 Founders Society Purchase, Robert H. Tannahill Foundation Fund © 1985 The Detroit Institute of Arts; figs. 53 and 57 National Portrait Gallery, London; fig. 60 Image courtesy of the Twining Collection, The Worshipful Company of Goldsmiths; figs. 61 and 81 © Royal Academy of Arts, London; fig. 65 and plate XV Reproduced by courtesy of the Trustees, The National Gallery, London; figs. 69, 71, 72 By courtesy of the Trustees of the British Museum, London; fig. 70 English Heritage Photographic Library; fig. 84 The John Carter Brown Library at Brown University, Providence, Rhode Island; fig. 85 Dean and Chapter of Westminster; fig. 86 Courtauld Institute of Art; figs. 97, 101 © National Maritime Museum, London; figs. 103, 105, 106, 107, 108, 109 and plate XXV Science Museum/The Science and Society Picture Library; fig. 111 Herschel Family Archive; fig. 112 Kulturstiftung Dessau Wörlitz; fig. 113 The National Gallery of Scotland, Edinburgh; fig. 115 By permission of the National Library of Australia; plate IX Fine Arts Museums of San Francisco, Gift of Mr and Mrs John D. Rockefeller III, 1979.7.104; plate XXII Yale Center for British Art, Paul Mellon Collection; plate XXIII Hirschl and Adler Galleries, New York.